THE KNOCKOFF ECONOMY

To my friend and mentor, with great affection.

THE KNOCKOFF ECONOMY

HOW IMITATION SPARKS INNOVATION

KAL RAUSTIALA
AND
CHRISTOPHER SPRIGMAN

OXFORD
UNIVERSITY PRESS

OXFORD
UNIVERSITY PRESS

Oxford University Press is a department of the University of Oxford.
It furthers the University's objective of excellence in research,
scholarship, and education by publishing worldwide.

Oxford   New York

Auckland   Cape Town   Dar es Salaam   Hong Kong   Karachi
Kuala Lumpur   Madrid   Melbourne   Mexico City   Nairobi
New Delhi   Shanghai   Taipei   Toronto

With offices in

Argentina   Austria   Brazil   Chile   Czech Republic   France   Greece
Guatemala   Hungary   Italy   Japan   Poland   Portugal   Singapore
South Korea   Switzerland   Thailand   Turkey   Ukraine   Vietnam

Oxford is a registered trade mark of Oxford University Press in the UK and certain other countries.

Published in the United States of America by Oxford University Press
198 Madison Avenue, New York, NY 10016

© Oxford University Press 2012

Library of Congress Cataloging-in-Publication Data
Raustiala, Kal.
The knockoff economy : how imitation spurs innovation / Kal Raustiala, Christopher Jon Sprigman.
p.   cm.
Includes bibliographical references and index.
ISBN 978-0-19-539978-3 (hardback)
1. Piracy (Copyright)—United States. 2. Piracy (Copyright)—Economic aspects—United States. 3. Copyright—United
States. 4. Intellectual property—United States. 5. Copyright—Music—United States. 6. Sound recordings—Pirated
editions—United States. I. Sprigman, Christopher Jon. II. Title.
KF3080.R38   2012
364.16'62—dc23   2012006974

1 3 5 7 9 8 6 4 2

Printed in the United States of America
on acid-free paper

For Lara, Clark, and Willem
For Anne, Arin, and Iain

CONTENTS

THE KNOCKOFF ECONOMY

INTRODUCTION

Every spring, millions of viewers around the world tune in to watch the Academy Awards. Ostensibly, the Oscars are about recognizing the year's best movies. But for many people the Oscars are really about fashion. Fans and paparazzi press against the rope line to see Hollywood stars pose on the red carpet in expensive designer gowns. The television cameras are there too, broadcasting the red carpet fashion show (and the inevitable fashion faux pas) across the globe. In the process, careers in both film and fashion are made and unmade.

For years, the designers at Faviana have been watching the Oscars as well—very closely. Faviana is an apparel firm located on Seventh Avenue in New York City. If you go to Faviana's Web site, you will see a link titled "Dress Like a Star."[1] That link leads to a collection of dresses that are direct copies of those worn by actresses on television, in movies, and, most important, at awards shows like the Oscars. In fact, the dresses are identified using photos of stars, such as Angelina Jolie and Sarah Jessica Parker, wearing the original designs.

Knockoffs like these are a significant part of Faviana's business, as its Web site somewhat immodestly makes clear: "For the past 7 years, the company's 'designer magicians' have been interpreting the red carpet looks of Hollywood's most glamorous stars." And the company does not try to hide that it does more than "interpret" these red carpet looks; it copies them. Indeed, Faviana trumpets this fact. "Ten minutes after any big awards telecast, the Faviana design team is already working on our newest 'celebrity look-alike gowns,'" crowed CEO Omid Moradi in an interview.[*]

Faviana's creations retail for between $200 and $500—not cheap, but much less expensive than the multi-thousand dollar designer creations they imitate. At these prices, even Faviana's "designer magicians" cannot replicate the expensive materials and workmanship of many of the originals. But for women who could never afford to buy the real thing, that does not matter. For them, a cheap facsimile is better than nothing. The company, which excels at the production of both knockoffs and PR catchphrases, refers to its work as "bling-on-a-budget."

The existence of firms like Faviana (or ABS, Promgirl, or any of a number of similar houses) raises fascinating questions about the relationship between creativity and copying. In most creative industries, copying is illegal. We all have seen this warning as we sit back on the couch to watch our latest Netflix arrival:

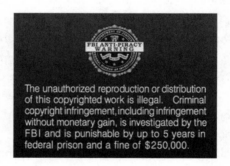

"Reproducing," or copying, a creative work like a film is against the law. Copyright law—and intellectual property law more generally—exist to prevent copying, on the theory that the freedom to copy would ultimately destroy creative industries. If others could simply copy the efforts of creators, few would bother to create in the first place. How then can a firm like Faviana get away with blatantly knocking off a dress that someone else has

---

[*] No one will be surprised that Faviana and its brethren do not stop at movie stars; detailed knockoffs of Kate Middleton's royal wedding dress, and even sister Pippa Middleton's bridesmaid dress, are available as well.

designed? And, even more important, why doesn't this rampant copying destroy the fashion industry?

Surprisingly, fashion designs are not covered by copyright law. What Faviana does is perfectly legal—and very common.[2] Fashion trademarks are fiercely policed; it is illegal to copy brand names such as Gucci or Marc Jacobs, and expensive lawyers aggressively sue those who try. But the underlying clothing designs can be copied at will. Firms both high and low in the fashion world knock off others' designs. Some merely take inspiration from or "reference" existing designs. Others copy far more blatantly. But all this copying is free and legal.

As a glance at the reliably thick September issue of *Vogue* will show, however, creativity in fashion has hardly ended. The development of new apparel designs continues every day at a dizzying pace. Indeed, the American fashion industry has never been more creative. All this copying has not killed the fashion industry. In fact, fashion not only survives despite copying; *it thrives due to copying.* This book is about why—and what the story of fashion, and of football, cuisine, finance, and a host of other unusual industries, can tell us about the future of innovation in a world in which copying is cheaper and easier than ever before.

Innovation is central to our contemporary economy. And many people believe that the rules about copying that fall under the banner of "intellectual property"—in particular, copyright and patent—are the basis of sustained innovation.[*] This belief in the power of intellectual property, or IP, predates the Internet, the computer, and even the lightbulb. It was also a central concern of the Framers of the U.S. Constitution. The Constitution explicitly grants Congress the power to create patents and copyrights for "limited Times" as a way to "promote the Progress of Science and useful Arts."

In a market economy like ours, of course, we depend on competition to keep the price of goods and services low and their quality high. And a lot of competition involves copying. (Think of Pinkberry, whose success spawned kiwiberry, Yogurt Land, and dozens of other stand-alone shops serving tart,

---

[*] When we refer to intellectual property in this book, we principally mean patent and copyright—the two forms that are focused on providing incentives to innovate. Trademark law has a different aim: to protect consumers by ensuring that they are buying what they think they are buying. We'll say more about trademark later in the book.

frozen yogurt with mix-ins). So why do we allow prohibitions on copying, prohibitions that constrain competition?[3] As the language of the Constitution suggests, we protect innovation from copying because innovation has good consequences, and restraints on copying are thought to be necessary for innovation to occur in the first place.

Some believe that these restrictions have an important moral dimension as well: copying the work of another, they say, is unfair and akin to stealing. The Framers generally took a different view.[4] As Thomas Jefferson famously wrote, ideas are not like tables or televisions:

> If nature has made any one thing less susceptible than all others of exclusive property, it is the action of the thinking power called an idea.... Its peculiar character, too, is that no one possesses the less, because every other possesses the whole of it. He who receives an idea from me, receives instruction himself without lessening mine; as he who lights his taper at mine, receives light without darkening me.[5]

In other words, if we take your car, we have it and you do not. But to copy an idea takes nothing from the creator; the creator still has it and so too does the copyist. And this makes the copying of ideas more morally ambiguous than stealing ordinary tangible property like a car.

The primary reason the American legal system regulates copying, in short, is not moral but practical. Both copyright, which protects books, songs, films, and the like, and patent, which protects useful inventions such as medicines, machines, and business methods, rest on the theory that the control of copying is necessary for innovation to occur. Innovation requires rules that allow creators to control who can make copies—either by making the copies themselves, or selling licenses to others. Creators, in short, need a monopoly over the right to make copies. In this book, we refer to this as the *monopoly theory* of innovation.[6]

Why is it thought that creators need a monopoly over their creations? Many innovations are difficult to invent but easy to copy. If copying is allowed, the monopoly theory holds, investment in new inventions and creations will be discouraged as copyists replicate the work of originators—and often more cheaply, since they do not bear the costs of creation. In Jefferson's terms, if everyone is constantly lighting their taper from our flame, we might not bother to light our own taper in the first place.

The argument that copying stifles creativity is intuitively appealing. Who is going to create if others are free to take? Proponents of this view tend to assume that it is self-evident that strong patent and copyright laws are essential to keep creative juices flowing, and that more protection is better than less.

This is one reason that the term of protection under American copyright law has increased from 28 years in 1790 to over a century today. It is also one reason the scope of patents has expanded from things like cotton gins and chemicals to cover a wide, some would say absurd, range of ways of doing business—such as the patent on "one-click" purchasing awarded to online retailer Amazon. (Only the naïve would ignore another reason for this expansion: there is a lot of money at stake in controlling innovations, and those who possess the relevant rights have every incentive to push to make them as strong as they can.)[7] The justification for the expansion of monopoly rights is simple: more intellectual property yields more protection, which in turn produces more creativity. Or so the story goes.

This book challenges the conventional wisdom about innovation and imitation. And it does so in a new way. Most of the debate on these issues has revolved around existing industries that are major proponents of strict rules against copying, such as the music business (copyright) or the pharmaceutical industry (patent). We instead explore a variety of industries and arts, like fashion, databases, and comedy, *in which copyright and patent do not apply, or are not used.* In other words, we ask, What happens when restrictions on copying are not part of the picture?

What we find is that even though others can freely copy in these industries, creativity remains surprisingly vibrant. In the pages that follow we will explore a clutch of industries in which copying does not necessarily kill or even impair creativity. In some, copying actually spurs innovation—an effect we call the "piracy paradox." In others, social norms protect the interests of originators and keep innovation humming. Imitation may also force innovators to structure their creativity in ways that make it less vulnerable to copying. The details vary, yet in all of these instances copying tends to lead to transformation rather than decimation.

Our main message is an optimistic one: surprisingly, creativity can often co-exist with copying. And under certain circumstances, copying can even be *good* for creativity.

This has vital implications in a world in which rapid technological advances have made copying easier and easier. Some believe we are entering an era of cultural and economic decay in which unrestrained copying by "digital parasites" destroys first one, then another, creative art.[8] Others foresee an impending utopia of the mind in which creativity and information are set free and available to all. We think the truth is more complex, but also more interesting, than either of these views. Copying can harm creativity and some rules are necessary; we are not IP-abolitionists.[9] But the effects of copying on creativity are not nearly as simple as the monopoly theory suggests. The industries we explore tell us that creativity is more resilient than commonly believed; that copying has unappreciated virtues; and that the rise of free and easy copying may, in the end, prove to be far less apocalyptic than many believe.

The industries we look at in this book are often surprisingly big and interesting. Understanding how they work, and *why* they work, is fascinating. We also want to draw out lessons for other industries, such as music and film, which increasingly struggle in the face of rampant, and rising, copying. These IP-dependent industries are certainly different from the industries we profile in the pages to follow.[10] Yet there are still useful lessons about how and when prohibitions on copying are necessary. This is especially true since copying appears increasingly difficult to stop, even as innovation becomes ever more central to our economy. In this new world, a close look at those industries that *already* survive and even thrive in the face of pervasive copying can help us judge whether the future of creativity is bleak or bright. For reasons this book will explain, we think the future is brighter than many realize.

Here are a few examples of the industries, and the stories, we examine in the chapters that follow.

CUISINE

Walking home one night in Los Angeles with his sister-in law, Mark Manguera had an epiphany. Mexican and Korean were two of L.A.'s street food mainstays. Could the tastes be combined? Maybe he could pull off the culinary version of a mash-up. What if he stuffed a tortilla with . . . Korean BBQ'd short ribs?

This was the birth of the now-famous "Korean taco": a concept that fused two of L.A.'s favorite cuisines—both associated with cold beer and good times—into one delicious combination. Within a month Manguera had teamed up with a friend and highly accomplished chef, Roy Choi. Choi took the idea and made it work. Together, they launched a business to sell Korean tacos out of a truck. They called it Kogi, a play on the Korean word for meat.

In L.A., food trucks are a common sight. But for decades trucks were limited to basic Mexican fare aimed at construction workers and residents of immigrant neighborhoods. Kogi's insight was to take the concept of a taco truck and tweak it. It was a flash of gastronomic inspiration to combine Korean BBQ with tacos, but it was also a flash of marketing inspiration to offer a more upscale and lively truck experience, one that would appeal to an entirely new demographic.

Still, Kogi's culinary mash-up was not an immediate hit. The truck parked in a busy part of West Hollywood, yet at first the team couldn't give their tacos away. But Manguera and Choi weren't deterred, and they tried some innovative strategies to get the attention of jaded Angelenos. The truck would park near offices by day, residential areas in the evening, and clubs and bars at night. Manguera would hand out free samples to the club bouncers, who loved the food and spread the word to those waiting at the rope lines. Manguera also reached out to L.A.-area food bloggers, and they reciprocated with glowing reviews. And Kogi benefited from the tech savvy of Manguera's sister-in-law, Alice Shin, who made extensive use of Twitter to help followers to know where the truck was at all times. But the overwhelming reason for their success was the creativity of the Kogi team, who cleverly combined two great tastes that had existed cheek-by-jowl in L.A. for decades, and, moreover, chose to "upscale" the plebian food truck rather than start a traditional brick-and-mortar restaurant.

The rest is food history. In 2010, Roy Choi was listed as one of *Food & Wine* magazine's 10 best new chefs, and today there are hundreds of gourmet food trucks in L.A. and nearly every other major city in the nation, offering everything from banana pudding to sushi. Inevitably, there are also many knockoffs of the Kogi taco. Even Baja Fresh, the fast-food Mexican chain, began offering one.

From an innovation perspective, cuisine is a lot like fashion. Recipes are unprotected by copyright, so anyone can copy another's recipe. Actual dishes—the "built food" you order in a restaurant—can also be copied freely. As anyone who has eaten a molten chocolate cake or spicy tuna on crispy rice knows, popular and innovative dishes do seem to migrate from restaurant to restaurant. The bottom line is that almost anything a chef does that is creative—short of the descriptions of the food in the menu, which are at least thinly protected by copyright law—can be copied by another chef.

Copyright's purpose is to promote creativity by stopping copying; if everyone could imitate, no one would innovate. By this logic, we ought to be consigned to uninspired and traditional food choices, since in the food world, it is easy and legal to copy. In short, the Korean taco should not exist.

But the real world does not follow this logic. In fact, we live in a Golden Age of cuisine. Thousands of new dishes are created every year in the nation's restaurants. The quality and variety of American cuisine today is very high, and much higher than it ever has been before. The so-called molecular gastronomy or modernist cuisine movement has innovated in myriad (and often bizarre) ways that have filtered down to more modest restaurants all over the world. But so too have the ideas of many "farm to table" chefs working in cities across America. Television shows such as *Top Chef* and *Iron Chef* challenge contestants to mix and match improbable combinations of ingredients with little warning or time. Our contemporary food culture, in short, not only offers creativity, it increasingly *worships* creativity—and many of us worship it right back. So how are chefs so creative when they know others can copy their recipes?

STAND-UP COMEDY

Louis C.K. is a "comic's comic," which is one way of saying that while his fellow stand-up comedians esteem him, he is not exactly a household name. That has begun to change in the last couple of years, however, not least because of his new television show, *Louie*. The show has received adoring reviews, and viewers are beginning to notice.

Dane Cook, on the other hand, is a stand-up comedy superstar. He has recorded five best-selling comedy albums, has a burgeoning film career, and has hosted *Saturday Night Live* twice. In 2007, Cook sold out two shows at Madison Square Garden in the same night. Dane Cook is the biggest thing that the world of stand-up comedy has produced in a very long time. He is, however, not well liked by some rival stand-ups. Some of the bad feeling may just be jealousy. But some is about Cook's credibility as a comedian. Cook has a reputation for stealing jokes. And the most persistent allegations revolve around three jokes that appear on Cook's 2005 album *Retaliation*, but which are remarkably similar to jokes on Louis C.K.'s 2001 album *Live in Houston.*[*]

Louis C.K. has never said anything publicly about the allegations against Cook. But other comedians and comedy fans certainly have. For the last six years or so, Cook's penchant for copying, and the specific allegations regarding Louis C.K., were detailed on comedy blogs and in a 2007 article in *Radar* magazine. And then there are the videos on YouTube, posted mostly anonymously, accusing Cook of imitating the routines of a number of other comedians. The allegations clearly have upset Cook. In a 2010 interview with comedian Marc Maron, an agonized Cook insisted that he "didn't steal anything from Louis C.K." "How can I really convey to people so that they understand?" Cook added. "I've never stolen anything in my life. . . . I'm not a thief."

And then, a couple of months after the Marc Maron interview, the Louis C.K./Dane Cook dispute took a fascinating turn: Cook appeared as himself in an episode of *Louie*. In the show, Louie wants to take his daughter to a Lady Gaga concert for her birthday. He approaches Cook, who shares a promoter with Gaga, for help in scoring tickets. The comedians meet in Cook's dressing room for a face-to-face discussion.

At first Cook is surprised and offended that Louie would ask him for a favor. But Cook agrees to get the tickets for Louie—on one condition: "All you have to do," Cook says, "is go on YouTube, and tell everybody that I did not steal your material."

Louie does not respond directly; instead, he denies ever accusing Cook of theft. Cook shoots back that what Louie has done is just as bad: he's allowed other people to make the accusations, without stepping in to deny them. And then Cook lays out how badly he's been hurt:

> You know what?—I'm excited that you're in this room right now, because I've waited four years to tell you this. . . .
>
> The year 2006 was the greatest year in my entire life. I had a double-platinum comedy album—first one ever to exist. I had a massive HBO special. . . . 2006—that should have been like my triumph. And I enjoyed it, Louie, for maybe two months. Two months before it started to *suck*. Because everything I started to read about me was about how I stole jokes from you. Which I didn't.

---

[*] One joke is about the strange names that parents give to their kids. A second focuses on how people get tongue-tied in moments of panic. And a third muses on the travails of having an itchy rear end.

"I kind of think you did," Louie shoots back. And then he tells what he thinks happened:

> I don't think that you saw me do those jokes and said "I'm going to tell those jokes too." I don't think there's a world where you're that stupid, or that bad a guy. . . . I think you saw me do them—I know you saw me do them—and I think they just went in your brain; I don't think you meant to do it, but I don't think you stopped yourself either. And that's why I never felt the need to help you not be hated by a lot of people.

An exasperated Cook asks Louie again for a public statement of absolution. Louie responds by asking whether Cook would be willing to admit that he did appropriate the jokes, even if inadvertently. Finally, Cook breaks down and says he'll get Louie the tickets. Nothing has really been settled, but each comic has had the chance to say his piece.

On one level, Louis C.K. and Dane Cook are simply actors playing parts in a TV show. But the dispute they're spatting over is real, and the on-screen confrontation also says something important about how comics behave out in the real world. When a comedian believes that a rival has used one of his jokes, he doesn't file a copyright lawsuit. Copyright law technically covers jokes. But because copyright protects the specific expression of a joke, rather than the underlying funny idea, it is very easy to sidestep the legal rule and simply tell the joke in a slightly different way. In practice, this means copyright just does not protect the work of comedians.

But that does not mean comedians stop creating new jokes: in fact, a big part of being a successful stand-up comic is churning out fresh material, not rehashing your greatest hits. The fact that copyright is essentially unavailable to comedians has not led to a decline in the invention of new jokes and routines. Instead, comedy is more pervasive than ever, with a flourishing world of comedy clubs and bars and even Comedy Central on cable television, featuring many stand-up acts. How is it that comedians have managed, without using the law, to reconcile creativity with copying?

FOOTBALL

When football started, it was a brutal game of straight-ahead running plays—the slow grind of "three yards and a cloud of dust." The results weren't always pretty, and indeed they were sometimes disastrous in an age when players wore little protection. In the 1905 college season, 18 players were killed and more than 150 badly injured. After viewing a photo of a mutilated player, President Theodore Roosevelt demanded change in the rules of the game. Football responded by innovating: teams introduced the forward pass into their offensive strategies.

The pass was thought to be less dangerous to players than the run, but some wondered whether it would ever count for much. A *New York Times* writer said, "There has been no team that has proved that the forward pass is anything but a doubtful, dangerous play to be used only in the last extremity."[11] Yet the pass not only caught on, it became, for many teams, the first tenet of their offensive doctrine. Passing changed football forever. Size mattered less; speed, smarts, and strategy much more. The pass added a range of previously unimaginable complexities to the offense, which demanded new defensive countermeasures. The result has been a continuous wave of innovation. And a just-as-continuous wave of copying.

Consider the "No Huddle Offense." In 1989, Sam Wyche, then coach of the Cincinnati Bengals, had the seemingly crazy idea of employing a "hurry-up" offense, typically used in a game's waning minutes, during the entire game. The offense became known as the "No Huddle," and it worked exactly as it sounds—Wyche's smaller and well-conditioned Bengals ran a very quick series of pre-scripted plays without huddles, all with the object of confusing and tiring the larger, less mobile players on the opposing defense. The strategy worked brilliantly and provoked anger among opposing coaches. In the days leading up to a playoff game against the Buffalo Bills, Bills coach Marv Levy angrily asserted that Wyche's innovation was equivalent to cheating. But anger soon gave way to imitation. The following season, Levy's Bills knocked off the no-huddle offense and went on to play in four straight Super Bowls.

So what does this mean? There is a lot of innovation in football. But there has been virtually no attempt to copyright or patent any of the innovations that have periodically roiled the game. There are some serious legal hurdles, but since American law already protects "choreographic works," copyrighting a football play is not as far-fetched as it may seem. Patent protection extends to new and useful "systems," and a novel football offense might be characterized this way. It might also be characterized as a "method of doing business"—a category of inventions which is also patentable (with some restrictions) under U.S. law. In short, IP law might conceivably step in to prevent copying, but it never has. So why do football coaches continue to innovate, even when they know that their rivals will study their innovations and imitate them?

Fashion, food, football, and comedy are all industries in which creativity is vibrant and the patent and copyright laws are either absent or irrelevant. There are many similar examples, as this book will demonstrate. Few have been studied as a source of insights about innovation. The best known involves open-source software. The entire purpose of open source is to keep code "open"—to allow others freely to copy and modify what previous programmers have created. The use of copyright law to prevent copying or modification of the code is not permitted. And yet creativity flourishes and open-source software products, such as Linux and Firefox, have significant market shares. Others have explored the story of open source in depth. Still, we will say a few things about it in the conclusion to point out just how important the overall approach of open source is to our understanding of how imitation and innovation mix.

There are many other fields in which IP plays little or no role in incentivizing innovation. Fonts are a vibrant creative area, with literally thousands available and many new fonts created every year. Copyright law does not effectively protect new fonts against copying. And the advent of digitization has made copying very easy. Rather than slow down the growth of new fonts, however, digital technology has actually accelerated it.

The financial industry—banking, investment management, insurance—is also a fertile ground for innovation, with new investment tools and strategies deployed (for better or worse is not clear) in a ceaseless competition to maximize returns, hedge risk, and lower costs. Some of these innovations are patented, but many—and many very valuable ones—are not. As a result, financial industry innovators are often knocked off by their competitors. Still, copying does not appear to suppress incentives to innovate very much.

The computer database industry—which provides a huge range of products that collect and organize information and make it searchable using a computer—is another innovative industry where an enormous amount of new work is produced with very little IP protection. The content in some databases is copyrightable—for example, the huge collections of news articles available via Lexis-Nexis or the DowJones "Factiva" database. In many other instances, the content of databases is composed of basic facts—like the price of houses—and under American law basic facts are uncopyrightable. This is a contrast with Europe, where factual databases *are* protected against copying. Yet the surprising thing is this: the database industry is growing on this side of the Atlantic, and stagnating on the other. The freedom to copy has not killed the U.S. database industry—if anything, it seems to have strengthened it.

These stories, and others, describe a world of robust creativity in the face of easy—and sometimes relentless—copying. These accounts are interesting in themselves. Taken together, however, they are more than just snapshots of particular settings in which innovation thrives without the incentives to create that IP is designed to provide. They raise wider questions about when, and how, restraints on copying are central to innovation in *any* setting.[*]

These questions are especially pressing now. Innovation is an ever more central driver of economic growth in today's economy. Rules against copying have a critical role to play in this economy.[12] Yet there are several reasons to think that having too much regulation of copying can pose as great a danger as having too little. IP rights come at a price. IP protects creators by limiting competition, and less competition means higher prices for books, films, music, drugs, and so on. They require enforcement, which is often expensive. And IP regulations can be a powerful tool for established firms and industries to squash newcomers, and new technologies, that could, if left alone, give rise to entirely new businesses and cultural products.

As this last point emphasizes, strong restraints on copying can inhibit as well as enable innovation. One of the key arguments of this book is that innovation is often an incremental, collective, and competitive process in which the ability to build on existing creativity is critical to the creation of new and better things. Apple took the idea of a mouse and an icon-based computer display from researchers at Xerox, tweaked it, and commercialized it. Disney's *Steamboat Willie* (and by extension Mickey Mouse) was a sort of proto-remix of Buster Keaton's Steamboat Bill. Thomas Edison's lightbulb imitated elements from over a dozen earlier bulbs. Shakespeare's *Romeo and Juliet* borrowed from earlier writers (and *Westside Story* in turn

---

[*] Smart defenders of rules against copying note—correctly—that these rules are not just aimed at creation but also at distribution. We say more about the role of intermediaries in the chapters to come.

drew heavily from Shakespeare). Since few creations are entirely new, laws that prohibit copying can block as well as spark innovation. The flipside is that open and easy copying can spark as well as block innovation.

To be sure, it is very hard to determine the optimal mix of imitation and IP in a given industry, let alone across the spectrum of our creative economy. The prevailing view, embodied in the monopoly theory, is that copying is a serious, even mortal threat to creativity. But perhaps the opposite is true: fewer restraints on copying could actually yield more innovation—or the same amount of innovation at a much lower cost. (That is the fundamental notion behind open source.) To date, there are few if any convincing tests of either of these propositions. Much of our regulation of copying, in short, is based on theory and intuition, not hard evidence.

Our central point is simply this: despite the widespread view that copying is a serious threat, when we stop and look at a broader range of creative industries, we see that imitation often co-exists with innovation. If the future is going to be one of more, rather than less, copying—and everything to date suggests that will be the case—these industries present a window on the ways in which innovation can continue to thrive.

And this has implications for how we think about the future of our increasingly ideas-based economy. Consider this example. In the 1980s the motion picture industry tried to use copyright law to eliminate a fearsome new technology—the VCR—that the industry's chief lobbyist, the famed Jack Valenti, in a congressional hearing memorably likened to the Boston Strangler.* That bid, spurred by the fear that Americans would begin copying films and television shows at home, just barely failed—the Supreme Court voted 5–4 to permit the VCR, and one vote going the other way would have resulted in the elimination of the home video market. Contrary to Valenti's prediction, that market became a huge moneymaker for Hollywood.[13] In subsequent decades the VCR, and then the DVD player, poured many more dollars into the film studios' coffers than piracy was ever able to steal away.

---

* Valenti did not stop there. The VCR, he predicted, would simply destroy Hollywood: "Now, we cannot live in a marketplace, Mr. Chairman—you simply cannot live in a marketplace, where there is one unleashed animal in that marketplace, unlicensed. It would no longer be a marketplace; it would be a kind of a jungle, where this one unlicensed instrument is capable of devouring all that people had invested in and labored over and brought forth as a film or a television program, and, in short, laying waste to the orderly distribution of this product."

As this history shows, getting our policies on copying right—or wrong—can have major economic impacts. And the story of the VCR illustrates that the relationship between copying and creativity is anything but simple. The film industry feared the VCR's ability to copy, but later discovered that copying created rather than killed markets, allowing the industry to grow and fueling future creativity.

Copying is not always so benign, or so lucrative. Rules about copying have an important, even essential role to play in our economy and our world. But that role is much more nuanced than many believe. Major industries survive and even thrive in the face of copying, and in some cases copying makes them richer and more productive. If we can begin to unlock that paradox, we can learn a host of important lessons about the future of innovation.

1

KNOCKOFFS AND FASHION VICTIMS

Oprah Winfrey: How do you keep reinventing?
Ralph Lauren: You copy. Forty-five years of copying; that's why I'm here.
—*Oprah Winfrey interviewing Ralph Lauren, October 24, 2011*[*]

In 2007, viewers of *The Late Show with David Letterman* saw celebrity Paris Hilton wearing a flower-printed dress designed by Foley + Corinna. Dana Foley, a one-time aspiring playwright, had begun making vintage-inspired women's clothing many years earlier. After Foley met Anna Corinna, a vintage clothing reseller, at the 6th Avenue flea market in New York City, the two women went into business together. They opened a store on the Lower East Side in 1999 and, several years later, another in West Hollywood. The design team eventually emerged as an industry favorite, but they also developed wider market appeal—according to the *New York Times*, in 2008 they sold over $20 million worth of garments and accessories.

* Eric Wilson, "O and RL: Monograms Meet," *New York Times*, October 27, 2011. Those present say that Lauren seemed to be at least partly joking, but of course what makes the quip funny is the knowledge that knockoffs are such a pervasive part of the fashion industry. And Lauren, a Jewish kid from the Bronx who built a spectacular career reinterpreting fashion designs associated with the WASP aristocracy, may well have hidden the truth in a joke.

After Paris Hilton's appearance on the David Letterman show, fast fashion retailer Forever 21 began selling a $40 dress strikingly similar to the Foley + Corinna design Hilton had worn.[1] The original dress was not expensive by the standards of high-end fashion. Yet it sold for about 10 times as much as Forever 21's knock-off. Shortly after the two dresses were shown, side-by-side, on some apparel Web sites, Anna Corinna was interviewed by the *New York Post*. "It's awful," she declared. "To me, the most awful part is that they're huge companies and they [employ] designers, and a designer's job is to design. . . . I totally understand being influenced by or inspired by, because everybody does that. But this obviously is neither. To me, they should be embarrassed. They're not designing, they're stealing it."[2]

Many of Forever 21's customers may have been unaware of Foley + Corinna's dress, and simply bought Forever 21's model because they liked it. Others may have been aware of the original but preferred the cheaper copy. As Ms. Corinna argued to the *Post*, "A lot of people don't know they're buying a knockoff, or they just don't care, they'd rather buy the cheaper one. . . . If you're in Forever 21 in whatever city, you see it and think, 'Oh, that's pretty,' and you buy it."

The story of Forever 21 knocking off Foley + Corinna is not unusual.[*] Every season—indeed, every day—clothing designs are copied, reinterpreted, and "referenced" by other firms in the apparel industry. Some well-known apparel companies, such as Allen B. Schwartz and Faviana, center their business strategies around copying striking designs. The practice is so widespread that the magazine *Marie Claire* features a regular section titled "Splurge vs. Steal" that pairs an expensive version of a given design (perhaps the original, but not necessarily) against a far cheaper version.[3] At times the two versions are virtually indistinguishable.

The ubiquity of knockoffs in the fashion world is the direct result of a gap in American copyright law. Copyright protection in the United States does not extend to fashion designs, and in the more than 200-year history of US

---

[*] Dana Foley and Anna Corinna nonetheless became poster children for a thus-far unsuccessful effort to ban fashion design copying, with Foley appearing alongside New York Senator Chuck Schumer at a press conference touting his proposed Design Piracy Prohibition Act. As we explain later, Congress has periodically considered, and thus far rejected, revising copyright law to address fashion designs. In December 2010, Schumer reintroduced this bill, recast as the Innovative Design Protection and Piracy Prevention Act. Hearings on a companion bill were held in the House in July 2011; as of this writing, the bill has not moved to a vote.

law regulating creative endeavors it never has. As we will explain in a moment, some elements of clothing, such as the label or the fabric print, are protected against copying. But for designs, it's a free-for-all. Anyone can copy or reinterpret a successful design, and there is nothing the original designer can do about it. In the case of Foley + Corinna, the Lower East Side designers received substantial attention from the incident, which struck a chord with reporters and bloggers alike. But they did not receive any legal judgment, nor could they stop Forever 21 from copying their work.

The standard justification for rules against copying is practical and purposeful. Since copying is cheaper than creating, the theory holds, creators will not create if they know that others will simply copy their ideas. Restrictions on copying are necessary to ensure that copying does not drive out creativity. Granting creators a monopoly over the right to make copies of their work is a strategy to achieve the goal of more innovation. We call this the *monopoly theory* of innovation.

The monopoly theory has important implications for the story of Anna Corinna, Dana Foley, and Forever 21. It suggests that the behavior at the heart of the dispute—the pervasive copying of creative designs—ought to precipitate a crisis in the fashion industry. Innovation should be driven out by the specter of fast and easy imitation, and investment should dry up. The industry should be in a freefall economically (something like what we see in the mainstream music industry today, perhaps). Yet quite the opposite has happened. The American apparel industry has boomed over the past 50 years in the face of uncontrolled copying, and it has been vibrantly creative.

What is perhaps most striking is that despite the ubiquity of copying, there is a greater diversity of designs available to consumers today than ever before. To be sure, some fashion insiders bemoan today's world of high-end fashion, in which designers are under relentless pressure to come up with something new.[4] But it is hard to contend that the contemporary world suffers from too few designs or too little creativity. New labels abound, clothing is cheaper than ever, and designs come pouring out of small niche firms and major international design houses alike.

Copying, in short, is commonplace in the fashion world, yet it has not destroyed the incentive to innovate. This is not to say that designers are not sometimes harmed by copying—perhaps Dana Foley and Anna Corinna might have sold more of their original design in a world without Forever 21's knockoff. But the industry as a whole has thrived.

Why do fashion designers continue to create in the face of such wide-spread copying? And what does this tell us about the nature of innovation?

A Very Short History of the Fashion Industry

The world of fashion—with its flamboyant personalities, ruinously expensive runway shows, and sometimes outrageous and borderline unwearable designs—strikes some as fundamentally silly. (Just watch *Zoolander.*) It is anything but. Conservative estimates suggest that worldwide the apparel industry sells more than $1.3 trillion of goods annually[5]—a number larger than the combined revenues of the motion picture, software, books, and recorded music industries. While not all of this fits most people's definition of "fashion," the world of apparel is large, rich, diverse, and truly global—with iconic brands, enormous advertising budgets, integrated international supply chains, and, increasingly, retail footholds in every corner of the world.

Fashion was not always a global industry. For a long time it was, in its higher forms at least, synonymous with Paris. The great couture houses operated there, and elites throughout the world looked to Parisian designers for guidance on how to dress.[6] Today, Paris is a major node in the contemporary fashion network, and remains the center of the relatively tiny market in elaborate, handmade dressmaking.

Traditionally, of course, all clothing was handmade and the market for "ready-to-wear" apparel—which today is essentially all clothes bought in the United States—was very small. The industrialization of apparel-making, which would ultimately transform the industry, began with the invention of the sewing machine in the mid-19th century. The United States was in forefront of the move away from traditional custom-tailored clothing to pre-made garments purchased off a rack. Indeed, by the early 20th century, America was the acknowledged world leader in ready-to-wear.[7] In 1902 a British apparel trade magazine presciently bemoaned the dangers of an American-led "ready-made invasion," noting that "a visit to America cannot fail to impress the stranger with the relative importance of the ready-made clothing industry there. . . . It seems ludicrous to say so, but there is a considerable and respected trade in ready-made suits."[8]

Over the course of the 20th century, handmade clothing essentially died out in the West, save for the ever-shrinking couture industry and a tiny slice of high-end custom menswear. The rise of ready-to-wear not only meant cheaper clothing, made using some of the same mass production techniques pioneered by Henry Ford; it also meant that average consumers were now presented with a wide range of predetermined choices aimed to entice them to buy. In this way, our contemporary idea of fashion—apparel produced for fickle consumers in an ever-changing array of styles developed by competing designers—was born.

The American apparel industry grew dramatically during the 20th century. As the Triangle Shirtwaist fire of 1911 illustrated, early in the century New York already had a large garment industry. The onset of the First World War meant that American editors and buyers could not travel to Paris to see the latest designs. American designers like Claire McCardell became overnight sensations as the nation increasingly looked to New York to fill the style void.[9] The industry grew further when, during the Great Depression, the federal government imposed punitive duties on imported clothes as an element of the infamous Smoot-Hawley tariffs.[10] By the Second World War the United States had become an important player in fashion, and many of the features of the contemporary fashion industry had fallen into place: an increasingly international set of brands; diversified, factory-based production of ready-to-wear clothing; and, over time, declining prices as the cost of production fell.[*]

For true luxury apparel, less had changed by mid-century. In the early postwar years France retained its central role in the high-end markets for women's fashion. (For men, Mecca remained further north, on London's Savile Row and Jermyn Street.) But as the world economy recovered in the early 1950s, Italian and American firms increasingly displaced Parisian firms as the central players in the burgeoning high end of the ready-to-wear market. And at the same time, brands and labels were replacing tailors and dressmakers at the center of consumers' attention. Early licensers, such as Pierre Cardin, tapped into this new mind-set to market an enormous array of goods that were manufactured by many different firms, but which all shared the (then-prestigious) Cardin trademark.

The postwar era was a time of continued growth and diversification for the American fashion industry. Established national brands such as Brooks

---

[*] This was also the birth period of standardized clothing sizes; in 1939 the US Department of Agriculture took the measurements of 15,000 women in an effort to arrive at standard sizes (each woman underwent 59 discrete measurements). Standardized sizes were ubiquitous by the 1950s.

Brothers, founded in 1818, were soon joined by a new wave of sophisticated homegrown (if not always home-born) postwar designers: Bill Blass in the 1950s, Halston (Roy Halston Frowick) in the 1960s, Ralph Lauren and Diane von Furstenberg in the 1970s, as well as associated editors and taste-makers, such as Diana Vreeland, Grace Mirabella, and Baron Nicolas de Gunzburg. New York, with its still-thriving garment district, increasingly became a world center of apparel design and brand management rather than mere assembly and tailoring.

During this era the high end of the fashion industry also became truly global. Expensive boutiques stocking the leading labels opened around the world, catering to an increasingly mobile and moneyed elite. In the 1970s, the Arab oil states became major destinations for fine clothing and helped keep the faltering—and now breathtakingly expensive—haute couture market alive in the face of an onslaught of top-quality ready-to-wear. For many major firms, couture functioned (and still does function) as a loss leader—a way to polish the image of an apparel brand and foster lucrative licensing opportunities, but not a business that itself makes money. Indeed, by 1993, Jean Francois Debreq, who engineered the purchase of Yves Saint Laurent's eponymous firm, would go so far as to joke that "if [Yves Saint Laurent] dies, I think I make even more money because then I stop the couture collections."[11]

Fashion continued to globalize and grow in the 1980s and 1990s. Italy became the new hotspot due to the dramatic rise (or rebirth) of firms such as Gucci, Giorgio Armani, Versace, and Prada. Japan too became a first-tier player, both as a source of innovative designs (Rei Kawakubo, Issey Miyake) and, for a time, the number one luxury goods market in the world. Russia, after the fall of communism, likewise became a major market packed with new money. And New York continued to grow as a center for design, with New York Fashion Week increasingly prominent among the global circuit of fashion shows. All of this growth fueled the introduction of tens of thousands of new designs every season by a very large number of fashion firms of all sizes. A small group of increasingly global brand names dominated the public consciousness: Armani, Chanel, Louis Vuitton, and the like. However, these firms, as famous as they became, have never comprised more than a small part of the industry's total turnover. The fashion industry has always been, and remains, competitive.

The economic boom of the 1990s produced many millions of new consumers with money to spend on fashion, and particularly on luxury ready-to-wear. Magazines such as *Vogue* and *Elle* grew fatter with advertising pages touting both global brands and high-end niche producers. Fashion also became a popular fascination, epitomized by the hit series *Sex and the City*'s silent fifth friend, Manolo Blahnik. Fashion grew ever more synonymous with coveted brands, which were applied most profitably to accessories rather than actual clothing. (The average price of a luxury handbag, which can sometimes cost as much as a new car, is 10 to 12 times the production cost.)[12] Just as couture had become a loss leader for many fashion firms, for some firms even ready-to-wear functions, if not as an actual money-loser, nonetheless as more of a vehicle for image management than an actual profit center.

The modern conception of the fashion industry—large factories rather than small ateliers; large firms rather than small family shops; the brand (protected by trademark law) the dominant value of the firm—was by the mid-1990s fully developed. In this system many labels were sometimes consolidated under one roof, usually with an acronymic name, such as GFT (Gruppo Finanzario Tessile), LVMH (Louis Vuitton-Moet Hennessy) and PPR (Pinault-Printemps-Redoute). These giants controlled a relatively small but important and highly visible slice of the industry. The mass market, however, was and is still contested by a welter of smaller firms producing for and selling through huge-volume retailers such as JCPenney, Walmart, and Old Navy.

At the same time, another front in the business of apparel was opening: the market in so-called fast fashion. By the end of the 20th century, rapidly shrinking tariffs and shipping costs meant that new labor sources, such as China and Bangladesh, could produce clothing at astonishingly low cost. Fast fashion retailers tapped into this global supply chain (as well as local producers closer to home) to churn out cheap but stylish articles at a very rapid rate. The Spanish firm Zara reportedly offers some 10,000 new products a year; UK-based Topshop perhaps 15,000.[13] Some of these firms have long histories—fast fashion darling H & M was founded in 1947 in Sweden—but others, such as Zara and Forever 21, only grew globally prominent in the 2000s. (Zara opened its first US location in 1989, in New York). By the end of the last decade, fast fashion retailers were challenging the established design houses on a surprising number of fronts.

Today, fast fashion is epitomized by Los Angeles-based Forever 21. Started by Korean immigrants who placed their first store, opened in the 1980s, in then-seedy downtown L.A., Forever 21 is today a nearly $2 billion business. As Anna Corinna and Dana Foley discovered, Forever 21 can quickly and fairly accurately ape a striking and salable design. Its ability to do this—and at amazingly cheap prices—keeps customers coming back for more on a regular basis. Not all the customers are 21; indeed, many are the mothers of 21-year-olds who navigate the store in an effort to stay on trend and inexpensively fill out closets. But as much as many consumers love Forever 21, some designers loathe it. At her Fall 2007 runway show, designer Anna Sui gave out T-shirts emblazoned with "Thou shalt not steal" and the likenesses of the co-owners of Forever 21, portrayed as wanted criminals.[14]

By the 21st century, fashion had become a popular obsession. Traditional fashion magazines are only a small part of the buzz around the industry. The Gray Lady's fashion reporting has expanded with the addition of the *New York Times* Style Section (now twice weekly). Many celebrity-driven magazines, such as *People* and *US Weekly*, feature substantial coverage of trends and designers. Blogs such as Fashionista and The Sartorialist are widely read and increasingly influential. Perhaps most striking is the rise of apparel-oriented television hits such as *Project Runway, What Not to Wear*, and *America's Next Top Model*, which, particularly in the case of the first, try to illuminate the creative process behind fashion design—and have millions of viewers. The same fascination with fashion and its workings is shown in the success of films such as *Unzipped, The Devil Wears Prada*, and *The September Issue.*

In short, over the 20th century, apparel was transformed from a largely small-scale, often handmade and relatively expensive craft to a much more diverse and creative industry producing garments in vast and far-flung factories for a global audience attuned to trends and on the hunt for something new. A tiny alternative world exists, exemplified by high-end menswear, which still adheres to the ideal of traditional styles tweaked by expert tailors into custom clothing. But for the vast majority of customers, ready-to-wear is the only thing they have ever owned. More than any other nation, the United States led the way to this new world of apparel.

Today, the fashion industry is a riotous blend of high and low: the extremely cheap (and largely disposable) clothing offered by firms like H&M standing side by side with stratospherically priced brands like Tom

Ford. Occasionally odd hybrids occur, such as *Vogue*-darling Rodarte designing a collection for mass retailer Target. Hunting and gathering at all these price levels are ever-more sophisticated fashion consumers, often armed with the latest magazine spreads and photos from their favorite street fashion blogs. Perhaps the signal feature of American fashion today is its dizzying diversity of design and style—and the frequency and speed with which appealing designs are knocked off.

WHY ARE KNOCKOFFS LEGAL?

Striking or popular fashion designs have long been reinvented, reinterpreted, and sometimes simply ripped off. Complaints about copying date back at least to the beginning of the 20th century, and probably further. Writing in the 1920s, Columbia business school professor Paul Nystrom declared that "the extent of the evil of copying is almost unbelievable. Every known device is used by the style creators to prevent their designs from going into the hands of imitators and copyists, particularly before the products of the design are offered for sale."[15] Yet in the United States, the copying of fashion designs has never been against the law and has remained legal even as a world-class fashion industry grew up in New York.

Why have fashion designs never been protected against copying? To explain this requires digging into some detail about the structure of our laws against copying. The lack of protection in American law does not arise from any conscious decision. Rather, it flows from a more general feature of the American approach to copyright law: so-called useful articles usually can be copied freely. Useful articles are goods, like apparel, furniture, or lighting fixtures, in which creativity is closely compounded with practicality. A painting has no functional use, whereas a dress is functional, even if it is also a work of art. Copyright law is generally aimed at art forms that either have no function (such as music) or have only the most minimal functional attributes.[16]

The useful articles concept leads to some curious results. Jewelry can be copyrighted, because it is considered ornamental, not useful. But an ornate dress that barely covers the body is considered functional, and consequently is not protected. A two-dimensional sketch of a fashion design is protected as a drawing. But the three-dimensional garment produced from that sketch is not protected. The same basic principle—two dimensions are protected, but three are not—applies to prints that appear on fabric. A printed fabric is protected, just as an ink print or drawing would be. But the cut and shape of the garment that employs the fabric can be copied at will.

Rules against copying are not totally inapplicable to apparel, however. Following the same basic principles, copyright law can sometimes apply when the garment's expressive component can be separated from its useful function.[17] For example, a jeweled appliqué stitched onto a sweater may be protected because it can be *physically* separated from the garment. It can also be *conceptually* separated in the sense that the appliqué does not contribute to the garment's utility. (The sweater is just as warm with or without it.) Very few fashion designs are separable in this way, however. The expressive elements in most garments are not "bolted on" in the manner of an appliqué but are instilled into the form of the garment itself—for example, in the cut of a sleeve or the shape of a pants leg. The bottom line is that most of the fashion industry's products, aside from fabric prints and some accessories, can be freely and legally copied.

While copyright is generally concerned with art forms that lack an obvious function, patent law is focused on functional inventions and new designs. At least in theory, novel fashion designs could be protected against copying via a "design patent." Design patents offer 14 years of protection for "new, original, and ornamental" designs. As a practical matter, however, design patents are rarely useful for clothing. Unlike copyright, which extends to all "original" expression (that is, to all expression not copied in its entirety from others and that contains at least a bit of creativity), design patents are available only for designs that are truly "new." As a result, design patents do not extend to designs that are merely reworkings of older designs.[18] Because so many fashion designs fail this test, they do not qualify for protection.[19]

Patents are also hard to obtain. The application is expensive, the waiting period lengthy, and the prospects of ultimately gaining protection uncertain. (The United States Patent and Trademark Office rejects roughly half of all applications for design patents.) Given the one or two season life of many fashion designs, design patents are simply too slow and unpredictable to be practical. The fashion industry's primary use of design patents has been in the world of handbags and shoes, which tend to have slower turnover in style and, as already noted, cost more, and are quite a bit more profitable, than the average garment.

What about other forms of intellectual property (IP)? Trademark is by far the most significant. Trademark law stops others from a using a mark—that is, a brand name or a logo—when that use would likely confuse consumers about the source of a product, or would dilute the value of the mark. For example, Adidas' famous three-stripe mark cannot be used by another firm in a way likely to confuse consumers about who made the shoe—as discount shoe purveyor Payless discovered to the tune of more than $50 million (reduced from an initial jury award of over *$300 million*) when Adidas sued it for selling look-alike sneakers with two rather than three stripes. Compared with confusion, dilution is a bit more difficult to imagine. Say that a manufacturer of kitchen appliances uses a three-stripe mark to identify its toasters. This might be considered dilution if a court finds that the use of the mark on toasters will weaken the mark's ability to help consumers identify Adidas' athletic shoes, even if the consumers don't actually believe that Adidas is the source of the three-stripe toaster.

Trademarks are critical in the fashion industry because they help to maintain a prestige premium for particular brands. As a result, many apparel firms invest heavily in policing their marks. (That said, many fashion goods sold by street vendors are counterfeits that plainly infringe trademarks, such as the cheap handbags and watches often found in areas such as Canal Street in New York and Santee Alley in Los Angeles.)[20] Trademark law does little to protect fashion *designs*, however. Occasionally a fashion design will visibly integrate a mark so that it becomes an element of the design. Burberry's distinctive plaid is trademarked, for example, and many Burberry products incorporate it into the design.

For this rare category of goods, the logo is part of the design, and as a result trademark law provides significant protection against design copying. But for the vast majority of apparel goods, the trademarks are either inside the garment or subtly displayed on small portions such as buttons. For these garments, trademark law is not a useful weapon against design copying.

Trademark law also protects "trade dress," a concept designed originally to protect distinctive packaging, but which has also been applied to product design. Like copyright, trade dress is limited to nonfunctional design elements.[21] Additionally, the design must signify the garment's *source or producer* to the consumer. [22] In other words, the trade dress must essentially function as a label. When a consumer sees the design, she must recognize it as the work of a particular producer.

As the Supreme Court has acknowledged, this rarely happens. In a case involving knockoffs of children's clothing, the Court said that product design "almost invariably serves purposes other than source identification."[23] As a result, a designer seeking trade dress protection must show that, "in the minds of the public, the *primary significance* of a product feature . . . is to identify the source of the product rather than the product itself."[24] Implicit in this approach is the idea that customers may admire a design, but they rarely link designs with particular brands. It is certainly possible that consumers may link some truly iconic designs with brands. For example, savvy consumers might associate with Chanel a group of trade dress elements consisting of contrasting-color braided piping along the lapels of a collarless, four-pocket woman's jacket. But few apparel design elements are likely to meet such an exacting standard.

The bottom line is that American intellectual property law presents a mixed bag for the fashion industry. Trademark is very significant, and many apparel makers work mightly to capitalize on their brands and cultivate an image of desirability. Patent counts for little outside of the important, but limited, world of accessories (and even there is used infrequently). Trade dress is mostly irrelevant. Copyright *could* be very relevant, but under existing law it simply does not apply to clothing, absent a few minor exceptions such as fabric design and appliqués. The result is a world of powerful and valuable fashion brands, but very extensive—and perfectly legal—copying of fashion designs.

Restraining Copying: The Fashion Originators' Guild of the 1930s

Proposals to amend American law to protect garment designs against copying are nearly as old as the American fashion industry. Writing in 1934, a federal judge in New York noted the prevalence of copying but stated that he could do nothing about it, because although "in recent years bills have been introduced in the Congress to amend the copyright statutes" to include apparel, none of the bills had yet passed.[25]

That same year, British economist Arnold Plant described in detail how copying worked in Europe—and what its effects were:

The leading twenty firms in the *haute couture* of Paris take elaborate precautions twice each year to prevent piracy; but most respectable "houses" throughout the world are quick in the market with their copies (not all made from a purchased original), and "Berwick Street" follows hot on their heels with copies a stage farther removed. And yet the Paris creators can and do secure special prices for their authentic reproductions of the original—for their "signed artist's copies," as it were.[26]

The British certainly had no monopoly on copying. During the 1930s and 1940s, American firms also copied designs widely, and some of the more upstanding ones paid a fee to Paris houses like Balenciaga and Dior that entitled them to send their best sketchers to France to copy original looks for manufacture back at home.[27]

It was against this backdrop that, in the 1930s, the burgeoning American apparel industry established an unusual cartel to limit copying, at least among their compatriots. The "Fashion Originators' Guild of America" registered American designers and their sketches and urged major retailers to boycott anyone known to have copied a registered design. Participants signed a "declaration of cooperation" in which they pledged not to deal in garments copied from American designers.[28] Guild members were left free, however, to knock off foreign designs.

To police this system, the Guild employed some 40 investigators to discreetly browse in member stores and ensure that the clothing for sale complied with the rules. Any store that defied the cartel was subject to "red-carding": its name was distributed to all the participating manufacturers, who in turn would refuse to fill its orders. Those who violated the boycott faced Guild-imposed fines.

The Fashion Originators' Guild was fairly effective at limiting copying among its members. And its membership was substantial. By 1936, over 60% of women's garments sold in the United States for more than $10.75 (approximately $177 in 2012 dollars) were sold by Guild-affiliated firms.[29] In all, nearly 12,000 retailers across the nation signed the Guild's cooperation agreements. The Guild, in short, made a difference in the market.

As with most cartels, however, the Guild faced internal conflict. Much of it turned on the differing interests of retailers and designers. The retailers wanted to sell as much clothing as possible, and, but for the threat of a boycott, would prefer to carry knockoffs in addition to original designs. So the retailers chafed against the cartel's rules. A signature example of this conflict—and one that ultimately led to the downfall of the Guild—is the lawsuit brought against the Guild by Wm. Filene's Sons Co., progenitor of the famous (and recently bankrupted) Filene's Basement chain of stores.

At the root of Filene's lawsuit was a disagreement over the scope of the cartel's rules. The conflict was sparked by what some retailers saw as "high-handed abuse of the Guild's position." As a contemporaneous story in *Time Magazine* colorfully recounted the events, the dispute began with a single incident in 1936: "one day last month at Strawbridge & Clothier, a swank Philadelphia department store, a Guild investigator became quietly uppish." The investigator demanded that "a certain dress, in her opinion a copy, be removed from the floor and that she be told the name of the manufacturer."[30] Strawbridge & Clothier's management refused, believing that they maintained the right to determine what was and what was not a copy.

Two days later, the store was served with notice that it had violated Guild rules and that it was now subject to a boycott. Within a few days the same had happened at Bloomingdale's in Manhattan and at R. H. White in Boston, a Filene's-owned department store. All three red-carded emporiums were members of the Associated Merchandising Corp., a buying coopera-tive. Soon, 16 out of 20 Associated Merchandising Corp. members had been red-carded. The Filene's suit against the Guild, charging a conspiracy in restraint of trade that violated American antitrust law, was a counterpunch.

"Five years ago the possibility of a group of dress manufacturers being powerful enough to draw fire on grounds of monopoly seemed so remote as to be funny," wrote *Time*. The garment industry in the 1930's was a "hodge-podge of feverishly busy small houses" competing intensely. "Dirty tricks" were ubiquitous. And aside from the prices, *Time's* description of copying could have been written last week:

> Among such tricks was the universal and highly developed practice of copying original styles. By the early Depression years it had gone so far that no exclusive model was sure to remain exclusive 24 hours; a dress exhibited in the morning at $60 would be duplicated at $25 before sunset and at lower prices later in the week. Sketching services made a business of it; delivery boys were bribed on their way to retailers.[31]

The Guild's purpose was to squelch this sort of behavior, though in its early years it concentrated solely on higher priced dresses (largely those wholesal-ing for more than $16.75—about $275 in 2012 dollars). The Filene's suit stemmed from the Guild's decision to start clamping down on copying of cheaper garments as well. As *Time* noted, high and low priced garments were seen by many industry insiders as different markets, with different rules. "It was one thing to guard against copies in expensive lines," wrote *Time*, "and another thing to give the same attention to lower-priced dresses, which are bought in greater quantities and sold to people who cared not at all whether they were copies or not. The retailers did not like the prospect of competing in these lines under Guild restrictions with the chain stores," which were not party to the Guild system.

In a narrow sense, the Filene's lawsuit against the Guild failed; a federal court held that the Guild's actions were legal. But the Guild won the battle only to lose the war. The Federal Trade Commission, which is tasked with protecting consumers from unscrupulous sellers, took notice of the suit. Agreeing with Filene's, the FTC decreed that the Guild was operating an illegal cartel and suppressing competition. In its defense, the Guild pointed to the difficulties of eradicating copying in the apparel industry. Its practices, the Guild's lawyers argued, "were reasonable and necessary to protect the manufacturer, laborer, retailer, and consumer against the devastating evils growing from the pirating of original designs and had in fact benefited all four."[32]

The Guild's view was rejected by the Supreme Court. In its 1941 decision in *Fashion Originators' Guild of America v. FTC*,[33] the Court acknowledged that rampant piracy might be a fact of life in the fashion world. However it did not give manufacturers a license to violate antitrust law and collude against competition. With that decision, the Guild was abruptly out of business.

The demise of the Guild did nothing, of course, to address the underlying issue of copying. But if the former Guild members could no longer organize a private cartel to stop copyists, perhaps they could have Congress do the work for them. Amending American law to protect fashion designs soon reemerged as a cause of some designers, just as it had been in the 1920s and early 1930s, before the Guild was organized. In the wake of the Supreme Court's decision, Maurice Rentner, the former head of the Guild, devoted himself to lobbying Congress to extend copyright protection to fashion designs. Unless Congress acted, he warned, resurgent fashion piracy following the fall of the Guild would "write *finis*" to the dress industry. Rentner urged Congress to adopt the French system of protecting garment design.

Others in the industry were less sure. Leon Bendel Schmulen, of New York's famous Henri Bendel department store, told the *New York Times* that design copying posed "no danger to the business" and was instead "a natural consequence of fashion." "By the time a design of ours is copied in the cheaper dress lines," said Bendel, "it's probably time for it to go."[34]

Leon Bendel and Maurice Rentner represent polar, and enduring, views in the long American debate over apparel and copying. Bendel believed that design copying was not only inevitable but perhaps even an essential part of the ecology of fashion. As he suggested, a design that was widely copied was a signal to start over and sell something new, and of course one made money by selling new things. This view has a distinguished pedigree in fashion; no less a figure than Coco Chanel claimed that "being copied is the ransom of success."[35] Maurice Rentner, on the other hand, saw copying as a serious threat that would eventually drive the industry under. Without protection, how could designers afford to keep designing? This view too had a distinguished pedigree, for it was the basis of the entire apparatus of copyright law in America (and much of the world) and it possessed an impeccable-seeming logic.

Nontheless, Bendel's view prevailed. Rentner's efforts to convince Congress to adopt French-style copyright protection for fashion went nowhere, despite his prediction that 500,000 American garment employees would lose their jobs due to piracy. And subsequent events belied Rentner's doomsaying. In the decades after the fall of the Fashion Originator's Guild, the US apparel industry boomed. Moreover, while in recent decades manufacturing has largely moved overseas in search of cheaper labor—leading to the decline of the manufacturing segment of New York's Garment District—American designers are more numerous and more successful than ever. Since the fall of the Guild, in other words, the American apparel industry has survived and even thrived despite widespread—and entirely legal—copying.

THE COPYING DEBATE TODAY

Copying has remained an issue of enduring interest within the fashion industry, even as the Guild and its red cards are a distant memory. In particular, the meteoric rise of fast fashion retailing in recent years has led to the renewal of the arguments first pressed by Maurice Rentner in the 1940s to amend American law to protect garment designs from copying.

These new calls for reform have arisen against a changed backdrop of American copyright law. In particular, over the past half-century, the strength and scope of restrictions on copying have markedly increased. Since Rentner's unsuccessful efforts, Congress has expanded rules against copying in a wide variety of areas, ranging from buildings to boat hulls. Congress has also expanded the breadth of rights granted to copyright owners. And Congress has expanded the length of copyright protection. In 1976, and again in 1998, the term of protection was markedly increased.[36] Adding force to these measures was a more powerful rhetoric of property rights, which increasingly characterized copyright (as well as trademark and patent) not as the regrettable-but-necessary government interventions into the free market they once were thought to be, but instead as a sacrosanct species of property that ought to be staunchly defended—not balanced against the value of wide public access to creative works, or other economic and social concerns.[37]

Against this backdrop, in 2006 the Design Piracy Prohibition Act (DPPA) was introduced in Congress. The DPPA was championed by the New York–based Council of Fashion Designers of America, and, in particular, by the group's president, wrap-dress impresario Diane von Furstenburg. The group pursued the reliably counterproductive approach, at least as far as the US Congress is concerned, of appealing—as had Rentner himself decades earlier—to the example of France. Proponents argued that because France and many other nations afforded copyright protection to apparel designs, the United States ought to as well, lest it lose out in the global fashion competition.[38]

Despite a determined lobbying campaign, the DPPA went nowhere. A revised version, now titled the Innovative Design Protection and Piracy Prevention Act (IDPPPA), was introduced in 2009. Representative Bill Delahunt of Massachusetts introduced the bill with this dire—and familiar—prediction: "One of our most vibrant industries—the fashion industry—is currently at risk because the copyright laws of the United States, unlike virtually all other industrialized countries, fail to protect fashion designs."[39] Updating Maurice Rentner's now six-decade-old prediction of catastrophic job losses (Rentner had predicted 500,000), Delahunt declared that 750,000 jobs were at stake due to design piracy, and that the proposed law would, in his words, promote and protect the nation's entrepreneurs "by ensuring a just and fair marketplace at home, and a level playing field abroad."*

As this book goes to press in 2012, the IDPPPA has failed to come to a vote in Congress, and its future is uncertain. But if it passes, it will mark a sea change in American law. For over 200 years the United States has treated fashion design as an unprotected form of creativity, there for the taking by any entrepreneurial passerby.

THE WORLD OF KNOCKOFFS

As our brief history of American apparel suggests, knockoffs have long been ubiquitous in the fashion world, and whether you're paging through Marie Claire's *Splurge vs. Steal*, perusing the newest Zara "lookbook," browsing the Web site of knockoff specialist Allen B. Schwartz (whose own biography states that he is "revered and applauded for the extraordinary job he does of bringing runway trends to the sales racks in record time"),[40] or just wandering around the mall, the point is clear: knockoffs are everywhere. Some are more fairly called derivative works—that is, designs that are inspired by the original, but which add some new creative elements. Others are really "point by point" (that is, exact) copies. All are easy to find.

If the ordinary rules of copyright law were applied to fashion, nearly all knockoffs would be illegal, and the guilty copyist would face substantial fines and penalties—including, in some cases, the possibility of jail time. Indeed, the practice of copying within the garment industry is so widespread that "normalizing" fashion within the regular copyright system (combined with America's lawsuit-friendly system and plentiful and entrepreneurial lawyers) would probably result in a staggering array of lawsuits, fines, and injunctions—which is why even strong proponents of amending American law acknowledge that fashion needs its own special and much more permissive rules.

---

* In touting the bill, neither the sponsors in Congress nor Steven Kolb, the head of the CFDA, denied that the American fashion industry was in great shape. In the press release trumpeting the act's introduction, Representative Goodlatte noted that "America's fashion design industry continues to grow." Likewise, Kolb declared that the United States was "the world leader in fashion" and nation's fashion industry was "growing steadily and adding jobs to our domestic workforce."

Two other points are worth noting about knockoffs. First, not all copying involves an entire garment. In many cases only a feature of a design is copied, and that feature may become part of that season's set of trends. Often these features are familiar, recycled elements that under no imaginable legal system would be protected: cap sleeves, kitten heels, peaked lapels, or an empire waist. But sometimes the feature is new—or newer—like the many mink, fox, rabbit, and raccoon stoles dyed in psychedelic colors that designers were showing for Fall 2011. Either way, it is the widespread copying of such features that often gives rise to (or evidences) a trend. Even the clichéd rise and fall of hemlines can be thought of this way.

This distinction between design feature and overall design is important, since many of the examples used in the debate over copying are really examples of overall designs copied more or less accurately. The Foley & Corinna/Forever 21 spat is a good example of this. But point-by-point copies like these, although they grab a lot of attention, are only a small part of the copying that goes on in the fashion industry. The relative amounts are hard to measure. But it is unquestionable that a large share of copying in the fashion industry involves design features, not the total design. The result is a range of garments that copy that feature in order to follow a trend, but which, unlike point-by-point copies, are easily recognized as different items.

Copying varies in scope but also in time. Some copying occurs in the same year or season that the original garment appears.[41] At times copying may even occur *before* the original arrives in stores.[*] Other copying occurs with a pronounced lag, and indeed this kind of copying is so common it is hardly noticed. Think of how often a style from a decade or two ago reemerges, usually slightly tweaked, on the runways in Paris or New York.

Viewed from the perspective of creative industries such as the music or motion picture industries, the ubiquity of copying in fashion is more than surprising. In these industries, every type of copying that is widespread in the fashion world is condemned as illegal piracy, and combating piracy is a

---

[*] Those concerned about copying have been making this claim since America was enduring Prohibition, and while it may have some degree of truth, we doubt it is pervasive or systematic—if for no other reason than that a truly accurate ability to predict what fashions will sell in advance would be a remarkable skill coveted by any buyer for a large department store or chain. Indeed, anyone who possessed this preternatural ability would likely earn more money picking the eventual fashion winners and selling them than actually doing the work of making copies themselves.

principal concern. This is clear to anyone who has followed the music industry's battle against online filesharing.

By contrast, the freedom to copy apparel designs—sometimes euphemistically referred to as "referencing" or "homage"—has long been taken for granted. Indeed, it is often accepted, and sometimes even celebrated, by a surprisingly large swath of the fashion world. Some designers are fatalistic: Alber Elbaz of Lanvin recently declared that "I don't care if people copy me," though he quickly added, alluding perhaps to the power of copying to inspire new creativity "well, I do care. For me, I create prototypes. They can copy yesterday but they can't copy tomorrow." Others view copying as a badge of honor. Tom Ford has said that "Nothing made me happier than to see something that I had done copied."[42] Prada CEO Patricio Bertelli was even blunter: "I would be more worried if my product *wasn't* copied." [43]

Not everyone agrees, of course. The fashion copying debate is often depicted as one that pits great artists (read: fashion press favorites) against sneaky pirates (read: Forever 21 and fly-by-night knockoff artists). But that's not a fully accurate picture. Famed designers don't just acquiesce in copying; they sometimes engage in it. In 2002, for example, Nicholas Ghesquiere, a heralded young designer for Balenciaga, admitted to copying point-by-point a vest originated some three decades earlier by a largely forgotten American designer named Kaisik Wong. As Cathy Horyn, the *New York Times* fashion critic, opined, this kind of incident was more commonplace than many realized:

> Were it not for Mr. Ghesquiere's fame and Mr. Wong's obscurity—were it not, indeed, for the recent examples of plagiarism in publishing and the continuing debate in the music and art worlds about sampling and ownership—this latest instance of copying might not merit special attention. After all, copying is part of the history of fashion. . . . Today, under the postmodern rubric of "referencing," copying flourishes so openly that nobody bothers to question it. And the practice isn't confined to the low end of the business, to knockoff kings like Allen B. Schwartz of ABS and Victor Costa. Tom Ford, Marc Jacobs and Miuccia Prada have all dipped into other designers' wells.[44]

None of this gainsays the fact that designers sometimes bridle when they believe they have been knocked off a bit too blatantly. Certainly Dana Foley and Anna Corinna did. On rare occasions, designers even sue one another. In 1994 Yves Saint Laurent sued Ralph Lauren in a French commercial court for copying a YSL design.[45] Saint Laurent's successful lawsuit took place in Europe, where copyright laws are, as Maurice Rentner long ago pointed out, far more protective of fashion designs. (And of course, the revered French designer prevailed and the parvenu American lost—a result Ralph Lauren later called "totally ludicrous").[46]

Whatever the rules in France, however, in the United States the law is different. Fashion designs are, for better or for worse, "free as the air to common use."[47]

The Piracy Paradox

To appreciate how striking the phenomenon of fashion copying is, think back again to the monopoly theory of innovation. The monopoly theory holds that copying is a grave threat to creativity. If a creator knows her creation will be freely copied by others, she will not invest in creation in the first place. Legal rights that give the creator a monopoly over who can make a copy are, consequently, essential. How then does the fashion industry remain so creative despite such extensive copying?

The answer turns on the unusual economics of fashion, and draws on a tradition of thinking about fashion that goes back at least to Thorstein Veblen's landmark work of social criticism, *Theory of the Leisure Class*.[48] For Veblen, much of social life turned on status, and the ways that many of us try to achieve and signal status to one other.

Status is certainly central to fashion. And in fashion, status can be signaled by expensive labels and materials. But it is also signaled by trends—specifically, by being on the leading edge of, rather than a late-comer to, a hot trend. Thinking about fashion as an industry driven by trends, and by people trying to acquire or keep status by discovering the new trends and discarding the old, can help explain why imitation in fashion is not especially harmful to innovation. Indeed, as we will explain, free and easy copying benefits the fashion industry more than it harms it.

The Fashion Cycle

People buy clothing for many reasons. The most basic is entirely practical—to cover our bodies and to stay warm. But of course even the simplest clothing can do that. So why will a woman spend thousands of dollars on a Balenciaga cocktail dress? Why will a man shell out thousands of dollars for a Thom Browne suit? These sorts of purchases are driven by the desire for expression and status.* Clothing is very personal, and it sends signals about the wearer, whether intended or not. Those signals are socially complex and context-dependent—in Los Angeles, the guy at the valet stand parking the Aston Martin is often wearing a tie, and the studio mogul who owns it a baseball cap. But the signaling features of clothing are omnipresent.

Put in economic terms, most kinds of clothing function as "positional goods." The *Economist* magazine helpfully defines positional goods as

> things that the Joneses buy. Some things are bought for their intrinsic usefulness, for instance, a hammer or a washing machine. Positional goods are bought because of what they say about the person who buys them. They are a way for a person to establish or signal their status relative to people who do not own them: fast cars, holidays in the most fashionable resorts, clothes from trendy designers.[49]

Positional goods purchases, in other words, are made based largely on the status the good is expected to convey. As a result, these purchases are interdependent. What we buy is partially a function of what others buy. Like parimutuel betting at the racetrack, the status payoff depends on the actions of others, actions that are not entirely predictable at the time of purchase. Fashion's positional nature is very powerful, and a consumer's attraction to a new design is often triggered not just by beauty or fit, but also by the status associations created by the producer's trademark, by stylish advertising, by seeing the garment worn by a famous actress or model, by a clotheshorse acquaintance, or even by a stylish stranger on the street.

The positionality of a fashion good is often two-sided, however. A trendy new design is most coveted when enough people possess it to signal that it

---

* The use of clothing to signal status is ancient; in her exploration of the luxury goods industry, *Deluxe: How Luxury Lost Its Luster*, Dana Thomas quotes an antiquities expert at the Getty Museum in Los Angeles who asserts that debates over status-signaling via apparel date back almost 3,000 years. The many "sumptuary codes" that once limited rights to wear certain clothing to members of particular professions or social classes are one manifestation of this long-standing concern.

is desired, but its value diminishes if every person on the street owns it. Nothing about the design itself has changed, except for its ability to distinguish its owner from the crowd. For fashion goods, in short, exclusivity is a large part of the appeal.[50]

Perceptions of beauty matter, of course. But these perceptions are not wholly divorced from perceptions of exclusivity. As Jean Cocteau astutely noted some 50 years ago, "Art produces ugly things which frequently become more beautiful with time. Fashion, on the other hand, produces beautiful things which always become ugly with time."[51] In short, consumers are drawn to a particular dress from Lanvin or a men's jacket from John Varvatos in part because stylish people have it and unstylish ones do not. The dress or the jacket will be coveted so long as it enables its wearer to stand out from the masses but fit in with his or her particular crowd. Many historical and sociological studies of fashion argue that this distinguishing quality is central. Fashion is "a vehicle which marks distinctions and displays group membership or individuality."[52] Consequently, as fashionable styles diffuse to a broader clientele their prestige diminishes. The style in question becomes unstylish, and eventually fades away.

This is the fashion cycle. New designs catch on, become trends, spread, become overexposed, and die. And then a new design appears, a new trend ignites, and the process repeats.

Fashion never stops, but it never goes anywhere either. Whether the fashion cycle is a good thing or a bad thing in its own right is an interesting question, but not the focus of our story here. It is fair to say, however, that fashion is routinely pilloried by intellectuals who view it as capricious, exclusionary, and socially wasteful. The rapid rise and fall of trends has been called "a symptom of intellectual, emotional, and cultural immaturity."[53] French cultural critic Jean Baudrillard went so far as to declare fashion "immoral."[54] Other commentators, however, have celebrated fashion designers as artists on par with any painter or composer. Indeed, this is one of the arguments used by advocates of copyright protection—that fashion ought to be treated like other great art forms.

For most of us, though, the fashion cycle is not a subject of great debate. It is just a fact of life; perhaps even an entertaining one that allows us to enjoy new clothes and occasionally scratch our heads at old photographs. Whatever its social meaning or ethical value, the fashion cycle is clearly a central feature of the apparel industry. Styles come and then they go. Soon after, many of us wonder what we were thinking.

An example of this ascent and descent is the Ugg, a sheepskin boot originating in Australia. Uggs, which date back to the 1930s, had sold steadily for years but became a must-have fashion item for many young women in 2003 and 2004. The style was then widely copied and gained broad distribution.[55] But soon a backlash began, with writers calling the shapeless and fuzzy Ugg a "human rights violation" and urging the fashion-conscious to give them up.[56] By 2005, the Ugg trend was, at least in some quarters, declared to be over.

In a 2006 *New Yorker* article about Los Angeles, writer Tad Friend described a telling story of the rise and fall of the Ugg. A local news helicopter was searching for actress Lindsay Lohan following a minor car crash on Robertson Boulevard, in which she was involved. The news dispatcher, Beth Shilliday, radios the chopper pilot:

"I know it's a long shot, but check the street for a skinny, movie-star looking woman. Channel 2 says she and her assistant ran into an antiques store across the way." [The pilot] panned down Robertson toward the Ivy [a West Hollywood bistro frequented by the L.A. celebrities]. "Problem is, every girl on the street kind of fits the profile. How's this?" He zoomed in on a Lohanish figure in dark glasses. "She's wearing Uggs," Shilliday pointed out. "Those are so last year, couldn't be her."[57]

One might quibble with the details of when (and, for diehard Uggs fans, even if) Uggs lost their cool.* Nonetheless, Uggs illustrate a basic point about fashion: the ruthless nature of the fashion cycle. In the fashion world, success can lead to the rapid diffusion of a design. But rapid diffusion typically dooms a design to decline and ultimately to death. Debut, diffusion, decline, death: that is the fashion cycle in a nutshell.

---

* Indeed, against all odds Uggs have appeared in some fashion-driven stores. In 2010 the window of Fred Segal on Melrose Blvd, ground zero for many fashion-conscious shoppers in Los Angeles (and less than a mile from the Robertson Boulevard site of the Lohan car crash), featured a large painted sign trumpeting the arrival of new styles of Uggs.

Induced Obsolescence

That styles rise and fall is of course not a new observation. Before Cocteau wrote his wonderful apercu about fashion and beauty, sociologist Georg Simmel noted the same process: "As fashion spreads, it gradually goes to its doom. The distinctiveness which in the early stages of a set fashion assures for it a certain distribution is destroyed as the fashion spreads, and as this element wanes, the fashion also is bound to die."[58] Even earlier than this, Shakespeare declared in *Much Ado About Nothing* that "the fashion wears out more apparel than the man."

What Cocteau, Simmel, and Shakespeare noticed was not merely the rise and fall of apparel designs. Instead, they highlighted the fact that *the rise actually led to the fall.* The fall was not merely inevitable, in the sense of a ball thrown into the air that gradually succumbs to gravity. They drew a causal connection: as fashion spreads, its distinctiveness is destroyed. That in turn destroys much of its value.

Of course, not everyone seeks distinctiveness in fashion. Just look at America's political class: for the men, an orange or purple tie is a mark of outright zaniness, and the women largely hew to pantsuits that look more like armor than fashion. But for the class of fashion early adopters, things are different. These early adopters seek to stand out, whereas the next tier of buyers seeks to "flock" to the trend.[59] As the flockers flock, the early adopters flee.

Again, the basics of the fashion cycle are well known. What has not been appreciated, however, is the crucial way that the fashion cycle interacts with the freedom to copy. *Legal rules that permit copying accelerate the diffusion of styles.* More rapid diffusion, in turn, leads to more rapid decline. And the more rapid the decline, the faster and more intense is the appetite for new designs. As they are copied, these new designs in turn spark the creation of new trends—and, as a consequence, new sales.

Copying, in short, is the fuel that drives the fashion cycle faster. It is essential to both the trend-making and trend-destruction processes. Copying speeds up the creative process, spurring designers to create anew in an effort to stay ahead of the fashion curve. This makes copying paradoxically valuable.

Copying also functions, in the fashion context, as a stand-in for something that many other creative industries depend on—improvements to their products. Cell phones clearly get more powerful and useful over time, leading us to discard our perfectly good old phones for the amazing new ones. Clothes, by contrast, do not improve in any clearly defined way. Garment makers rarely can tout the great new features of their products as improvements—and indeed in practice, unlike cell phone makers, they do not claim this season's offerings are qualitatively better than last season's.[60] For the most part, clothes just change, and that change is what drives buyers to the stores. In this environment, the rise of a new trend is the functional equivalent of a great new feature on a cell phone: the thing that makes a consumer discard a perfectly useful item and go out and buy something new.[61]

We call this process *induced obsolescence*—that is, obsolescence induced by copying. A design is launched and, for some reason that few can predict (or even explain), it becomes desirable. Early adopters begin to wear it and fashion magazines and blogs write of it glowingly. Other firms observe its growing success and seek to ape it, often at lower price points. As the now-hot design is copied and tweaked, it becomes far more widely purchased and hence even more visible. For a time, the trend grows. Past a certain point, however, the process reverses course. The once-coveted item becomes anathema to the fashion-conscious, and, eventually, to those who are somewhat less style-focused. The early adopters move on, and the process begins again.

The key point is that fast and free copying is fully legal—and the widespread copying that flows from this rule induces more rapid obsolescence of designs. Obsolescence would probably happen anyway, eventually. But the fashion cycle is driven *faster* by widespread and legal copying, because copying more rapidly erodes the positional qualities of fashion goods. The result has profound effects on the apparel industry. Piracy paradoxically benefits designers by inducing more rapid turnover and greater sales—a process we call the "piracy paradox."

If we drill down a little deeper, we can understand the role of copying in this story in at least two broad ways. First, copying allows the marketing of less expensive versions, pricing-in consumers who otherwise would not be able to afford to purchase the design. A middle-class woman might be able to put a Louis Vuitton handbag on her credit card occasionally, but absent extraordinary measures (or very sticky fingers) it cannot be done regularly. Copying permits the design to spread to lower income consumers, who are far more plentiful than the top income tier of consumers to whom the most exclusive fashion goods are marketed.

Second, copying facilitates variations on an attractive design—what lawyers refer to as "derivative works." These are garments that use the original design, but tweak it in some new way. Under standard copyright law, the originator has the exclusive right to make or authorize derivative works. The legal rule for fashion is the opposite, and the many variations on a theme this makes possible means that the stores will be full of countless versions of a popular design.

As we mentioned earlier, sometimes only a particular feature of a garment is copied—a certain sleeve or cut—and sometimes the entire garment is copied. And what is copied is not necessarily part of a hot trend. Consider the Foley + Corinna story that opened this chapter. The dress in question was striking and somewhat popular, but it was not the Must-Have-Item of the season. Still, the basic dynamic we describe applies. The Forever 21 version surely sold at levels that Dana Foley and Anna Corinna could only dream of. The Foley + Corinna customers, many of whom trekked to the Lower East Side for their dress, were not wild about seeing that dress in shopping malls across the suburbs and on the backs of thousands of more women.[62] So they decamped for a new design or new trend earlier than they would have absent the copying.

The key point remains the same: existing rules, by permitting this kind of copying, act as a kind of turbocharger to the fashion cycle. And that spurs designers to create anew so as to ride the next wave of trends.

There is, of course, a downside to all this. While induced obsolescence generally helps the industry sell more goods over time, widespread copying can and does harm particular originators in particular cases. Certainly that is the view of Dana Foley and Anna Corinna. But the effect of a system of free and easy copying, across the fashion industry and over time, is beneficial. Because this effect is spread out over many products, it is less noticeable than the losses suffered by individual designers. But in the aggregate, it is much more significant. It creates more demand, and therefore more designs and more sales.

We now have some more precise and targeted data to back this observation up. We recently spent a few months working (with the help of our crack research assistant, Charlie Murry) at the US Bureau of Labor Statistics (BLS) in Washington, DC.[*] The BLS is the federal agency that, among other things, assembles the official measure of US inflation. To do this, BLS employees collect price data every month on millions of goods and services.

---

[*] This research was conducted with restricted access to BLS data. The views expressed here are our own and do not necessarily reflect the views of the BLS.

Among the data they collect are many thousands of apparel prices. We looked at these data to see if the changes over time in the prices of apparel suggest any significant effect on elite designers from the knockoffs that often imitate high-end looks at lower prices.

To do this, we collected data on the prices of women's dresses from 1998 to the present. We then divided the dresses in this dataset into 10 categories, or deciles, ranging from the cheapest 10% of women's dresses, such as the stuff on the racks at Walmart, to the most expensive 10%, such as Prouenza Schouler's latest design.[63] Now, take a look at the graph.

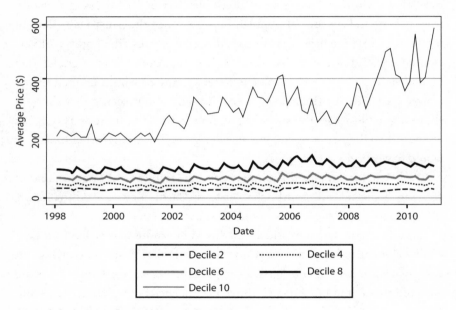

FIGURE 1.1 Average Prices-Women's Dresses.

What you see is price stability over the entire period for every decile pictured—except for one—the top decile—that is, the most expensive women's dresses. What happened there? The average price of the most expensive 10% of women's dresses went up, substantially. The top decile of dresses increased in price by over 250%. Even adjusted for inflation, the prices of the top-end dresses still almost doubled. But everything else either stood still, or even got a bit more affordable (adjusted for inflation).

So what does this mean? Virtually all knockoffs are cheaper than the high-end garments they imitate. And if a substantial number of consumers who would have purchased the original bought the knockoff instead, we would expect to see that competition have an effect on the prices of those high-end garments. In short, competition from knockoffs ought to depress the prices of originals, just as greater supply generally lowers prices. But that doesn't appear to be the case in fashion. The high-end items are the only ones that have any price growth during the period—and the price growth of this segment is very healthy indeed.

The official federal data on prices, in other words, is consistent with what the piracy paradox predicts. Over the long term, knockoffs do not harm the industry as a whole. Rather, knockoffs are actually a key part of the industry's success. More copies mean a faster fashion cycle; a faster cycle means more designs and more sales. Debut, diffusion, decline, death—and then it starts over again.

Anchoring

The legal freedom to copy not only induces a faster fashion cycle; it also helps consumers figure out how to stay in style. In economic terms, copying lowers consumers' information costs. It does this via a process we refer to as *anchoring*. Anchoring, like induced obsolescence, helps the fashion industry remain creative even in the face of extensive copying.

Despite a flood of new designs available at any one time, identifiable trends eventually emerge and define a season's style. What drives these trends is hard to untangle. Trends are not chosen by committee, nor are they simply the accreted musings of god-like designers, as Meryl Streep famously suggested in the "cerulean sweater" scene in *The Devil Wears Prada*.[*] Instead, trends evolve through an undirected process of copying, referencing, and

---

[*] In the film, Meryl Streep's character (reportedly an approximation of long-time Vogue editor and fashion industry kingmaker Anna Wintour) berates the fashion magazine intern played by Anne Hathaway for her lack of respect for the industry's hidden influence over her style choices: "You go to your closet and you select . . . I don't know . . . that lumpy blue sweater, for instance, because you're trying to tell the world that you take yourself too seriously to care about what you put on your back. But what you don't know is that that sweater is not just blue. It's not turquoise. It's not lapis. It's actually cerulean. And you're also blithely unaware of the fact that in 2002, Oscar de la Renta did a collection of cerulean gowns. And then I think it was Yves Saint Laurent . . . wasn't it?, who showed cerulean military jackets? . . . And then cerulean quickly showed up in the collections of eight different designers. And then it, uh, filtered down through the department stores and then trickled on down into some tragic Casual Corner where you, no doubt, fished it out of some clearance bin. However, that blue represents millions of dollars and countless jobs and it's sort of comical how you think that you've made a choice that exempts you from the fashion industry when, in fact, you're wearing the sweater that was selected for you by the people in this room from a pile of stuff."

reworking, coupled to communication with key retailers and commentary in the press. Insiders often talk of the convergence of designs as a reflection of the *zeitgeist*. Like a school of fish moving first this way and then that, designers follow the lead of other designers and tastemakers in a process that, while bewildering at times, results in the emergence of particular trends—as a quick look through any fashion magazine or blog will make clear.

We wouldn't perceive fashion change nearly as well without fashion trends. And every hot trend, almost by definition, involves some copying. A trend is a series of things that look alike and that are widely sold in the marketplace. Unless many designers magically arrive at the same design or theme simultaneously, this necessarily must involve copying. In this way copying is essential to fashion. As one astute early observer noted, "If there were not imitation there could be no fashion."[64] Just as copying is necessary to a trend's birth, however, it is also a predicate to its death. Copying first makes the trend, and then makes the trend obsolete.

Copying creates trends by anchoring the new season to a limited number of themes—themes that are freely workable by all producers. For trendy consumers to follow trends, they need to be able to identify them. Anchoring thus encourages buying by conveying to consumers important information about the season's dominant looks.

Again, we can't explain the sudden emergence of a trend—if we could, we would have stopped writing this book and gone to work in New York or Milan. But somehow, trends emerge; firms copy from one another, spin out variations, and diffuse them widely. The result anchors a season's innovation around a small set of designs, and this helps drive consumption by defining, in a literal sense, what is and is not in style that season. We also see this process at work within a large adjunct to the fashion industry—magazines such as *Glamour* and *Vogue*, television shows such as *What Not to Wear*, and fashion blogs of various stripes, all of which (to differing degrees) provide fashion advice to consumers. These proclamations do not always take root, but they are a constant.

In the fall of 2005, for example, the *New York Times* described the appearance of a large number of women's boot designs. The article highlights the unusual existence of *multiple* designs at once:

> There are 60s styles a la Nancy Sinatra; 70s styles a la Stevie Nicks; 80s styles a la Gloria Estefan; and 90s styles a la Shirley Manson. It is a puzzling

sight for fashion seers used to declaring that one style of boot—Midcalf! Thigh high!—is The One for Fall.[65]

The writer's expectation—which the style promiscuity of 2005 violated—is that the industry will anchor narrowly. And it usually does.

This is not to say that the styles produced by closely watched designers always resonate with consumers, or with retailers that must make decisions about purchases well before the clothes hit the racks. But it is undeniable that particular designs are identified as anchoring trends—"Midcalf boots are The One for Fall"—and that these trends wax and wane, only to be replaced by the next set of themes.

To summarize, copying plays two central but counterintuitive roles in fashion. By allowing others to imitate and rework successful designs, copying acts like a turbocharger that spins the fashion cycle faster. Designs quickly go up, and then even more quickly they come down. We call this induced obsolescence, and this process forces designers to innovate anew. Apparel designs don't become obsolete because a "better" design comes along. They become obsolete because they become too popular. Copying also wraps the incredibly varied output of the fashion world around a few key trends—and it is through the emergence of trends that most of us understand what to wear that season or year. We call this process anchoring.

These twin forces have dished up a huge, vibrant, innovative market—with lots of copying. In fashion, the freedom to imitate turns out to be a very powerful economic spur to innovation. Copying helps to kill popular designs and birth new ones. And copying helps to reduce the search costs of style. This is the piracy paradox—and it is the primary way in which fashion reconciles imitation with innovation.

NORMS AND FIRST-MOVER ADVANTAGE

Let's briefly consider some other arguments that might explain why fashion creativity thrives despite copying. The first focuses on the possible effect of social norms, which play an important role in some other industries we explore in this book. Norms have been the subject of a lot of academic research. The impact of social norms in the fashion industry, however, appears to be far more modest compared with other areas we look at later, such as comedy and cuisine. We are skeptical that norms meaningfully influence either the level or type of copying that takes place in the apparel industry.

The second possible argument relates to what economists call "first-mover advantage": the notion that a first mover in a market can reap enough benefits before others move in to compete to make innovation worthwhile. While first-mover advantage appears to have some role to play in fashion, that role is also relatively small. Finally, we take up some possible implications of our arguments about copying's paradoxical effects, in particular the implication that if we are correct, fashion designers ought to sometimes knock off their own designs.

Social Norms

Some creative industries remain innovative in the face of imitation due to the power of social norms. These norms act as extra-legal checks on copying; they keep copying within certain bounds or act to exact costs for copying that goes "too far." Do such norms matter among designers?

At the high end of the fashion world overt copying is sometimes frowned upon. To be derided as overly derivative can derail an ambitious designer's career. A recent analysis of knockoffs argues that the American fashion industry indeed operates in a norm-based system. The norms about copying, it is said, constitute an effective control system which "can render stiff penalties on offenders, such as critical disparagement or neglect from the American fashion media, that can ultimately harm their brand name and their bottom line."[66]

The evidence that norms really constrain copying by fashion designers is, however, pretty thin. As the example we gave earlier about Nicholas Ghesquiere and Kasik Wong illustrates, leading designers do copy. Fashion insiders can name many other examples, both high and low. Of course, the sheer fact that a norm is violated does not mean the norm has no power. And to be sure, Ghesquiere's point-by-point copy of a lesser known (and dead) designer is, as a practical matter, different from copying the work of a living, breathing fashion titan such as Marc Jacobs.

Yet the Ghesquiere affair suggests that norms against copying among the fashion elite are not especially powerful. According to the *New York Times*, Ghesquiere not only spoke candidly about the matter; he also didn't seem embarrassed. "I'm very flattered that people are looking at my sources of inspiration," he said, comparing what he did to the practice of sampling in the music industry. "This is how I work. I've always said I'm looking at vintage clothes." He didn't think the incident would hurt his reputation. "No, I'm known for many things," he said.[67]

Moreover, the *Times* suggested, Ghesquiere was not alone in his optimism that the incident would produce no lasting harm. "Although Julie Gilhart, the fashion director of Barneys New York, expressed astonishment when she saw how similar the two garments were, she said: 'I don't think this diminishes Balenciaga's creativity at all. How many people have copied Yves Saint Laurent? My question is always: Who can do it better? We're all savvy enough to know what's been borrowed and what hasn't.'" [68]

Ghesquiere is just one designer, albeit a well-known one, and so we cannot rest much on this particular vignette. But a look around at the fashion press suggests that he is hardly alone in either his actions or his views. Marc Jacobs has been widely accused of being derivative of the work of John Galliano, Chanel, Martin Margiela, and others. (Jacobs himself offered an interesting defense to this charge: "I'm attentive to what's going on. . . . I have never insisted on my own creativity, as Chanel would say.").[69] In 2008, the design team of Proenza Schouler was criticized for riffing too much on Ghesquiere's work at Balenciaga. Earlier, Calvin Klein was said to rip off Helmut Lang and Giorgio Armani. And so on. Top designers are not infrequently accused of lifting from their rivals. The accusations don't appear to deter them, nor are the copyists held to account by their peers in any way that we can detect.[*]

Interestingly, some designers even see parallels with chefs, whom they perceive as largely reinterpreting the work of others rather than copying. Christian LaCroix opined that "a designer has to at least put his or her own twist on a look." "Inspiration is not enough," he said. "You have to bring your own strength, energy and imagination to push further. It's like cooking. When you cook directly from a book, you just copy a recipe. When you adapt it, adding this spice or that ingredient with your own fantasy or intuition, you make the dish your own creation."[70]

It is inherently difficult to assess the power of social norms, but responses like these make it hard to believe that they play a substantial role in restraining copying—at least aside from point-by-point copying—among leading designers. And of course the sheer fact of extensive and often open copying

---

[*] To all this, Vera Wang offered her own riff on the famous "nobody knows anything" line of Hollywood screenwriter William Goldman: in fashion, she said, "Nothing has never been done before."

is very hard to explain if the norms against copying are strong. For these reasons, we doubt that social norms explain all that much about how fashion designers remain so creative in the face of extensive copying.

First-Mover Advantage

Perhaps fashion designers remain innovative in the face of wide-scale imitation because the benefits that accrue to the "first mover" are large enough to sustain innovation.[71] If a clothing designer can sell enough units before copies begin to flood the market, the return may be sufficient, on average, to make continued innovation profitable.

We think that first-mover advantage does have some effect in fashion. But there is little evidence that it is the center of the story; rather, first-mover advantage appears to add to the incentives that the piracy paradox already provides. What do we mean? If first-mover advantage was the best explanation for the fashion industry's ability to create in the face of copying, designers would need to have an appreciable time gap before copyists moved in—in other words, a gap, perhaps only a couple of months, during which they could sell versions of their designs before copyists got to it. As we noted earlier, however, copying in the industry is very fast. It is often claimed that today copyists are as quick, or maybe even quicker, to market than originators. If true, this casts doubt on the power of first-mover advantage to make a difference in the fortunes of designers, since the copy might come out right after the original—or might even be first to market.

Let's dig a little deeper. There is no good study of the speed of copying, and so it is hard to know the exact length of any first-mover advantage that might exist. Still, it seems plausible, given changes in technology, that copyists are faster today than they were the past. At least, this view is widely held. It is often given as a reason that, whatever the failures of Maurice Rentner in the 1940s to convince Congress to amend American copyright laws to protect fashion, such an amendment is necessary *now*.

Yet there is good reason to be skeptical that copying is much quicker now than it was in the past. Indeed, for a very long time the copying of fashion designs has been easy and fast. Well before Al Gore invented the Internet, ordinary photos combined with a fax machine allowed copyists to begin work within hours of photographing or sketching the original. Even before that, transcontinental air travel allowed designs to be copied in a matter of days, and for designs produced domestically, less than a day. *Time* magazine wrote in 1936 that "by the early Depression years [copying] had gone so far that no exclusive model was sure to remain exclusive 24 hours; a dress exhibited in the morning at $60 would be duplicated at $25 before sunset and at lower prices later in the week."[72]

So very fast copying is actually many decades old. And people have been predicting doom from fast copying for just as long. Back in 1940, a *Harvard Business Review* article about design piracy noted that fashion producers have, "within the past 50 years," been complaining "that modern, high-speed methods of communication" have made copying much quicker and therefore more harmful to originators.[73] If the industry moved that fast during the 1930s and 1940s, the speed of copying has hardly changed meaningfully in the decades since. In fact, even the claim that copyists are beating originators to market, which sounds like an artifact of our whiz-bang Internet-meets-Globalization 21st century world, is old news. Close observers of the industry were sounding the alarm about this alleged peril when Herbert Hoover was just starting his run for the presidency.[74]

In short, claims about the impact of fast copying sound grave and new but have been around a very long time. Fast copying is old hat. And in the intervening (many) decades, the American fashion industry has grown enormously successful. The bottom line is that there doesn't seem to have ever been a golden age of first-mover advantage, in which designers could reap the benefits of originality before copyists swooped in. Given that, it is hard to believe that first-mover advantage explains why copying doesn't kill creativity in fashion.

Nor, by the way, is there much evidence that fast copying causes serious harm to the fashion industry overall. If fast copying is a really serious problem, it is hard to explain the industry's commitment to its runway schedule. A lot of new fashion designs debut in the major spring and fall shows in New York, Paris, Milan, and London. The "spring" shows are actually held the preceding fall. And the "fall" shows the preceding spring. If first-mover advantages were crucial, and rapid copying deadly, we would not expect to see such a significant lag between the runway and retail. The industry would rely more on secrecy and speed to protect first-mover advantage. That the major players do not suggests that first-mover advantage is not the mainspring of innovation incentives for the industry as a whole.

Still, first-mover advantage probably does play some role in the creative success of the apparel industry. But it is more important to *consumers* than to producers. What do we mean?

It may be easy to copy a design quickly, but that doesn't mean the public is going to *buy* quickly. There is a lag as consumers figure out what they like and what is trendy that season. The lag that exists between debut and diffusion allows early adopters to differentiate themselves from the crowd. Fashionistas adopt a new design, and then, in a few cases, it begins to spread. The freedom to copy a design that is becoming hot helps to create a trend and, ultimately, expand the market for that design. For this process to unfold, however, the design must become hot in the first place. And as a practical matter, styles become hot over time, not instantly (and of course most remain very cold). In short, some lag between creation and *widespread* copying almost always exists, and this lag is an essential element of the piracy paradox. But that is not the same as saying the reason fashion designers stay creative in the face of copying is because they have a meaningful first-mover advantage.

In sum, the trick to being a successful fashion copyist isn't just copying. It's copying *winners*. And that almost always requires waiting.

CONCLUSION: SHOULD DESIGNERS KNOCK OFF THEIR OWN DESIGNS?

The paradoxical effects of piracy in fashion have an interesting implication. If free and legal copying propels the fashion cycle forward ever faster, leading to more rapid turnover in styles and more sales, why do individual designers leave the copying to others? In other words, shouldn't designers knock off *their own* designs? The more designs diffuse, after all, the quicker they die—and hence the quicker new designs can debut.

Indeed, some have provocatively suggested that smart firms ought to give away cheaper, visibly inferior versions of their products.[75] We are not aware of anyone who gives away bad versions of their clothes. And there is a good reason. Brand protection—the desire by trademark owners to maintain the exclusivity of their very valuable high-end marks—stops this from occurring in the real world. But we do see a careful version of self-knockoffs: what insiders call "diffusion" or bridge lines.

Diffusion lines are clothes by a famous designer that sell at lower price points under a distinctive but related label. A good example is Marc by Marc

Jacobs—clearly identifiable as something designed (supposedly) by Marc Jacobs, but not the same as the top end Marc Jacobs. To be sure, using a well-respected trademark at multiple price points runs the risk of diluting the value of that mark. While some fashion insiders stress the danger of these lines blurring a brand's identity and tarnishing a mark—and cite the story of Halston, whose fall from grace and fortune was dramatic after he tried marketing clothes under his name to the masses at JC Penney—many well-known design houses have a second or even third line that is lower priced. One way to understand the phenomenon is precisely as a strategy to knock off one's own signature designs, so that consumers who can't afford the real thing can at least get a piece of it—and that desirable label.

A very prominent user of this strategy is Giorgio Armani, which has up to five distinct lines, depending on how one counts. Most fashion firms, however, do not go this deeply into the diffusion world. Why the Armani approach is not more common is an interesting question. But it is clear that at least some degree of self-copying occurs throughout the industry.

We suspect the reason true self-knockoffs—in which the same basic design is offered at different prices—are rare revolves around the great power of trademarks. Tarnishing a brand is perilous, as Halston and Pierre Cardin taught the fashion world. Moreover, different labels even within the same house—Armani Exchange, Armani white label, and so forth—have different identities, and it is dangerous to blur them. Customers at the high end will not appreciate it; it is one thing to see a favored designer's work knocked off by Forever 21, and another for the designer to do it herself. Given this, fashion firms are wisely cautious. It is usually better to have someone else do the copying.

Let us return to where we began. Fashion is a huge industry in which imitation is everywhere—and completely legal. The fashion world ought to be in an economic freefall, since our conventional view of innovation tells us that widespread copying destroys creativity and kills markets. Yet the apparel industry is not just surviving—it is thriving. Extensive and legal copying accelerates the fashion cycle, banishing once-desired designs to the dustbin of apparel history (perhaps later to be dusted off and reintroduced) and sending the fashion-conscious off in search of the new, new thing. And copying allows trends, the cornerstone of contemporary fashion, to develop and spread. The result is an American fashion industry that is dynamic, innovative, successful, and full of copying.

CUISINE, COPYING, AND CREATIVITY

In the spring of 2007 a chef named Ed McFarland opened a restaurant on Lafayette Street in downtown Manhattan called Ed's Lobster Bar. For years McFarland had been the sous-chef at the very successful Pearl Oyster Bar on Cornelia Street in Greenwich Village. Pearl Oyster Bar was a small place, but it was well known and always packed. The chef and owner, Rebecca Charles, had built an avid following based on a simple formula: a short list of excellent seafood, elegant but spare New England coastal décor, a signature Caesar salad with English muffin croutons, and plenty of oyster crackers on the tables.

Eventually Ed McFarland sought to strike out on his own, and when he did, he took with him a lot of ideas drawn from his years working at the Pearl Oyster Bar. At least, so claimed Rebecca Charles. Shortly after Ed's Lobster Bar opened less than a mile from Pearl, an angry Charles filed suit in the federal court in lower Manhattan. In her suit she claimed that McFarland had "pirated Pearl's entire menu; copied all aspects of Pearl's presentation of its dishes; [and] duplicated Pearl's readily identifiable décor."[1] According to Charles, Ed's Lobster Bar was "a total plagiarism" of her well-known restaurant. Perhaps most galling to Charles was the Caesar salad. When she taught

McFarland how to make her signature Caesar salad, she told him "you will never make this anywhere else."[2] Ed's Lobster Bar menu nonetheless featured a Caesar salad somewhat tauntingly dubbed "Ed's Caesar."

McFarland saw things differently. "I would say it's a similar restaurant," he told the *New York Times*. "I would not say it's a copy." McFarland pointed to some differences between the two establishments. Ed's Lobster Bar, he asserted, was "more upscale . . . a lot neater, a lot cleaner, and a lot nicer looking." Moreover, Ed's had a skylight (Pearl had none) and a raw bar (though at the time, and still today, Pearl served oysters and clams on the half shell, as well as a shrimp cocktail). McFarland also noted that much of the décor in Pearl Oyster Bar was in fact common to seafood bars in New England, which was the ostensible homeland for the menu and the design of both Pearl Oyster Bar and Ed's Lobster Bar.* Nonetheless, it was undeniable that Ed's Lobster Bar looked a lot like Pearl Oyster Bar. It was casual but crisply designed, with a long and narrow room and a bar as the centerpiece. The menu looked quite similar too, though Ed's, as befitting its name, featured lobster more prominently.

The suit between Rebecca Charles and Ed McFarland was eventually settled out of court. But the issues it raised continue to vex the culinary community. What rights does a chef have to her creations? What makes a dish original? When does homage cross over to theft?

These questions, and others like them, are unsettled, but the stakes are not small. Like the fashion industry, the restaurant industry is very large— sales at American dining establishments alone were estimated at nearly $604 billion in 2010.[3] Also like fashion, the world of cuisine features extensive imitation—call it borrowing, copying, or, if you prefer, piracy. And, in a situation similar again to fashion, for the most part American law grants chefs very limited rights over their creations. For all practical purposes recipes, no matter how original, cannot be copyrighted. So while a cookbook can be copyrighted as a whole, the individual recipes can be borrowed and republished by anyone—as a brief tour of the Internet, and popular cooking Web sites like Epicurious, will make clear.

---

* Not to mention the venerable Grand Central Oyster Bar, which opened its doors (and raw bar) to shellfish lovers in 1913. Perhaps worth noting too is that in a recent visit to Pearl Oyster Bar, a waiter, asked to describe the Caesar salad at issue in the suit, said it was "a normal Caesar, nothing different about it."

Perhaps more important, the "built food"—the edible dish itself—cannot be protected either. However good Rebecca Charles's Caesar salad is, there is nothing in the law that stops the Ed McFarlands of the world from reproducing it. Anyone can taste a dish they like, apply their expertise to reverse-engineer it (by recognizing the taste and appearance of primary ingredients and reconstructing the steps taken to prepare them), and then recreate it elsewhere, including in a competitor restaurant. As any connoisseur of good food knows, this kind of copying happens all the time.

The contemporary culinary scene is nonetheless astonishingly creative. Globalization has brought us an ever-expanding palette of new ingredients from around the world, and made them ever more affordable. And new cooking techniques, such as those pioneered by the "molecular gastronomy" or "modernist cuisine" movement, abound. It's no wonder that new dishes are invented and refined every day. In many respects we are living in a golden age of cuisine, with more choices and more creativity than ever before.

In short, cuisine presents much the same puzzle as fashion. How do chefs remain so creative while enjoying so little legal protection for their core product? Why doesn't the mainstream view of copying—that it will squelch creativity—seem to apply in the kitchen?

A Very Brief Culinary History

For millennia, chefs throughout the world have labored to create delicious food. Yet for most of that history they labored in obscurity. In the West, only in the nineteenth century did a few great chefs, like Antoine Careme and Auguste Escoffier, achieve a public persona and some measure of fame. For many decades after these pioneers first entered the public eye, chefs were rarely treated as artists on par with their peers in the visual or literary arts, and for the most part restaurants, well into the 20th century, hardly noted their chefs. Today, of course, star chefs seem to be everywhere. Food lovers follow chefs from restaurant to restaurant, famous "consulting chefs" license the use of their names to kitchens that they may have never entered, and the Food Network has spawned an entire industry of chef contests and celebrities. The *New York Times* dining section documents the comings and goings of chefs as if they were baseball stars traded from team to team.

While countries such as France, Italy, and China have ancient and storied food traditions, for much of its history the United States lacked a robust culinary culture. Local cuisines have long flourished in obvious places like New Orleans, as well as in less obvious spots, such as the low country of South Carolina, where traditional ingredients and dishes were passed down and cherished. But for the most part it is fair to say that compared to Europe, the United States was a culinary wasteland for a very long time. In his engaging history of contemporary American food culture, *The United States of Arugula*, David Kamp recounts the story of James Fenimore Cooper, the novelist, returning in 1833 from several years in France. Commenting on the differences between the French and American diets, Cooper called Americans "the grossest feeders of any civilized nation ever known," and a people who subsisted on a "heavy, coarse, and indigestible" diet.[4] While by the Gilded Age of the late 19th Century it was clear that the rich in the major cities ate very well—think Diamond Jim Brady and his Brobdingnagian feasts of oysters, terrapin, and roast duck—there was no mass culture of food appreciation in the United States. Fine dining in restaurants existed in places like New York, but until the end of the Second World War most Americans seldom ate in restaurants.

This began to change by the middle of the 20th century. The 1939 World's Fair in Flushing Meadows, New York, was arguably the birthplace of contemporary fine French dining in the United States; it was the source of Henri Soule's Le Pavillon restaurant in Manhattan, which, until its closure in 1971, was the sun around which postwar haute cuisine revolved in New York—as well as the training ground of many top chefs.[5] In the same era, the influential chef and food writer James Beard nurtured a growing appreciation of traditional American cooking and ingredients. The burgeoning American interest in fine cooking was exemplified by, and stoked by, Julia Child's television show *The French Chef*, which debuted in 1963 and quickly became a cultural icon. The nation, increasingly richer and blessed with more leisure time, embraced cooking as a pastime and even a passion.

By the 1970s a new wave of chefs, both in New York and in California (as well as in France), was redefining fine cuisine, emphasizing local ingredients, lighter treatments, and more casual service. Americans in due course discovered hitherto-exotic provisions such as goat cheese, baby greens, and sundried tomatoes. Lawyers Nina and Tim Zagat introduced their populist (in the sense that they reflected the views of many discerning customers, rather than a single critic) restaurant guide in 1979, as Americans began eating out in greater and greater numbers. By the 1980s a full-blown culinary revolution was taking place, led by names that are now well known: Wolfgang Puck, David Bouley, Danny Meyer, Alice Waters. Slowly, chefs were becoming celebrities and restaurants a site of art appreciation on par—in the view of many—with the museum and the opera house. Even the US Department of Labor took note of these shifts, changing their classification of chefs from "domestics" to "professionals" in 1976.[6]

The "chef revolution" of the late 20th century coincided with, and was driven by, changes in how great cooking was understood and evaluated. Creativity has always been a part of fine cooking, alongside skillful and precise preparations of time-honored classics. But increasingly, culinary reputations were being made by innovative and bold new dishes. A well-known example is Wolfgang Puck's much-imitated smoked salmon pizza. Pizza had been around for a long time, but it took Puck, an Austrian working in tradition-flouting Los Angeles (and to a large degree—perhaps a very large degree—working with the assistance of his original Spago pizza-man, Ed LaDou) to create something truly new in the pizza world.[*] Puck's success spawned a rash of imitators, and pizza has never been the same. Along the way Wolfgang Puck became a very rich and famous man.

In short, from the 1960s onward, and especially during and after the 1980s, American food culture underwent a remarkable flowering. Across the board, a wealthier and more time-starved nation increasingly chose to eat out rather than cook in. To be sure, Americans overwhelmingly ate at fast-food restaurants, or at one of the thousands of simple Chinese take-out joints that dot the continent.[7] (There are more Chinese restaurants in the United States than there are McDonald's.) In parallel, however, the nation developed a more sophisticated restaurant scene, along with an increasingly food-knowledgeable populace that yearned to eat innovative, challenging cuisine.

Today, it is not too much of an exaggeration to say we live in an unprecedentedly food-centered nation—not for everyone, to be sure, but for a large

---

[*] LaDou went on to develop the menu for the very successful California Pizza Kitchen, as well as start his own restaurant, Caioti Pizza Café. In a bizarre twist Caioti became most famous not for its pizza but for a different innovation: its salad, known as "The THE Salad" (with a copyright symbol appended) which is alleged to have supposedly labor-inducing qualities and is often consumed by past-due pregnant women from all over Los Angeles.

slice of affluent Americans. For these fortunate people, the search for crea-tive and unusual meals is a way of life. Food is now art as well as sport.

The rise of the regular weekly restaurant review in the 1960s and 1970s perhaps best encapsulates this new reality. While the *New York Times* long had a food editor for what was known as the "women's pages," it was only with the advent of the legendary Craig Claiborne as food editor in 1960 that the make-or-break starred restaurant review, today so familiar a feature, came into its own.[8] With it came a culture of seeking entertainment and pleasure from chefs, who now competed for public and private acclaim and the dollars a worshipping public brought. To do so, increasingly, ambitious chefs sought to either introduce novel cuisines to Americans or innovate within traditional idioms. And all the while the restaurant industry boomed: from $43 billion in food and drink sales in the United States in 1970 to over $600 billion today.[9]

Over time, nearly every great foreign cuisine, and many minor ones, became available, first in major American cities and then in smaller cities and towns, both in traditional and modern, tweaked, form. "American" food, usually dubbed New American, also became a religion for many as it updated traditional regional cookery to achieve a new, more sophisticated cuisine. A vibrant culture of culinary innovation took hold. Moreover, this culture was increasingly global, with chefs around the world frequently collaborating and sometimes borrowing from one another (or, less charitably, stealing). To be sure, some of this innovation has been less in the actual food than the atmosphere or design of the restaurant. (There is a restaurant in Brussels where diners are suspended in mid-air in a crane, and one, unsurprisingly now closed, in Tel Aviv where diners "pretended" to eat but paid with real money).[10] But none of this flim-flammery gainsays the tremendous diversi-fication of dining in the United States and around the world. Today, revered chefs such as Thomas Keller are known not just for their excellent restau-rants but also for specific dishes they invented—such as Keller's famous "Oysters and Pearls": caviar-topped oysters on a bed of tapioca pearls.

The apotheosis of this trend toward extreme culinary innovation is what is often termed the "modernist cuisine" movement.[11] Practitioners, such as Ferran Adria of the recently closed El Bulli restaurant in Spain and Homaro Cantu of Moto in Chicago, use complex and highly inventive processes to create flavored foams, liquid "olives," edible inks, and various other savory special effects.[12] Many of these dishes push the envelope of good taste; a few are bizarre and arguably inedible. But they are unequivocally novel, and people pay dearly to experience them.

Even outside this rarified world, however, creativity in cuisine is prized in a way that contrasts sharply with the past. Chefs frequently seek to charge jaded palates through novel combinations of flavors, ingredients, and technique. The *Wall Street Journal*, for example, noted in 2006 "a big shift in high-end restaurant culture. . . . The past decade has seen the focus shift to innovation" and away from the apprentice-driven reproduction of classic dishes that anchored cuisine (especially French cuisine) for many decades.[13] Not all restaurants pursue this approach, by any means, and the largest concentrations of highly innovative chefs are found in major cities like New York, Los Angeles, and Chicago. But creativity and variety are now prominent elements of culinary scenes throughout the nation. In short, it is difficult to dispute the proposition that we are living in a golden age of cuisine, with a far greater diversity of dishes—both innovative and traditional—available to us than ever before.

COPYING IN THE KITCHEN

This tremendous output of creativity in contemporary kitchens has been accompanied by substantial copying, or more charitably, borrowing, among chefs. Now-ubiquitous dishes, such as molten chocolate cake or miso-glazed black cod, did not just pop up like mushrooms after a storm. Each debuted in a specific restaurant but soon migrated outward in slightly altered form. The putative inventors (Jean-Georges Vongerichten in the case of molten chocolate cake, Nobu Matsuhisa for miso black cod)* can claim no royalties on their creations. Nor can they effectively halt the interpretation of their creations by others.[14] Indeed, today a molten chocolate cake is even on the menu at a mass-market chain such as Chili's. (In fact, a recipe claiming to be for Chili's Molten Chocolate Cake is readily available on the Internet).[15]

---

* Though Nobu Matsuhisa is informally credited with inventing this dish, insiders note that it is a traditional preparation for black cod in Japan. See, for example, Mark Bittman of the *New York Times*: "Black cod with miso was not invented by Nobu Matsuhisa, the chef at Nobu in Tribeca, but he certainly popularized it." Mark Bittman, "The Minimalist," *New York Times*, April 14, 2004.

FIGURE 2.1 Molten chocolate cake © *Shutterstock.com*

Why are dishes like molten chocolate cake (or less common ones, like Oysters and Pearls) not protected against copying? In the United States, copyright law protects only "original works of authorship fixed in any tangible medium of expression." In principle, there is no obvious reason why a culinary creation is not a work of authorship. It has an author (the chef), and it is certainly fixed in a tangible, albeit edible, medium of expression— the recipe is "fixed" in the food itself.[16] A painting of a molten chocolate cake would clearly receive copyright protection; so too would a sculpture of one.* But as we will explain, under current law the molten cake itself would not be protected.

At the outset it is important to distinguish between the *recipe* for a given dish and what we referred to as the "built food." The recipe is the ingredients and instructions: what a reader might clip out of the newspaper or pull up on Cooks.com. The built food is the actual, edible version that appears on a plate. This distinction is in many respects no different from that of the sheet

---

* A fascinating case is that of "food artist" Jennifer Rubell, whose shows, or installations, include paintings that pour cocktails out of spigots and "honey paintings" created by 50,000 bees. Art, or dinner? The first is copyrightable, the second not. Rubell also worked for a time as the "vegetable butcher" in Mario Batali's Eataly store in Manhattan.

music for a song versus the sound recording of that same song, or the architectural plans of a building versus the actual building that you can enter and live in. As it happens, both sheet music and performed songs are protected by copyright. The same is true for architectural drawings and actual buildings. (In the case of buildings, this was the result of a specific amendment of American copyright law, the Architectural Works Copyright Protection Act, enacted in 1990).[17] But despite the similarities to music and architecture, neither recipes nor built food are currently protected by copyright. And there has been no serious push to promulgate a "Culinary Works Copyright Protection Act" equivalent to the Architectural Works act.

Let's consider recipes first. In 1996, the Meredith Corporation sued a company called PIL for allegedly poaching recipes from its cookbook *Discover Dannon—50 Fabulous Recipes with Yogurt*. The 7th Circuit Court of Appeals agreed that the recipes in the two books were very much the same. As the court stated,

> There is not really any dispute that that salient PIL recipes are functionally identical to their counterparts in Discover Dannon. . . . [T]here are certain differences in the listing of ingredients, directions for preparations and nutritional information. However, it doesn't take Julia Child or Jeff Smith[*] to figure out that the PIL recipes will produce substantially the same final products.[18]

Yet as the appeals court noted a few pages later, American law does not protect every act of creativity. Copyright protection does not extend to any "idea, procedure, process, system, method of operation, concept, principle, or discovery." A recipe certainly looks like a procedure or method of operation: it tells the cook how to combine a set of specified ingredients using a number of specified techniques, and in what order. And indeed most courts and commentators that have considered the issue have held recipes to be procedures. Consequently, recipes are not generally copyrightable. Again the 7th Circuit:

---

[*] The one-time *Frugal Gourmet*, famous to many in the 1980s and '90s for his popular televised cooking show. (And presciently invoked by the Beastie Boys on their 1992 *Check Your Head* album: "I've got more spice than the Frugal Gourmet.") After sexual assault charges were raised against him by two of his teenage male assistant chefs, Smith and his show disappeared from view.

The identification of ingredients necessary for the preparation of each dish is a statement of facts. There is no expressive element in each listing; in other words, the author who wrote down the ingredients for "Curried Turkey and Peanut Salad" was not giving literary expression to his individual labors. Instead, he was writing down an idea, namely, the ingredients necessary to the preparation of a particular dish.[19]

Meredith v. PIL expresses the dominant view of recipes in American law. Recipes are functional guides, not creative expressions. Nonetheless, the *Meredith* court was careful not to create any blanket or overly rigid rule. The recipes copied by PIL from *Discover Dannon* were not copyrightable, the court declared, because they did not contain "even a bare modicum of the creative expression" necessary for copyright to apply. This phraseology appeared to leave the door open for recipes that do contain such a "bare modicum" of creative expression.

What does this all mean? The court implicitly rejected the idea that a *recipe itself* can be creative—even if it combines hitherto-uncombined ingredients, such as sea urchin and ice cream. But, it suggested, some recipes might contain enough creative expression to be copyrighted. The US Copyright Office—the federal agency that administers copyright law—has taken a similar position: any "substantial literary expression" that accompanies a recipe "in the form of an explanation or directions" may be copyrightable.[20] So writing that comments or expands upon the recipe, as distinguished from the list of ingredients and the bare description of the steps taken to prepare them, *is* copyrightable.

An example from English food personality and chef Nigella Lawson's cookbook, *Nigella Bites*, illustrates this distinction between recipe and expression. In a prologue to her recipe for "Double Potato and Halloumi Bake," Lawson claims that this seemingly simple dish has unappreciated virtues:

> I first made this for a piece I was writing for *Vogue* on the mood-enhancing properties of carbohydrates. . . . It's a simple idea, and as simple to execute. What's more, there's a balance between the components: bland and sweet potatoes, almost caramelised onion and garlic, more juicy sweetness with the peppers and then the uncompromising plain saltiness of the halloumi (which you should be able to get easily in a supermarket)—that seems to add the eater's equilibrium in turn.[21]

This passage is protected against copying, and Lawson's musings on the mood-altering qualities of the dish probably comprise part of the cookbook's appeal. Indeed, cookbooks are generally full of such passages, which provide color and context and help tell a story about the dish and perhaps the chef or author. The addition of these sorts of discussions also transforms a cookbook from a collection of recipes—"mere listings of ingredients"—into a copyrightable book.[22] Still, the parts of Nigella Lawson's recipe that seem the most valuable—the actual instructions on how to prepare the Double Potato and Halloumi Bake—can be copied at will.

If we step back, however, we might ask: Are recipes really just procedures? The simple answer is yes. The very point of a recipe is to tell the reader how to recreate the dish in question. Yet as the legal scholar Chris Buccafusco points out, treating recipes as uncopyrightable procedures is not consistent with how we treat another widely used set of instructions: sheet music. Recipes tell cooks how to reproduce a dish for someone to taste; sheet music tells musicians how to reproduce a song for someone to hear. There is no obvious reason to treat a sheet of paper with a recipe and a sheet of musical notation differently.[23]

What would happen if recipes were treated like sheet music? Because sheet music is protected by copyright, public performances of the music by anyone but the creator require a license. Likewise, if recipes were copyrightable, then the public preparation of that recipe by another chef would require a license.

Such a system would not be hard to implement. Many restaurants are already required to pay license fees to publicly perform musical works when they play a CD for the entertainment of their customers. There is no obvious reason that they should not also pay a fee when they entertain their customers with someone else's original recipe. After all, the food, rather than the music, is the restaurant's primary product. Of course, all this is conjectural; at the moment, there is no copyright protection for recipes, nor any notable effort under way to expand copyright to cover recipes.

"Built" food, recipes made tangible on a plate, is even more removed from current copyright law than are recipes. Copyright is meant to protect creative expression. The dominant view of food in American law, however, is that it is a functional item, much like clothing is functional. We eat food because we are hungry, and the qualities of a dish are thought to be dictated by functionality, not aesthetics. A foie gras mousse with burnt caramel sauce and Maldon sea salt, by this reasoning, is not an expressive statement, but instead a vehicle for a specific function: the ingestion of needed (or unneeded) calories.

This view of food has long roots. Well before the 7th Circuit Court of Appeals decided *Meredith v. PIL*, the influential legal treatise *Nimmer on Copyright* opined that recipes were unlikely to be protected against copying "because the content of recipes [is] clearly dictated by functional consider-ations, and therefore may be said to lack the required element of originality, even though the combination of ingredients contained in the recipes may be original in a noncopyright sense."[24] Though the Nimmer treatise did not consider the status of built food, presumably the same reasoning would apply. A dish is useful, not artistic; therefore it is not within the scope of copyright. This perspective—known generally as the "useful articles doctrine"—is one that we have seen before in the context of fashion, and is foundational in American copyright law.

Some have challenged the application of the useful articles doctrine to food, on the grounds that there is nothing functional that dictates the con-tent of striped bass wrapped in potato with a Barolo wine sauce or maple-bacon ice cream. These dishes were invented by someone, and exhibit as much originality as any painting or short story. They surely serve a function— satiating appetites—but people don't seek out haute cuisine to feel full. They do so for the aesthetic experience.

Indeed, the same is true of clothing. A woman who purchases an expen-sive and elaborate dress does so because she likes the way it makes her look, not because it might also keep her warm. Despite this, the law deems the dress a useful article, effectively the same as a smock. Whatever its aesthetic appeal or originality, under current law the fact that a dress, or a scoop of sorbet, might serve a useful function is sufficient to strip away all copyright protection.[25]

In short, the copying of recipes and dishes is entirely permissible. And since there is no law stopping it, copying is—as you might expect—not unknown in the culinary world. Chefs around the globe imitate the innova-tive and popular creations of others. Copying is similarly ubiquitous in cookbooks and in prepared foods. And though it is difficult to measure, some of the chefs we interviewed think that copying is more common than ever. The rise of the Internet has made copying easier; one no longer need eat a particular dish to copy it, at least when the dish is described and photographed with enough specificity on a food blog or magazine page. Yet, in an interesting twist, at the same time the Internet has made copying easier to identify, since the same photo + blog combination allows originators to quickly ascertain whether their signature dishes have been referenced, or simply recreated, by someone else. What is clear is that the combination means more debate over the topic of copying.

The spat between Pearl Oyster Bar and Ed's Lobster Bar, in other words, is noteworthy not because the underlying behavior was unusual. Instead, the dispute stands out largely because Rebecca Charles, the chef and owner of Pearl Oyster Bar, decided to sue her former sous-chef. Increasingly, however, chefs are following her lead and trying to assert some rights, however thin, over their creations. While the dominant story in this chapter is one of copying creative works, there are nonetheless some barriers to copying in the kitchen. Before more closely analyzing the patterns of copying among chefs, we need to understand what legal tools do exist to limit copying.

LIMITS ON COPYING

Chefs can copy recipes and dishes from one another. But they cannot copy the look and feel of entire restaurants. Nor can they freely use trademarked names or phrases, such as "Spago" or "I'm Lovin' It!"[*] In the Pearl versus Ed's dispute, for instance, the press focused extensively on the idea that Ed McFarland had stolen recipes and dishes from Rebecca Charles. That was certainly part of the claim made by Charles in public. But a closer look at the actual legal complaint filed tells a somewhat different story. Charles's lawyers, cognizant of the novelty and near-impossibility of claiming ownership over a dish—especially a type of Caesar salad—instead stuck to safer ground. They claimed that the "trade dress" of Pearl Oyster Bar had been appropriated.[26]

We discussed trade dress briefly in our tour of the fashion world. Trade dress is a legal concept akin to trademark. The idea is that the look or feel of a product (or service) can, like a brand name such as The Palm or Taco Bell,

---

[*] Trademarks sometimes show up in the cooking world in ways you wouldn't expect. For example, Food Network star chef Emeril Lagasse's stock phrase "Kick it up a notch!" is actually a trademark owned by an oil and gas company from Sugar Land, Texas.

signify the creator or maker. That feature makes the trade dress valuable to the owner and, most important, to the consumer who wants to purchase the item. As with trademark law, trade dress law aims to protect consumers from confusion. If a particular trade dress is associated with a particular producer, its use by a different producer might confuse customers about what exactly they are buying and who is responsible for it. At the same time, of course, trade dress law also protects creators from others who might closely imitate their products.

Trade dress disputes are nothing new in the restaurant world. The issue in these disputes is generally whether the design and décor of a given restaurant is generic, or instead somehow distinctive enough to evoke that particular eatery and no other. If the design and decor is distinctive enough, it is illegal to copy it.[27] When San Antonio-based Tex-Mex chain Taco Cabana alleged that its Houston-based rival, Two Pesos, copied the distinctive Mexican-themed décor and open-kitchen layout of its restaurants, for instance, the Supreme Court had to decide the reach of trade dress law in restaurants.[28]

Considered today, the Taco Cabana trade dress looks fairly generic. But from the perspective of the Supreme Court back in 1992, the appearance of the Taco Cabana restaurants seemed distinctive enough. Two Pesos, the Court said, had illegally copied. (And the following year, Taco Cabana bought Two Pesos).[29]

Following the Supreme Court's decision in *Two Pesos v. Taco Cabana*, many restaurants have asserted trade dress claims to prevent imitation of their décor, which can be as important to the restaurant's appeal as the food. More generally, chefs can use the law of "unfair competition"—rules governing business conduct that are both broader and less specific than the rules of copyright and patent—to challenge the actions of those who take, or are overly inspired by, their restaurant's look and motifs. A good example is the ongoing dispute between the Mr. Chow restaurants, famous along the New York-Los Angeles axis for very expensive Chinese food, and the upstart Phillipe Chow restaurants, which operate in the same pricey Chinese food niche. Phillipe Chow was started by a former employee of Mr. Chow named Chak Yam Chau; Chau was sued by Chow for a series of trademark and unfair competition violations.[30] (Mr. Chau apparently changed his name to Phillipe Chow at some point prior to developing the restaurants.) The suit, which sought $21 million in damages, illustrates the economic importance of trademark and trade dress to restaurateurs.

The law of trade secrecy is another useful tool for chefs. Trade secret law protects valuable business information, which can include unpublished recipes. The most famous example is the formula for Coke. That formula has remained a well-guarded secret—even within the company, knowledge of the formula is restricted to a few key individuals—and none of Coke's rivals have ever succeeded in perfectly replicating it. The law protects trade secrets against theft by those owing some sort of duty to the owner, such as an employee or business partner. Still, nothing in trade secret law prohibits a competitor from reverse-engineering the way a particular risotto—or soft drink—is prepared.

In short, American law already protects some of the key features of a restaurant via trademark and unfair competition law, and it provides some (usually narrow) measure of exclusivity over unpublished recipes and special ingredients via trade secret. Restaurant names ("Pearl Oyster Bar") and the names of specific dishes—examples include Chili's Big Mouth® Burgers, or, more exotically, the Crack Pie® and Compost Cookies® served in David Chang's famous Momofuku restaurant in New York—can be trademarked. A restaurant's design and décor might be protectable by trade dress, if they are distinctive and well enough known to the public.

The other major form of intellectual property (IP), patent, has not escaped the notice of chefs and restaurateurs either. In the commercial food industry, patenting is a central business tool, deployed widely—many would argue too widely—to protect inventive industrial processes and products. (One company has even tried to patent the peanut butter and jelly sandwich, albeit an allegedly special crustless version).[31] Among restaurant chefs, patenting is much less common, but it is not unknown. The most frequently noted example is Chicago-based chef Homaro Cantu, of the Moto and ING restaurants. Cantu, who cultivates a sort of mad-scientist persona, is famous for highly innovative dishes often made with complex tools and techniques. At one time Moto even featured a laser in its dining room used for preparing certain items. Cantu has sought numerous patents on his dishes, cookware, and techniques. Consulting closely with attorneys as he works out new creations, Cantu seems to have taken the most aggressive approach to intellectual property protection of any major American chef.

Perhaps the most talked-about innovation at Moto is edible paper embedded with particular flavors. For example, Cantu has served small sheets of this paper imprinted with an image of cotton candy. The paper itself tastes of cotton candy. Edible, flavored paper is interesting enough, but what is arguably most striking is what is printed below the image:

Confidential Property of and © H. Cantu. Patent Pending. No further use or disclosure is permitted without prior approval of H. Cantu.[32]

This (edible) language is intended to serve as a novel form of license. The language invokes intellectual property law, but the provision's real force is not IP, but the customer's *agreement* to Cantu's terms. Cantu, in other words, has made creative use of contract law to protect his innovations and confirm the rules under which the customer may enjoy them. Like the more familiar "click-wrap" license, which we encounter every time we download a software update or buy an item on the Internet, this license employs the law of contract to limit the use of an invention by others. Cantu's lawyer cleverly calls it "sit-wrap" (though it may be just as apt to call it "eat-wrap.") This kind of license has never been tested in court. But most courts have enforced click-wrap licenses, and so the sit-wrap license is far from crazy. The effect of the license is, moreover, likely to be substantial even if it is never tested in litigation. It communicates the rules of the restaurant. Most customers, once they understand the rules, are likely to abide by them.

THE DEBATE OVER COPYING IN THE KITCHEN

Sit-wrap licensing has not yet caught on in the restaurant community, but it illustrates a more general point. Cuisine gets copied. And increasingly, chefs are asking why their creations are not the subject of the same level of protection enjoyed by other artists. A few are seeking creative means to ensure that their work does receive improved treatment. While these chefs may not be interested in the details of copyright law, they recognize that there are good reasons to question the widely varying treatment of different art forms. A recent tempest over copying in the kitchen illustrates how the issues are being debated inside the industry today.

In 2005 a restaurant in Melbourne, Australia, called Interlude began serving food of a sort never seen before down under. Interlude's young chef, Robin Wickens, was already well known when he started shaking up the Australian culinary scene, but the highly creative dishes he served—such as pureed shrimp turned into noodles—were unlike his earlier work. (Indeed, a 2004 review of Interlude in the Australian newspaper *The Age* chided the original menu for being a bit stodgy.)* Soon commentators on the Web site of the eGullet Society—which includes among its members and readers many famous chefs and food professionals—pointed out that the new dishes appeared to be direct copies of those served in famously innovative American restaurants such as Alinea in Chicago and WD-50 in New York. And as it turned out, Wickens had volunteered (a practice known in the industry as "staging") for a short period at Alinea just a few months earlier.[33]

A volcano of hostile commentary soon followed on eGullet, with staff from Moto, Alinea, and many other top restaurants weighing in. Ultimately, a chastened Wickens removed several dishes from his menu, declaring that "I never tried to claim them as my own," and apologized to Grant Achatz, the chef of Alinea.[34] The eGullet fracas that led to this decision, however, is worth recounting because it reveals the emerging debate within the culinary community over exactly what sort of copying is permissible and what is not.

Less than an hour after a self-proclaimed "Australian chef" posted on eGullet that many dishes at Interlude appeared to have been copied directly from several innovative American restaurants, Wickens mounted a defense. Because the discussion on the site is so interesting and revealing, we quote it at length in its original (that is, often ungrammatical) form. First, Chef Wickens:

> *Thought i should post my reply. with regards to the prawn noodle dish this came about after getting hold of some 'transglutiminaise'. Rather than just throwing it radomily into food, we had a recipe for the prawn noodles and started there, we then played around with recipes and new recipes to see what we could come up with. We now use it in completely new and original dishes. My trip to America and staging at Alinea gave me ideas and i saw new techniques that after cooking for over ten years in some pretty good restaurants i had seen before.*

---

* Those well versed in cuisine would have noticed the review mentioned a dish strikingly similar to one made famous in the United States by Daniel Boulud (though some discern an even earlier provenance in France): "A piece of mulloway—the farmed variety from the same South Australian producers who send us the Hiramasa Kingfish—is roasted with crisp potato 'scales,' sat upon creamed leek and finished with a tart, fruity Barolo sauce with just the right level of acid for the fish." Like many other noteworthy gustatory creations, this one is now found at many fine restaurants around the world.

When i got back to my own kitchen of course we played around and saw how we could use these techniques in our own food. . . . We are always coming up with new and evolved dishes for our menus. I totally agree that Chefs Achatz [of Alinea], Cantu [of Moto] and Dufresne [of WD-50] are some of the top chefs in the world but I am sure they would agree that true originality comes from inspiration itself. If they do come up with a new technique as say someone like Ferron Adria [of El Bulli] has in the past. Of course people are going to imitate it and evolve it.

Many commentators on eGullet were highly critical of Wickens's defense. One wrote:

Saying that replicating these dishes verbatim and then adding them to your menu (for profit, I might add) is the first step in an evolution would be like if I were to re-record Miles's Davis' "Kind of Blue" note for note, retitle it "Sort of Blue," make no reference to the original composer, turn around and sell it for a profit, and later claim that it was just part of my evolution as a musician.

As this comment rightly points out, it is generally forbidden to remake a copyrighted work in a new form without first obtaining a license. It is not, however, impossible, especially if a court finds that the reworking is a parody of the original. Alice Randall famously rewrote *Gone With The Wind* from the point of view of a slave as *The Wind Done Gone*, and was slapped with a lawsuit in return. But she escaped when a federal appeals court ruled that her book was a parody and therefore "fair use."* Similarly, the rap group 2 Live Crew likewise was sued for remaking Roy Orbison's "Oh, Pretty Woman" song in 1989, but it too prevailed before the Supreme Court on the grounds that the remake was a parody.[35] While these instances suggest that remakes are possible, it is a dicey strategy and defending oneself in court is expensive. In any event, because copyright does not apply to food, reworkings of others' recipes are generally permitted. But what is legal is not necessarily ethical—at least in the eyes of many chefs.

---

* The court in *The Wind Done Gone* case seemed to (perhaps intentionally) misread the book—the Randall work was more frontal assault on the morality of *Gone With the Wind* than any sort of parody. In any event, the court's fair use ruling led to a settlement favorable to Randall, under which Randall's publisher made a donation to Morehouse College, a historically black college in Georgia. The book's cover has a large red circle on it that reads "The Unauthorized Parody."

The tradition of staging in restaurants—in which a young chef works essentially as an intern under the tutelage of another chef—was widely recognized as part of the problem in the Wickens affair, because it created fertile terrain for this kind of behavior. As one commentator noted,

> *The tradition of welcoming stages into the kitchen is long held. The idea is that chefs can learn from one another, grow, and move the art forward. Chef Achatz has both benefited from this tradition, and now welcomes chefs from all over the world into Alinea's kitchen.*

But, several other participants in the debate pointed out, the stagiere system requires a set of rules about when and how to copy, since it is inherent in the staging tradition that the stagiere learn something useful to take with her. Unsurprisingly, then, the issue of attribution was central to many comments. For example:

> *I don't believe the issue is that he copied the dishes or that he is unoriginal. The real issue is one of a lack of attribution. The apparent dishonesty is in claiming the creation of the dish for oneself. It seems that Chef Robin is indeed a fine technician and can run a fine kitchen. I very much doubt that we would be reading about this right now if he gave proper credit.*

Alinea's managing partner then weighed in, agreeing that from the perspective of the restaurant as a whole, the real issue was indeed one of attribution, not economics:

> *The stagiere tradition is long held, and by welcoming chefs into his kitchen at Alinea, Chef Achatz honors that tradition. The idea is to freely share information with others to promote the art and craft of cooking—and move cuisine forward. Visiting chefs learn technique, and then go home to apply these ideas to their own style of cuisine. The problem in this case is, for Alinea, not an economic one or a legal one. I don't personally believe that we have anything to gain economically, nor do I think we have any sort of legal case. Even if we had one, we would not pursue it. What is at stake is another issue. A chef at Alinea said to me a few days ago, "The thing that bothers me the most, is that if a diner went to Interlude first and then dined at Alinea, that diner would think that we were copying him." It would, however, be a loss for the industry if such a violation of*

unwritten ethical guidelines endangered the "open source" nature of the industry and the stage tradition. I for one don't believe it will—if anything, the freedom of information presented on the internet will tend to have the opposite effect.

While many commentators on *L'affaire Wickens* agreed that norms about attribution were central to the profession, others could not resist drawing comparisons with other art forms, as the preceding excerpts suggest. Several debated the similarities and differences with more conventional copyright disputes, such as in the music world. One thought Wickens's copies were akin to the practice of sampling in songs, which is legally actionable in many circumstances. But another commentator thought that was not quite the right analogy:

The difference between sampling and this is that sampling is more like if I bought some food at Alinea and then took it to my own restaurant, reheated it, and sold it as part of one of my dishes. What's happening here is more like George Harrison rewriting "He's So Fine" as "My Sweet Lord" without licensing (which he somehow mostly got away with).[*]

Still another noted that the conversation was based on a set of named dishes and photographs, and that virtually no one outside of Melbourne had actually tasted these dishes. Who knew whether they tasted half as good?

Ultimately the eGullet Society editorialized on the issue, opining—accurately we think—that the debate over Robin Wickens's menu had tackled a major frontier in the industry: *"We believe the Interlude controversy is not a simple matter of a lone Australian restaurant copying a few dishes from halfway around the world. Rather, it's one of the most significant issues facing the global culinary community today."* Many of the chefs we interviewed for this book had a similar view on the phenomenon of copying. But there was by no means unanimity among chefs on how big a problem copying was, or whether laws regulating the copying of food were a good—or workable—idea.

As David Chang, of the famed Momofuku empire, declared—echoing the views of many others we spoke with—"There is nothing new under the sun. Our job is just to make [existing dishes] better." Josiah Citrin of Melisse

---

[*] In fact, Harrison was found liable for copyright infringement in *Bright Tunes v. Harrisongs Music*, 420 F. Supp. 177 (S.D.N.Y. 1976).

in Los Angeles was similarly dubious about the role of creativity: "we are all taking from the wheel and reinventing it," he said. "The wheel goes around. It's very hard to say what is a copy and what is not a copy." As this suggests, many great chefs are uncomfortable with the notion of true culinary invention. In an interview given in another setting, Thomas Keller of the French Laundry identified the central issue of origin in describing his very famous— and widely copied—salmon cornets:

> Look at the cornets for example. Where did it really come from? . . . Did I really invent it? Did I create it? Or was it an inspiration from an ice cream cone that I just looked at differently? Do I have the right to say that this is mine and nobody else's? I don't know. . . . What happens to my salmon cornet if they copyright it? Does someone have to get my permission to use it? Does somebody have to pay me royalties? . . . I kind of have a problem with that. I really do.[36]

Charlie Trotter likewise said that "I honestly don't care [about copying]. It doesn't bother me because we did [it] first [. . . .] It's our point of view, and I think people know what's up."[37]

Even those chefs who are more positive about the idea of copyrighting food were generally skeptical that it is workable in practice. It is "too simple to change a few ingredients in a dish," said Joachim Splichal of the Patina group.[38] Laurent Torondel of the Bistro Laurent Torondel empire likewise thought copyright could not work in culinary world. (And in Torondel's BLT restaurants, the complimentary—and addictive—popovers are even served with the recipe helpfully attached.) Tourondel echoed the views of several chefs in saying that while creativity was very important, "execution is everything."[39]

Where this debate will end up is anyone's guess. Perhaps the law of intellectual property will inevitably embrace the creations of fine chefs. Maybe there will be an amendment of the copyright statute to embrace recipes and built food—as has been done in the past for buildings and boat hulls. Or maybe through creative lawyering and the massaging of existing legal doctrine, chefs will obtain a bit more protection over their creations and recipes, as chefs such as Homaro Cantu are attempting to do. Such prognosticating is, however, not our primary interest in this book. We are instead interested in what we can learn from the creativity of the culinary world. How has innovation thrived—indeed, arguably accelerated—absent meaningful legal protection for new creations? And what lessons can be drawn for other innovative industries?

Why Are Chefs So Creative?

Like many areas we explore in this book, culinary creativity has been largely ignored by those who study innovation.[40] The challenge is to understand how creativity survives in the face of copying, and to map out the mechanisms that support this process. As with the fashion designers we met in the previous chapter, creativity among chefs seems to defy the notion that imitation kills innovation. Despite extensive copying, chefs continue to create at a high rate. Next we consider several arguments that together may help explain the unusual relationship between cuisine and copying.

Norms

One possible explanation for why copying in the culinary world appears to have few bad effects is that copying is actually less prevalent and less blatant than one might expect. Yes, it is generally legal to copy. But despite the weakness of legal controls, there is not a copying free-for-all. The relevant restraints are not generated by law, however, but by extra-legal forces: high-end chefs, at least in some places, self-police the most egregious copying via social norms. The result is some copying, but not an overwhelming amount. And the copying that is permitted by these norms is generally not very harmful. Legal scholar Robert Ellickson famously wrote about "order without law" among the cattle ranchers of Shasta County, California.[41] Perhaps the same is true among high end chefs.

The best evidence for chefs' use of social norms to police copying comes from a fascinating study of elite French chefs by two economists, Emanuelle Fauchart and Eric von Hippel.[42] Fauchart and von Hippel studied French chefs who worked in Michelin starred and "forked" restaurants—that is, those restaurants especially renowned for their food.[*] These chefs were all

---

[*] In the fabled and influential (at least in France) Michelin Guide, forks are given to "good gastronomic restaurants" that are generally good values. Stars, however, are the true coin of the realm, which, Fauchart and von Hippel note, chefs have likened to "winning an Olympic medal."

very good and well regarded; some were famous beyond the confines of the culinary world. Fauchart and von Hippel conducted a number of interviews; they also sent out a detailed questionnaire asking about the prevalence of copying among French chefs, and about likely responses when copying comes to light. The researchers concluded that an effective system of social norms operates to restrain and police copying among the elite chefs of Paris. They identified three main norms that are in play in the world of French haute cuisine:

1. Accomplished chefs expect that other chefs will not copy their recipes exactly.
2. Accomplished chefs expect that chefs to whom they reveal information will not pass that information on to others without permission.
3. Accomplished chefs expect that chefs to whom they reveal information will acknowledge them as a source.

These three norms are fairly simple. The first does not proscribe any and all copying, just copying which is "exact." As we discuss further, "exactness" in the culinary context is hard to define, and indeed Fauchart and von Hippel note that the boundary between an exact copy and a permissible reinterpretation can be blurry. But it is easy to see a link here to the debate in fashion over point-by-point copies versus mere homage.

The second norm shaping the behavior of French chefs essentially mimics the law of trade secrecy. The *creator* can reveal information to whom she likes, but there is an understanding that the *receiver* of the information will not spread it further without the approval of the creator. Moreover, the economists found that in many instances recipes and techniques were traded with the expectation that the recipient would reciprocate with something useful of her own—an arrangement sometimes dubbed "informal information trading."[43] This I-scratch-your-back, you-scratch-mine system helps promote both innovation and collective learning among the participants.

The third norm, that of attribution, is sometimes enforced by chefs through public acts against rule breakers: the wronged chef may write a public letter identifying herself as the true creator of the dish, or may simply let others know informally that she, and not someone else, is the originator. Often action by famous chefs is unnecessary since their work is well known and copies that transgress the rules are easily recognized by other chefs. The threat of public exposure is enough in most instances to deter copying.

Together, Fauchart and von Hippel argue, these three simple norms provide an important bulwark against blatant copying. They deter most uncredited appropriation of signature dishes, and they ensure that at least some of the rewards for innovation go to the putative originators. And while the economists' study only establishes that these norms operate among French chefs, similar norms may well exist more widely.

Formal codes of professional ethics within the industry support, or at least are consistent with, these norms. The Code of Ethics of the International Association of Culinary Professionals, for instance, states that a chef should credit a source for a recipe if only minor changes are made. If more major changes are made, one should indicate that the recipe is "based on" or "adapted from" another.[44] And whether or not customers have read the Code of Ethics, as the Interlude saga shows, many intuit or appreciate the basic ideas of attribution and inspiration (as opposed to total imitation) and also work to police those norms through food blogs, outlets like Chowhound, eGullet, and Eater, and word of mouth.

Legal scholar Christopher Buccafusco has undertaken another study examining the norms of elite American chefs. He concludes that at least some American chefs think much the same way as their Parisian peers—a viewpoint that the pillorying of Robin Wickens amply illustrates. Inspiration and homage are fine, or at least accepted, but attribution is crucial, and blatant and exact copying without attribution is bad. Our own conversations with chefs working on this side of the Atlantic broadly reflected this position as well. But not all chefs agreed that norms existed, or that they governed behavior effectively, or that they were as well defined and widely shared as those among the French chefs.

Again, social norms grounded in attribution and confidentiality certainly do not block all imitation. But they may provide enough of a check on copying to maintain adequate incentives to continue to create and to dampen any initiative to alter the existing legal rules. As we've seen, our culinary culture continues to create many fine and innovative dishes. Something explains the remarkable creativity of contemporary chefs; we suspect that norms play some role.

There is a broader lesson here. Social norms that operate alongside or in place of legal rules have long attracted interest from scholars. If social norms are powerful enough, they can achieve much the same outcome that legal regulation would—they keep honest people honest, even if they fail to stop the determined violator, and they express the rules of a given community about what is allowed and what is not. Norms can probably achieve this at a lower cost to society than legal rules do, though measuring this is very hard to do.

Is this the case in the world of cuisine? Since a copyright system for recipes or "built food" is necessarily conjectural—as far we know, no nation has implemented such a system*—we cannot directly compare the relative efficacy or efficiency of norms versus laws. But we do know a little bit about one side of the ledger. Informal discussions with chefs support the view that a legal prohibition on copying would be difficult to create and perhaps ineffective in practice. A 2006 *Food & Wine* magazine story on copying in the kitchen, for example, quoted Grant Achatz of Alinea restaurant, whose cuisine is often emulated by others (such as by the ill-fated Robin Wickens). Achatz declared flatly that "chefs won't use [a copyright system.] Can you imagine Thomas Keller calling me and saying, 'Grant, I need to license your Black Truffle Explosion so I can put that on my menu'?"[45] Perhaps Achatz is unusual in his views, but our discussions with chefs, and those in other studies, suggest that he is not. Most chefs do not seem to want a legal regime against copying.

But how effective are social norms at policing copying? A common critique of norm-based approaches to social regulation is that they lack effective enforcement. In Fauchart and von Hippel's study, enforcement of the norms was largely accomplished via informal retaliation by other chefs. As one interviewee explained, "If another chef copies a recipe exactly we are very furious; we will not talk to this chef anymore, and we won't communicate information to him in the future."[46] This not merely a loss of reputation,

---

* The distant past provides an interesting counterexample. The first recorded evidence we have of an IP system comes from third-century AD Greek author Athenaeus, who, quoting an earlier writer, reports that in the sixth century BC, the inhabitants of Sybaris, the largest of the ancient Greek city-states, enforced short-term exclusivity in recipes:

> If any caterer or cook invented a dish of his own which was especially choice, it was his privilege that no one else but the inventor himself should adopt the use of it before the lapse of a year, in order that the first man to invent a dish might possess the right of manufacture during that period, so as to encourage others to excel in eager competition with similar inventions. Athenaeus, *The Deipnosophists*, Vol. 5, Charles Burton Gulick, trans. (Harvard University Press, 1927), 348–49.

in other words; the sanction is also denial of access to other innovations, and some degree of social shunning to boot. For the very best chefs, who by definition are a small group, this is likely to be an effective strategy. The more a chef sees herself as a member of a profession, with its own standards and mores of behavior, the more likely it is that norms enforced by social sanction and reputational penalty will effectively police her behavior.

As this suggests, however, there are obvious limitations to norm-based systems of control. Norms are generally thought to become less effective as the size of the relevant group grows. As chefdom rapidly becomes more global—think Britain's Gordon Ramsay opening a restaurant in Los Angeles, or France's Joel Robuchon (among many others) in Las Vegas—the group grows larger, social ties grow weaker, and the effectiveness of norms is very likely to decline. Moreover, the tradition of staging in fine kitchens, combined with a more international market for talent, creates significant scope for those tempted to knock off existing dishes—especially when they do so in faraway places where they may not be noticed (at first) or which are distant enough that the pain of social pressure and lost reputation are simply not sufficient to deter them from close copying. Indeed, this may have been Robin Wickens's story.

Consider, however, whether far-away copying is a threat to the creative incentives of most chefs. The restaurant business is intensely local. With the exception of a small class of wealthy super-foodies, people rarely travel far simply to eat in a restaurant. They eat near their home, or near wherever they find themselves when traveling. For this reason, a restaurant in Paris is competing mostly with other restaurants in Paris. As a result, the fortunes of a Parisian chef will often be unaffected by copying elsewhere. Indeed, as we discuss further later in this book, the copying may well enhance her reputation, stamping her as a pioneer worthy of imitation—and spurring food fans to seek out the original.

Consider also a principal point illustrated by the Wickens affair: the power of new technologies to enhance the norms-based policing of copying. The existence of the eGullet community provided a communications platform for word of copying to spread and for the community's norms to be expressed. Communication is vital to the functioning of norms—to be persuasive, norms must be articulated often, and widely, among the relevant community. And there must be a way that accusations of violations can spread—the threat of public exposure is the stick that the norms system relies upon for its power. Web sites like eGullet bolster norms by making detection more likely, and public shaming more pervasive and (importantly) permanent. The Internet never forgets.

As we will discuss in the next chapter, we see some of the same dynamics at work in the world of stand-up comedians. In comedy as in cuisine, technology can be a powerful tool for originators, one that allows them—or their fans—to discover copyists in far-flung and unusual places. We see more and more detection of copying by fans in the food world. Today, passionate diners routinely post digital photographs of every course in a meal on their blogs, often accompanied by detailed critiques. In this world it is hard for more blatant copies to go unnoticed. This is especially true since the skill involved in recreating many fine dishes is in short supply, and hence these recreations, or derivatives, are most likely to be found in reasonably ambitious and expensive restaurants. It certainly did not take long for the discussion on eGullet to lead to charges of theft and plagiarism—though the conversation revealed significant uncertainty in the culinary community over what was and was not permissible.

In short, social norms are no doubt important checks on certain forms of copying, at least in some contexts and among some communities. But there is little reason to think norms alone explain the continuingly high level of creativity in the culinary world. There is still a substantial amount of copying taking place among chefs; the key question is why this copying does not destroy the incentive to innovate in the first place. An additional constraining force, we believe, lies in the nature of a copy.

Analog versus Digital, Product versus Performance

American copyright law does not address itself only to perfect or exact copies. Rather, it is illegal to take more than an insubstantial amount of creative expression from a previous work. In copyright argot this rule is referred to as "substantial similarity"—but the word "substantial" has been construed by the courts very expansively. Many copies that ape only a small portion of someone else's copyrighted work have been declared illegal. In fact, in one case, a federal appeals court held that a song violated copyright law for sampling just *three notes* of another composition.[47]

In cases like that, where the copying is far from exact, the infringing work is unlikely to serve as any kind of substitute for the original. In other words, the two songs are not really competing in the market. As a result, the case for harm to the originator's incentives to create is much weaker, overall, than in instances where copying is exact. Digital goods, like songs and movies, lend themselves to essentially perfect copies. For these goods the copy really is the equal of the original for almost any plausible purpose.

In cuisine, almost no version of a given dish is indistinguishable from another. The exact ingredients may vary. Or their quality may change from season to season. The composition may be tweaked subtly, and the execution will surely not be the same each time. Indeed, because in a fine restaurant each dish served is in essence a hand-crafted item, one that is purpose-built for each customer, even versions by the same chef on the same evening will vary. And of course in many high profile restaurants the ostensible chef and creator is not necessarily behind the stove every evening, or even any evening. As noted chef Bobby Flay once quipped, "For a celebrity chef, cooking means handing someone a recipe."[48] Even for noncelebrity chefs, in a kitchen of any size there are many chefs, and often the executive chef is merely supervising the process.

As a result, even in the finest restaurants the original version of a dish is subject to change. Variation is inherent in this system. Food, in short, is more like an analog technology, in which copying is never perfect. Think of an LP copied to a cassette tape—analog copying technologies like these generate copies in which quality degrades in an obvious way. Copies of famous recipes are like cassettes—they can be good, but they are never perfect (though unlike a cassette tape, the copy might be better). This is very different from the case of a digital technology, like an mp3 music file, which can be copied *perfectly*. For this reason, the norm against perfect copying that Fauchart and von Hippel identify among French chefs is, in a sense, enforced by the nature of cooking itself. Because perfect copies are almost impossible in cuisine, their values are also not the same as that of the original. Again, as Laurent Torondel told us, "execution is everything."

This point may seem obvious, but it is significant because it helps explain the generally forgiving nature of both legal rules and social norms against culinary copying. If ostensible copies are not true copies, are they really competing in the same marketplace? Consumers who buy and eat the "copy" are in many respects enjoying something distinct from the original; perhaps better, perhaps worse, but certainly different. Those differences can give them something to argue over: whose version of gargouillou is best—Michel Bras' or one of the many imitators? Differentiation can defang copies, and indeed can even make the copy a form of advertisement for the original: if you love the molten chocolate cake at Local Bistro X, don't you want to try Jean-George Vongerichten's signature version? Looked at this way, being copied is a strong signal of success, one that can reinforce a valuable reputation as an innovator.

Moreover, the entire experience associated with consuming a given dish varies tremendously, and from a consumer standpoint the overall experience is what is being purchased. It may be possible to copy a recipe faithfully, but it is very rarely possible to copy the experience of consuming it.

Thomas Keller's famed Oysters and Pearls, for example, is a great creation. The recipe itself can be reproduced. Yet the experience of eating it at Keller's famous Yountville, California, restaurant, the French Laundry, cannot be. Those who consume Keller's version are participating in a larger event, which features exceptional service, a special ambience, and the pleasure of a first-class night out. Together with the expertly prepared food, these hard-to-copy elements of the French Laundry experience lead many diners to desperately call the reservation line months in advance. (And a Keller meal is not cheap: as of April 2012, the prix fixe menu at the French Laundry began at $270 and escalated rapidly from there.) Finding the same dish in a local haunt, no matter how skillfully reproduced, is not a true substitute.

In a way, the same might be said about digital copies: owning a pirated music file is not the same as owning the actual, legal file. With the legal version you get a virus-free file that is what it claims to be. The pirated version may fail or infect your computer. Compared with a digital good like a music download, however, the differences between original and copy that arise for a complex product like a plate of fine food are far greater.

Moreover, the central item created by a chef—food—cannot be easily disentangled from the "packaging" of the restaurant in the way that songs can be separated out and sold, or traded, as discrete digital files. (And the importance of "packaging" is one reason trade dress disputes among restaurants crop up.) At many top restaurants you cannot order home delivery of a meal, or for that matter even order takeout. The dish you crave must be purchased as part of a larger, multifaceted transaction, replete with various courses, beverages, and side dishes. There are ambience, service, energy, and other intangibles in the mix. All of these factors work together. Copying one aspect—the main dish—may be easy. Copying the experience in full is virtually impossible. The experience is less one of buying a product and more that of enjoying a performance.

Consequently, the mere fact that a recipe is copied does not necessarily threaten the originator. And as we suggested a moment ago, the copy might even serve as an advertisement of sorts, trumpeting the value and specialness of the original. In this way, copying may serve as a signal of quality and a building block of something else that is often valuable: reputation.

Reputation

There are many reasons for chefs to ignore or even welcome copying of their creations. One is the desire to acquire or maintain a reputation among other chefs for bold and unusual cooking. When a great or particularly inventive dish is pioneered, its creator frequently becomes well known and respected in the community of chefs, restaurateurs, critics, and writers. For many chefs, that acclaim is a powerful inducement to create.

Indeed, in their study of French chefs, Fauchart and von Hippel note that the leading chefs in France will sometimes openly reveal the secrets and methods behind their creations in a public forum. According to their interviews, these chefs expect a number of benefits from disclosure. Among them are that disclosure will increase their personal reputation; generate publicity for their restaurant; inform potential patrons about what is offered in their restaurant; enable them to claim the "innovation space" before another chef gets a related idea; be an enjoyable experience for them; and be an opportunity to promote regional products.[49]

Whether chefs' expectations about the positive effects of sharing are likely to pan out in every case is hard to say. But these are certainly plausible rationales for revealing things that could otherwise be kept as secrets, and they help explain the relatively open culture of innovation that exists among many chefs.

Of course, a chef's reputation can grow even if he or she doesn't publicly reveal the secrets of a hot new dish. Great dishes get talked about; this means their creators get talked about too. And because chefs generally hew to a norm of attribution, most everyone who matters will know who the creator is. Identifying creators is a necessary step in the development of reputations for creativity. But even in the absence of a strong attribution norm, a reputation for innovation can develop among peers. It is often easy for insiders to recognize a copied dish, and the originator's peer reputation may grow even when copyists fail to acknowledge, or try to hide, the provenance of their creations.

Chefs care about their reputation among peers, but they also care about their broader public reputation. In fact, today public renown can be more valuable to a chef than respect from insiders. In recent years leading chefs have increasingly become celebrities; some argue that "being a chef now is like being a rock star."[50] In 2006 the Food Network—an enormously popular channel which on many nights has more viewers than any cable news outlet[51]—even debuted a show called *Chefography*, devoted to biographies of famous chefs and food personalities.[52] Much of this intense interest in chefs is created and sustained by other television shows devoted to cooking, ranging from competition shows such as *Iron Chef* and *Top Chef* to how-to shows such as *Secrets of a Restaurant Chef* and *30 Minute Meals*.

Feeding all of this is a mass culture of food appreciation that is increasingly about consumption of creative food rather than cooking. As food writer Michael Pollan has noted, Americans have a waning interest in actually cooking their own meals. "The historical drift of cooking programs— from a genuine interest in producing food yourself to the spectacle of merely consuming it—surely owes a lot to the decline of cooking in our culture."[53] Indeed, the competition-style cooking shows that air on television are far more popular than the how-to cooking shows and, as a result, are much more likely to air in primetime. Consumers of shows like *Top Chef* may not cook much themselves. As avid fans, however, they increasingly are educated about gustatory detail and exotica. Learned connoisseurs of eating are in turn more likely to prize creativity when they go out.

In short, wider public interest in the work of chefs is high, and as a result garnering public as well as peer attention is increasingly valuable to chefs. Attention is the route to fame and riches: a lucrative cookbook contract; reviews from critics; a profile in one of the many food-oriented national magazines.

Most valuably, public attention is the critical entrée to television. To be sure, this brass ring is grasped only by a precious few. But like many markets characterized by winner-take-all dynamics, the existence of this prize is a powerful inducement to innovate. And having one's creations widely copied is a testament to one's influence and creative power. This not only helps explain the equanimity with which many chefs greet copying. It also helps explain the otherwise perplexing level of desire to produce highly risky, innovative food, which may not turn out to be all that tasty and, more important, may not sell well.

A *Wall Street Journal* article captured these complex incentives well. After noting the work of daring chefs such as Richard Blais of Atlanta—whose creations include such non-crowd-pleasers as tableside-prepared mustard ice cream and raw-lamb meatballs—the *Journal* opined,

> The goal of this edgy fare is not just to shock; these chefs want to create new food that is delicious to eat. But it's aimed at an audience outside the restaurant, too. The rise of food media—from television's "Iron Chef" and cooking magazines to a small army of self-styled epicures writing blogs on the Internet—means that a couple of offbeat dishes can win attention that mastery of French culinary technique can't buy. Restaurants . . . may flame out, but the chef becomes a celebrity. . . . It's no wonder that more young chefs are modeling themselves after stars such as Ferran Adria, the guru of avant-garde cuisine in Spain, and thinking of themselves as artists rather than artisans.[54]

Whether this dynamic is producing successful restaurants is a separate question: the public's taste for creativity on their dinner plate may be limited. (Indeed, Richard Blais's first restaurant flamed out quickly.)* But it unquestionably is producing substantial innovation. In a field where innovation for centuries was seen as incremental at best and undesirable at worst, this is a noteworthy development.

To summarize the argument so far, we have explored three reasons that chefs continue to create even though their central creative work—their

---

* The same might be said about contemporary art: innovation doesn't sell on a mass scale or even a moderate one. Thomas Kinkade is surely America's favorite (recently deceased) artist; his work is said to hang in 5% of American homes. But the self-proclaimed "Painter of Light" (dubbed "the King of Kitsch" by the British newspaper *The Independent*) never has been classed among the avant-garde.

recipes and the food they cook from them—can be freely and legally copied:

- Because widespread copying can burnish a chef's reputation for creativity, which is increasingly valued by diners and the broader public;
- Because copies in the culinary world are necessarily reinterpretations, not exact copies, and hence do not readily compete with originals and may even serve as advertisements for originals;
- And because social norms among skilled chefs restrain the most egregious forms of copying and thereby blunt its impact.

Together, these arguments help to explain why the widespread copying of new dishes is not viewed as much of a threat in the culinary world. Copying in the kitchen has both positive and negative effects, and the balance between the two varies from case to case and chef to chef. But the key point is simply that copying does not inevitably kill creativity, as the conventional wisdom about copyright law assumes. Warren Buffet (supposedly) once said that his investment approach works in practice, but not in theory. The situation here is not so different. We know that copying does not kill creativity among chefs because chefs remain enormously creative even though the rules against copying barely apply to them. But until now, there have been few attempts to explain why, or how, this is possible.

The Open Kitchen

A deeper take on how chefs continue to create in the face of copying begins with a more frontal challenge to the premise that copying is anathema to creativity. Perhaps copying is not, on balance, much of a threat to innovation, but instead a valuable tool to achieve it. To consider this, step back to the basic justification for regulations on copying. As we explained at the outset of this book, monopoly rights in creations are said to be the price we pay to ensure that creations keep coming. As the Supreme Court declared in a famous music case from the 1970s, copyright exists "to stimulate artistic creativity for the general public good."[55] The underlying policy behind these rules is forward looking and results oriented.

This does not, however, necessarily entail a focus on preventing copying. The real goal is *incentivizing innovation*; stopping copying is just a means to that end. If copying does not diminish innovation, it is not a problem in itself. The standard view considers it self-evident that copying is harmful to innovation. The worlds of fashion and food, however, give us substantial reason to doubt that copying is inevitably harmful.

There are other, similar, examples, to which we will soon turn. Probably the best known is open-source software—software designed collaboratively by large groups of (sometimes otherwise unconnected) individuals. Software and food are very different, and we will talk more about open source in the Conclusion to this book. But some of the principles underlying open-source software also have a surprising resonance in cuisine. Chefs often say that culinary change is largely the product not of large inventive leaps, but of collective, incremental processes of innovation. If so, spreading and sharing innovative ideas is essential to creating them. Legal prohibitions on copying may indeed incentivize some creations, as the traditional view of copyright assumes. But by impeding sharing, these restrictions threaten to squelch other creations. That is the big idea behind open source: innovation is better served through open collaboration and unimpeded propagation and use than via enforcement of property rights.

This dynamic might also explain why creativity in the kitchen continues to flourish in the face of extensive copying. In short, perhaps copying is not the problem, but instead is part of the solution. Freedom to copy enables chefs to learn from one another, and thereby to keep incrementally improving their offerings.

Indeed, in their "Statement on the 'New Cookery,'" famously inventive chefs Ferran Adria, Heston Blumenthal, and Thomas Keller declared that "culinary traditions are collective, cumulative inventions, a heritage created by hundreds of generations of cooks."[56] If they are correct, the application of standard rules of copyright to dishes and recipes would create more problems than it might solve. Not only would chefs have legal costs to bear—protecting their erstwhile innovations while defending themselves against (perhaps frivolous) claims of copying. They would also face new barriers to their engagement in the centuries-old "collective, cumulative" process that Adria, Keller, and Blumenthal salute.

That process has successfully produced a world of great food. And it is hard to see how food could be much *more* creative than it already is. Like fashion design, culinary creation is not a problem to be fixed. It is instead a window on an important and overlooked understanding of innovation.

Conclusion: The Creative Cocktail, or Why Drinks May Tell Us More about Dinner

Step down into Crif Dogs, a tiny, unassuming hot dog spot on busy St. Mark's Place in New York City, and you may notice—if it is after 7 PM or so—a small knot of slightly anxious people clustered by a vintage pay phone on the wall to your left. If you pick up the phone, a woman will answer and a hidden opening will appear. Beyond the opening you may glimpse the dim confines of the modern-day speakeasy known as PDT (short for "Please Don't Tell"). If you don't have a reservation you probably will have to wait an hour or more for entrance—the hostess will even take your number and call you when your seat is ready. But once inside you'll be glad you did. PDT serves some of the best cocktails in New York, a famously besotted city where serious bars compete to attract serious drinkers.

Part of PDT's appeal is obviously its retro-speakeasy vibe and its dark interior filled with stuffed squirrels and other bizarre decor.[*] But equally important are the excellent cocktails served there. Like a lot of new bars in cities such as New York, Los Angeles, Chicago, and San Francisco, PDT serves impeccably made and innovative drinks. PDT and its brethren combine two important trends in 21st-century bar culture: secrecy and creativity.

The secrecy part—the unmarked doors, the fake phones—harks back to the Prohibition era, but without the risk of arrest. The creativity part is obviously what interests us in this book. Bars like PDT (and today there are many) certainly serve their share of simple martinis and Manhattans. But they also offer some pretty creative cocktails, many of which feature unusual and handcrafted bitters, carefully sourced and shaped ice and freshly infused elixirs of various kinds. Put together in unusual ways, the fine ingredients and meticulous mixing make for excellent and interesting drinking.

Indeed, like cuisine, it is fair to say we are living in a golden age of cocktails. And as a result, many of the same questions that we raised in this chapter about cuisine apply to cocktails. Like great dishes, great drinks can be very innovative—more so than many people may realize. Consider a few examples.

---

[*] And, in a stroke of genius born of proximity, you can order Crif Dogs and waffle fries from inside PDT, served to you thru an even-tinier trap door in the wall behind the bar. Some of the dogs served here are named after famous chefs—including regular patron David Chang of Momofuku, whose signature dog is covered in a kimchi relish.

In Los Angeles, the Tar Pit serves the Prude's Demise, made with overproof rum, kumquats, kaffir lime leaves, black pepper agave syrup, velvet falernum (a kind of tropical flavoring), and lime juice. Similarly, Death & Co. in New York serves a Cortado: two kinds of rum, coffee-bean infused vermouth, white crème de cacao, demarara sugar, angostura bitters, and mole bitters. Aviary in Chicago makes a Hot Chocolate with tequila and Fernet Branca that involves smoking milk over a burning cigar. At the now-closed Tailor in New York City, cocktail empresario Eben Freeman offered "solid" cocktails, including a Ramos Gin Fizz marshmallow and "White Russian Breakfast Cereal"—cereal soaked in Kahlua, half and half, and vodka, then dehydrated and served in a small bowl.[*]

Even in lesser known drinking meccas, like Charlottesville, Virginia, the business of high-end cocktails is booming. Charlottesville's Blue Light Grill makes many of its own ingredients, including house-made tonic. One drink recently on offer at the Blue Light featured a mix of bourbon and sugar syrup painstakingly infused with the flavor of expensive tobacco. The goal, according to the bartender-innovator, was to capture the taste of whisky and cigarettes without the need to light up. Not every innovative cocktail is a success—some, indeed, are quite difficult to swallow. Yet, in their creativity and care these drinks push the envelope well beyond the world of the frozen margarita or Long Island iced tea.

Like great and inventive dishes, great and inventive drinks can and often are copied by others, sometimes as overt homage but often simply because they are great, and people want to drink them. For some, creative cocktails are the chief draw not only in bars but also in restaurants. Indeed, as the Pulitzer prize–winning food critic Jonathan Gold argued with regard to Los Angeles, "In some of the best restaurants in town now, the bartender may be as well-known as the chef and even more creative."[57] Molecular mixology and molecular gastronomy often blur. At Bazaar, the celebrated Los Angeles restaurant of Spanish chef Jose Andres, his dirty martinis are served with a spherified olive—olive oil and olive essence in a gel-like robe—and his mojitos are poured over a kind of cotton candy. The afore-mentioned Aviary,

---

[*] We can't leave out the notorious McNuggetini, made with vanilla vodka and a McDonald's chocolate milkshake, with the glass rim coated in barbecue sauce and a Chicken McNugget garnish slapped on. For an instructional video (watched nearly 150,000 times), see www.youtube.com/watch?v=iX8Hzxu7C1g. We draw the line at the Ham Daiquiri, however.

a spinoff from the acclaimed Alinea restaurant in Chicago, even dispenses with a bar, instead making drinks in an open kitchen.

Can creative cocktails be protected from copying? Recipes, as we discussed, can be freely copied. Nonetheless, some are trying to use other legal rules to protect their liquid creations. In 2010, Painkiller, a tiki bar in New York City, was threatened with a cease and desist letter by the makers of Pusser's rum, who claimed a trademark in the Painkiller cocktail (dark rum, orange juice, pineapple juice, and coconut cream, topped with nutmeg).[58] Gosling's Black Seal rum, based in Bermuda, likewise claims a trademark in the Dark 'n Stormy, a simple mix of rum and ginger beer.

"We defend that trademark vigorously, which is a very time-consuming and expensive thing," said Malcolm Gosling Jr., whose family owns Gosling's rum. "That's a valuable asset that we need to protect." Not all see it the same way, as an article in the *New York Times* explained,

> But a trademark-protected drink—especially one as storied and neo-classically cool as a Dark 'n' Stormy—seems anathema to the current bartending practice of putting creative individual spins on time-tested drinks. Drinks like this one undergo something like a wiki process: a tweak here, a substitution there, and the drink is reimagined.[59]

For the most part, bartenders tend not to keep their inventions secret. Like chefs, they often freely pass their recipes and techniques on to others. Still, there is some resistance to the culture of copying that exists in the high-end cocktail world. Eben Freeman, the originator of the solid cocktail at Tailor, also claims creation over a technique called "fat-washing," which involves mixing a melted fat with a spirit of some kind and then chilling it, so the fat rises to the top and can be skimmed off, leaving only the flavor.[60] "In no other creative business can you so easily identify money attached to your creative property," said Freeman in a recent interview. "There is an implied commerce to our intellectual property. Yet we have less protection than anyone else."[61] However hyperbolic this last claim, it is true that copying is common in the mixology world. Yet as Freeman himself illustrates, there is substantial innovation taking place.

In short, cocktails look a lot like cuisine: creativity absent copyright, coupled to vibrant competition. And many of the same factors that we argue shape innovation in the kitchen apply across the restaurant in the bar.

First, cocktails are hand-crafted, often right in the front of the customer, and technique and ingredients matter substantially. So like food, an individual drink is not reliably the same from maker to maker, and may even vary at the same bar in the same night. This is especially true of today's often rococo cocktail creations, which demand precision and often arcane inputs.

Second, cocktails, even more than cuisine, are a performance as much as a product. A bar, fundamentally, is at least as much about atmosphere as it is about actual drinking. So the copyist of a particular cocktail isn't necessarily going to compete with the originator. Of course, if the bar itself were copied—the entire look and feel of the place—the copyist would be vulnerable to a trade dress lawsuit, just as one restaurant cannot copy the entire look and feel of another.

Third, bartenders, Eben Freeman notwithstanding, tend to believe in sharing as an ethos—perhaps even more so than chefs. Take the crucial issue of technique. For years, well before the classic cocktail craze took off in the United States, Japanese bartenders had been meticulously recreating American drinks. One of the most famous is Kazuo Ueda, who invented the "Hard Shake" method of mixing drinks. Though it appears to have been taken down now, until recently Ueda operated a Web site called Cocktail Academy, where he explained the Hard Shake as well as his overall philosophy of drink making (and philosophy is not as much of a stretch as it may seem—the site included entries such as "The Way as an Art of Cocktail," referencing the classic Japanese Cha-do, or "Way of Tea").

Ueda's willingness to share the Hard Shake technique[*] certainly doesn't prove that bartenders are an especially collaborative group. But taken in context, it is consistent with virtually everything else we found about cocktail (and culinary) culture. Openness, sharing, and innovation are generally seen as going hand in hand, and not as inevitable antagonists.

Kazuo Ueda also underscores another area of tangency between bartenders and chefs. Like celebrity chefs, who have many, and growing, options to make money outside of the kitchen, celebrity bartenders can work as consultants and even teach others in special bartending academies.

---

[*] Interestingly, Eben Freeman, despite his dissatisfaction with the limited IP protection available for cocktails, has a video in which he demonstrates the Hard Shake, as taught to him by a disciple of Ueda. http://videos.nymag.com/video/Eben-Freemans-Hard-Shake#c=XR4JYD0V7W83M87K&t=Eben%20Freeman%27s%20Hard%20Shake.

Ueda himself came to New York City in 2010 for a special appearance in which he explained (through an interpreter) his approach to bartending and of course taught the assembled guests his famed Hard Shake. Tickets were $675. As this suggests, an ethos of openness and sharing doesn't preclude making some money along the way.

COMEDY VIGILANTES

One day Milton Berle and Henny Youngman were listening to Joey Bishop
tell a particularly funny gag. "Gee, I wish I said that," Berle whispered.
"Don't worry, Milton, [said Youngman,] you will."[1]

Late one Saturday night in February 2007, Joe Rogan decided to take the
law into his own hands. Rogan, a well-known comedian and host of the popular reality program *Fear Factor*, was on stage at The Comedy Store, a vener-
ated club on the Sunset Strip in Los Angeles. Rogan had heard from fellow
comedians that an even more famous stand-up, Carlos Mencia, had copied a
joke from one of Rogan's friends, a relatively obscure comedian named Ari
Shaffir. Rogan spotted Mencia in the audience and called him out in front of
the crowd—insulting him as "Carlos Menstealia" and accusing him of
stealing jokes. Mencia rushed the stage to defend himself, and there began a
long, loud, and profane confrontation.[2]

The Rogan/Mencia blow-up was caught on video, and if you can tolerate
a bit of rough language, it is well worth watching.[3] In the course of a high-
volume duel of insults, with the angry comics standing inches from each
other, Rogan laid out the details of Mencia's alleged offense, including the

joke allegedly lifted from Ari Shaffir[*] and other material Rogan accused Mencia of ripping from rival comedians George Lopez and Bobby Lee. Mencia angrily denied stealing, declaring that Rogan was a "whiny bitch" motivated by jealousy. As the argument grew more intense, Shaffir himself jumped on stage to support Rogan.

Eventually, the comics left the stage, but Rogan continued to press his case against Mencia in interviews. In the following weeks a number of other comics joined in the feud, most siding with Rogan. Perhaps more important, Rogan posted video clips of the confrontation on YouTube along with examples of Mencia's alleged joke thievery. These videos have been viewed more than 5 million times.[4]

The last number should catch your attention. *Five million views* for You-Tube clips recording a public argument between two comedians over copying jokes. What's going on here?

In this chapter, which draws on a two-year study that one of us (Sprigman) conducted with University of Virginia colleague Dotan Oliar,[5] we look closely at how creativity and copying work in the world of stand-up comedy. The story is fascinating on its own. More broadly, the world of comedy provides important insights into how some creative communities develop informal and extra-legal rules of conduct—which we have referred to in this book as social norms—to control copying and limit the harms it may cause. For many decades copying was an accepted part of the comedy world. But since roughly the 1960s, when stand-up comedy began to move away from strings of one-liners and toward longer, more personalized routines, social norms have played an important role in regulating copying among comedians.

Comedy differs in some important ways from the worlds of cuisine and fashion we described in the previous two chapters. Much more so than chefs, comedians are fairly united in their opposition to copying. More so than the fashion industry, the comedy industry has a strong set of social norms that effectively constrain copying. But as is true of both food and fashion, legal rules about copying play almost no role in comedy. While jokes and comedy routines are technically subject to copyright protection—another area of difference with food and fashion—as a practical matter

---

[*] The joke in question was about the security wall proposed between the United States and Mexico, meant to keep out illegal immigrants. The punch line: "well, who's gonna build that wall?" We say more about this joke later in the chapter.

copyright law is almost useless. (And patent simply does not apply.) Cuisine, clothing, and comedy, in short, are all arenas in which copying is effectively uncontrolled by the law. Yet in all three, creativity thrives.

We explain why legal rules are irrelevant to comedians and how, despite this, comics remain so creative. What the story of comedy shows is not so much that innovation can occur despite extensive imitation—though that was true in the early days of stand-up comedy—but that is the law is not the only way to restrain imitation. Like fashion and food, comedy demonstrates that legal rules about copying are not always necessary for creativity to thrive.

Before we examine how comedians' system of social norms works, however, we have to pull back a bit—to the beginnings of modern stand-up comedy, and, along with it, the once very common practice of joke copying.

A Very Brief History of Stand-Up Comedy

The roots of American stand-up comedy can be traced to variety theater and especially vaudeville, America's primary form of entertainment in the late 19th and early 20th centuries. A ticket to a vaudeville show bought a stew of singing, dancing, juggling, acrobatics, magic, animal performances, pantomime, and comedy. Comedy in vaudeville was presented in a theater format, where funny elements would be intertwined with drama or dance or singing, and occasionally with other talents such as magic or throwing lassos.

Straightforward joke telling was not unknown in vaudeville, but it was not common until the late 1920s, when vaudeville moved closer to modern stand-up by placing increasing emphasis on the character of the "master of ceremonies," or "emcee." The emcee's short jokes (they had to be brisk so as to not slow down the quick flow of the bill) set the standard for the post-vaudeville generation of "one-liner" comics. Early vaudeville performers freely borrowed funny material from other performers. Originality was not a priority.

Vaudeville declined in popularity during the 1930s for various reasons, including the impact of the Great Depression and, most important, the emergence of radio and film. Vaudeville performers began to move to these new media, as well as to independent stand-up shows in nightclubs, casinos, and resorts concentrated in areas such as upstate New York's "Borscht Belt."

Comics like Milton Berle, Henny Youngman, Jack Benny, and Bob Hope represent the transition from vaudeville, where comedians played a relatively minor role in the greater variety show, to a new form, where stand-up comedy was offered as a stand-alone performance. These performers carried with them much of the vaudeville aesthetic—fast-paced gags, wordplay, remnants of theater (song, dance, and costumes), and physical humor. This was the golden era of the one-liner. The basic unit of humor was the joke, and comedians loaded scores of them into their quiver and shot them, rapid-fire, at the audience.

Phyllis Diller, perhaps the fastest worker in the post-vaudeville cohort, could keep up for her one-hour act a constant pace of 12 punch lines a minute. Diller and her fellow post-vaudeville comics worked to master the art of timing the audience and feeding them a new zinger—or perhaps just as often a clinker—as soon as the laughs or groans from the previous joke were starting to wane. This style of stand-up, characterized by strings of jokes that ranged over a wide variety of topics and had little connection to one another, was dominant until the mid-1960s, and remains a part of the comedy world today.

Participants in this seminal era of stand-up had to have a large number of jokes at hand. Not surprisingly, many maintained significant joke archives.[6] Phyllis Diller had over 50,000 jokes, carefully organized by topic.[*] (The Diller archive is now at the Smithsonian Museum.) Approximately half of the jokes in Diller's file were obtained from one of the large groups of writers she used. Looking at the file, it appears that she freely borrowed from other sources, such as comic strips. For example, a number of jokes about Diller's dysfunctional marriage to her fictional husband "Fang" seem to have been inspired by the comic strip, "The Lockhorns," which she followed obsessively. The Diller joke files contain hundreds of "Lockhorns" panels mounted on index cards[7]

In this era, straightforward copying of jokes, as well as the "refinement" of other comedians' materials, was still prevalent. A history of Borscht Belt "Toomlers," or joke-slingers, notes that "[Henny] Youngman's style of delivery

---

[*] Diller also reworked her jokes frequently. One index card in the file featured a joke about the law. "What has 18 legs, 9 heads, and 4 boobs?" she wrote. Punch line: "The Supreme Court." She then crossed out the original joke and rewrote it in pen below, reflecting changes on the Court. "What has 18 legs, 3 boobs, and one black asshole?"

kept him joke broke. Like all Toomlers his need for new, fresh material was complicated by the fact that he worked to repeater guests season after season. The usual method of obtaining material . . . was to lift from the best. Any opening day at Loew's State or the Palace found a dozen comics in the audience, pencils akimbo."[8]

Milton Berle was one of the most famous practitioners of the one-liner era, and also such a well-known joke thief that rivals referred to him as the "Thief of Bad Gags." Berle openly admitted to a penchant for copying, and even made jokes about it—for example, Berle's famous gibe, made on stage at the Beverly Hills Friar's Club, that the prior act "was so funny I dropped my pencil." As Berle explained in 1948, copying was just how business was done: "You say that I, Milton Berle . . . steal from Bob Hope? You don't understand, that's just high finance. . . . I take a joke from Bob Hope . . . Eddie Cantor takes it from me . . . Jack Carson takes it from Cantor . . . and I take it back from Carson. . . . [T]hat's the way it operates, it's called *corn exchange*."[9]

Around the time of the Kennedy presidency, however, stand-up comedy began to make a significant turn. Reflecting larger trends in society, and the growing presence of the baby boomers in American cultural life, a new generation of comics began to explore politics, race, and sex as part of a general move toward increasingly personalized humor. Many comics began to shift from one-liners and short jokes to longer monologues, with a more distinct narrative thread that reflected the individual comedian's life and point of view. Stock, shared jokes on topics like mothers-in-law were increasingly out; individual observations and peccadillos, sometimes woven into long stories, were increasingly in.

Mort Sahl and Lenny Bruce led this new wave of work. Sahl's act was explicitly political and intellectual; Bruce's profanity-laced commentary pushed at social convention, especially race, religion, and sex. Sahl and Bruce were hugely influential; their descendants comprise the majority of working comedians today. And like those seminal artists, most of the current generation—which includes comics as different as Jerry Seinfeld, Chris Rock, Zach Galifianakis, Patton Oswalt, Lewis Black, Louis C.K., Margaret Cho, and Sarah Silverman—work within well-developed comic personalities.

The mainstream of post-1960s comedy, in short, embraced a more conversational style with jokes and funny asides woven into a very personal monologue.* One result is that there is greater variety of styles in comedy than ever before. Whereas earlier comics tended to stick to prescribed themes and types of jokes, today's combine a much greater diversity of approaches and subjects into their routines. And whether the stage personas of comedians are real or invented, routines often reflect an established personality that fans come to love and expect.

Alongside the shift in the last 50 years in how comedy is performed was a parallel shift among comedians in their views about creativity. The copying culture of Borscht Belt comedians was a victim of this new style. Copying was commonplace in the 1940s and 1950s. But it appears to be far less common today—or at least, much less accepted by comedians themselves. Today, comedians who rely on generic joke telling are often derided as "hacks." Originality is prized—indeed, it is the first criterion by which comedians judge other comedians—and imitation is condemned. As we explain below, this shift in views about copying is probably not unrelated to the shift in comedic style that occurred in the same basic period.

One other change is worth noting. As the comedy industry changed in both style and attitude from the 1960s onward, it also grew much larger. A national circuit of comedy clubs spread to most every major city and quite a few smaller towns. Comedians began to release recordings of their performances—and some of these sold massively. Comedians also gained more and more television exposure, both from late night shows and regular sitcoms. In more recent decades, this exposure accelerated, to the point that today we see not only channels like HBO carrying a lot of stand-up, but even a dedicated cable channel, Comedy Central, that features many comedians in many formats. Comedy, in short, is everywhere.*

---

* Of course, there remain a number of comedians who specialize in the older one-liner style. But even with modern purveyors of the one-liner, there is an emphasis on persona and the performative elements that establish persona, such as Steven Wright's monotonic delivery of nuggets of first-person surrealism. In short, contemporary stand-up tends to be pretty clearly stamped with the persona (whether real or invented) of the comedian actually on stage.

* Indeed, whereas once the most trusted newsman in America was Walter Cronkite, today it may well be a former stand-up comedian: Jon Stewart of the *Daily Show*.

Copyright's Irrelevance to Stand-Up Comics

Jokes and routines are literary works, a category that copyright law clearly protects. And yet, despite the many examples of joke theft that exist, there has been only a handful of lawsuits over copying—and none that we could find in the past half-century involves a dispute between stand-up comics. There is also no evidence of threatened litigation or settlements between stand-ups.

Why does the law seem to have so little relevance in the comedy world—even back in the days when copying jokes was as common as breathing? One reason is the expense of enforcement. Comics considering a copyright lawsuit quickly discover that legal fees often mount into tens and even hundreds of thousands of dollars. Yet there are other, arguably more significant, obstacles to a successful suit. The most important of these is copyright's distinction between original expression, which is protected, and the creative ideas underlying the expression, which are not.

This idea-expression distinction is central to copyright law. What this means for comedy is that the particular wording of a bit is protected, but the underlying idea or premise that makes it funny is not. Copyright law permits a rival comedian to take that funny premise, reword it, and create his own version of the joke. This principle of copyright law leaves comedians with little practical protection, because often it is the idea or premise conveyed by a joke that causes the audience to laugh, and that premise can be expressed in several different and equally funny ways.

Another important barrier is the difficulty of proving that another comic actually engaged in copying, rather than creating his or her joke independently. Unlike patent law, which creates monopoly rights that are good against all later-comers to a patented invention (whether they copied that invention or not) copyright *only protects against actual copying*. In most creative fields, this usually isn't an issue in practice; it is virtually impossible to imagine that two authors have written the same play, or two painters produced the same painting. But it is a harder issue when the material in question is a joke. Jokes often are based on premises that are sufficiently topical that a number of comedians will come up with very closely related bits based on the same premise at about the same time.

A good example of this is the very joke over which Joe Rogan went to war with Carlos Mencia. At least four comics have told a similar joke about the construction of a border fence between the United States and Mexico. The first, Ari Shaffir, was recorded telling the joke at a "Latin Laugh Festival" in March 2004:

[California Governor Arnold Schwarzenegger] wants to build a brick wall all the way down [to the] California/Mexico border, like a twelve-foot high brick wall, it's like three feet deep, so no Mexicans get in, but I'm like "Dude, Arnold, um, who do you think is going to build that wall?"[10]

Here are three other comics telling different versions, all in 2006:

Carlos Mencia (January 2006): Um, I propose that we kick all the illegal aliens out of this country, then we build a super fence so they can't get back in and I went, um, "Who's gonna build it?"

D. L. Hughley (October 2006): Now they want to build a wall to keep the Mexicans out of the United States of America, I'm like "Who gonna build the motherf***er?"

George Lopez (November 2006): The Republican answer to illegal immigration is they want to build a wall 700 miles long and twenty feet wide, okay, but "Who you gonna get to build the wall?"[11]

Comedians admit that it is often hard to say whether one comic copied another or whether both converged on the same idea—a fact that makes lawsuits unlikely to succeed. The "Mexican border fence" joke is an apt example. Inspired by events in the news, many comedians working independently could have written similar jokes based on the same premise.

The bottom line is that legal rules against copying seem like a useful tool, but in practice they hardly matter in the comedy world. Yet, while contemporary comedians often hash out funny ideas cooperatively, creating substantial scope for imitation, they value originality and oppose copying. The way they keep this all together is through an unusually well-developed system of social norms. These norms are entirely private and informal. But they restrain copying, allowing for some kinds but not others. And although there is no legal basis for these norms, they are surprisingly effective.

MODERN STAND-UP COMEDIANS AND THEIR SOCIAL NORMS

In the study that is the principal source of what we write here, one of us (Sprigman) and UVA law professor Dotan Oliar interviewed many successful comics about originality and innovation, and especially about what comedians do when they believe that a fellow comic has lifted a bit from them.[12] In other words, the study sought to find out what the norms were and why they existed. Some of these norms mimic the rules of copyright law: for example, the major norm that prohibits publicly performing another stand-up's joke or bit. Others, however, deviate from the ordinary rules of copyright. For example, copyright protects expression but not underlying ideas, but comedians' norms protect expression *as well as ideas*.

We will dig into these norms in a moment. But it is important to note that comedians' norm system includes informal but powerful punishments. These start with simple bad-mouthing and ostracism. If that doesn't work, punishments may escalate to a refusal to work with the offending comedian. Occasionally, comedians threaten joke thieves and even beat them up. None of these sanctions depend on legal rules—indeed, when comedians resort to threatening or beating up other comics, that's obviously against the law. Yet these tactics work. Within the community of comedians, allegations of copying can cause serious harm to the reputation of a comic—remember the example involving Dane Cook from the introduction to this book?— and may even destroy a showbiz career.

The upshot is simple but profound: using informal norms, comedians are able to limit copying. They assert ownership of jokes, regulate their use and transfer, impose sanctions, and maintain substantial incentives to invest in new material. As with fashion designers and chefs, this story presents a puzzle for the monopoly theory of innovation. Since there is no effective legal protection against copying jokes or routines, the monopoly theory predicts that copying should be common and creativity should dry up. Yet thousands of stand-ups keep cranking out great new material night after night.

If you talk with comedians, they seem to agree on one thing: Carlos Mencia steals a lot of jokes. We began this chapter with one well-known example— Mencia's altercation with Joe Rogan. Here's another. On his 2006 album "No Strings Attached," Mencia performed a bit about a devoted father teaching his son how to play football:

> He gives him a football and he shows him how to pass it. He shows him every day how to pass that football, how to three step, five step, seven step drop. He shows him how to throw the bomb, how to throw the out, how

to throw the hook, how to throw the corner, he shows this little kid everything he needs to know about how to be a great quarterback, he even moves from one city to the other, so that kid can be in a better high school. Then that kid goes to college and that man is still, every single game, that dad is right there and he's in college getting better, he wins the Heisman trophy, he ends up in the NFL, five years later he ends up in the Super Bowl, they win the Super Bowl, he gets the MVP of the Super Bowl, and when the cameras come up to him and say "you got anything to say to the camera?" "I love you *mom*!" Arrrgh . . . the bitch never played catch with you![13]

Compare this to a bit from Bill Cosby's 1983 hit album "Himself":

You grab the boy when he's like this, see. And you say, "come here boy"— two years old—you say, "get down, Dad'll show you how to do it." "Now you come at me, run through me," (boom!). "There, see, get back up, get back up—see you didn't do it right now come at me," (boom!). See, now we teach them—see now you say, "go, attack that tree, bite it, (argh!) come on back, bite it again," (argh! argh!). You teach them all that: "tackle me!" (bam!). And then soon he's bigger and he's stronger and he can hit you and you don't want him to hit you anymore, and you say, "alright son." Turn him loose on high school and he's running up and down the field in high school and touchdowns, he's a hundred touchdowns per game and you say, "yeah, that's my son!" And he goes to the big college, playing for a big school, three million students and eight hundred thousand people in the stands—national TV—and he catches the ball and he doesn't even bother to get out of the way, he just runs over everybody for a [touchdown] and he turns around and the camera's on him and you're looking and he says, "hi *mom*!" Ah . . . you don't mind that. You know who taught him.[14]

Mencia has denied copying Cosby's football routine—indeed, he's denied ever hearing Cosby's routine prior to performing his. But that's hard to believe. Cosby is an icon in the comedic community, and *Himself* has sold a huge number of copies and is still on sale 25 years after its release. Given these facts, it's unlikely that Mencia never heard it. And given the striking similarity of the two routines, it's a fair inference that Mencia copied. Cosby, who has denounced copyists but who has also admitted to having once copied comedian George Carlin,[15] has taken no action against Mencia.

Comedian George Lopez has not been as generous. In 2005, Lopez accused Mencia of incorporating 13 minutes of his material into one of Mencia's HBO specials. And Lopez retaliated: he grabbed Mencia at the Laugh Factory comedy club, slammed him against a wall, and punched him.[16]

Yet if a hard punch is a legitimate response among comics to joke stealing, then perhaps Lopez should also beware. Speaking at the 2008 Grammys, Lopez noted how pleased he was to see a woman (Hillary Clinton) and an African American (Barack Obama) competing for the Democratic presidential nomination. He worried, however, that the first female or black president might be assassinated. The best thing to keep them safe, he suggested, would be to choose a Mexican vice president. "Anything bad happens," Lopez promised, "Vice President Flaco will live in the White House."

Funny, but eight years earlier, in his 2000 HBO special "Killing Them Softly," Dave Chappelle declared that he would not be afraid if he were elected the first black president, even though he knew that some people would want to kill him. The reason? Chappelle would choose a Mexican vice president "for insurance." Chappelle's punch line: "So you might as well leave me and Vice President Santiago to our own devices."[17]

Did Mencia copy Cosby and Lopez? Did Lopez copy Chappelle? We don't know for sure: in these, as in many other cases, it is possible that one comedian has imitated another, or that each came up with the joke independently. There are scores of examples that suggest that a joke has been copied— but the evidence is rarely definitive.

The "Mexican Vice President" joke helps to explain why there are fewer lawsuits over imitation than one might otherwise expect. It can be hard to figure out who is an originator. But it's still a puzzle why there are none, since not all—or even most—comedy is based on topical issues like elections. The utter absence of suits is not just a result of copyright's poor fit. It is also a consequence of comedians' social norms system. Let's get more specific about what these norms are.

Thou Shalt Not Covet Thy Neighbor's Jokes, Premises, or Bits

The most important norm is a basic one: a widely shared taboo against copying. This norm is so fundamental that a popular guide for new stand-ups, *The Comedy Bible*, puts the following as the first of its Ten Commandments to the novice: "Thou shalt not covet thy neighbor's jokes, premises, or bits." Other "how to" guides convey the same message.[18]

One obvious question is what exactly this norm prohibits. Does it apply only to exact copying, or all the way to imitating another comic's funny idea? As we've seen, standard rules of copyright prohibit the use of expression that is "substantially similar" to a protected work, but do not protect the underlying idea. The social norms of comedy do not draw the same distinction. They protect both expression *and* ideas.

One comedian illustrated this with an example of a joke about a person having sex in a church. The idea is so general, the comic said, that it should remain open to rival comics. Add, however, even a minor bit of specificity (the comedian posited a joke about a person having sex in a church who is caught by a priest) and both the particular joke embodying that idea, and the idea itself, are off limits to anyone else. Along these same lines, many comedians say that borrowing even general premises—anything that is not "stock" or "commonplace"—is objectionable.

In other words, comedians' norms system extends to the type of behavior usually thought of as *plagiarism*. From a legal perspective, copyright infringement and plagiarism are quite different. Copyright infringement involves the unauthorized copying of protected expression. Plagiarism is a broader concept: it means either the unattributed copying of another's expression (which may also violate copyright law), or unattributed copying of another's *ideas* (which would not violate copyright or, in the vast majority of cases, patent). Of course, copying ideas without proper citation is regarded as a serious offense by certain institutions, such as universities and publishing companies, and certain social groups, such as writers or academics. But these rules against plagiarism are not legal rules—no one can be sued for plagiarizing an idea. Rather, the punishments for this sort of plagiarism are either found in institutional rules like university codes of academic conduct, or they are part of the informal norms of some particular professional group (such as journalists).

Many comedians use the word "plagiarism" to refer to the copying of funny ideas. And, interestingly, they do this whether the idea is attributed to its creator or not. That is a significant step further than the usual approach to plagiarism, which applies only where the original author *is not credited*. Think of academic writing, where it is fine to copy another idea as long as the author is credited in the text or even in a footnote. (Indeed, academics like us love when someone copies our ideas—as long as we get the citation).

Why would comedians take this extra step and bar even the copying of attributed ideas? Maybe it is because audiences want new, fresh material every time they see a favorite comic, and so a comic who tells another comic's joke, even if credited, hurts the originator by over-exposing the material. And maybe (and a related point) it is because comics are committed, as a community, to originality as the defining characteristic of a comic. A person who makes a living telling other people's jokes is simply not a stand-up comedian—at least according to other stand-ups.

But as we explained earlier in this chapter, it hasn't always been this way. In an earlier era, funnymen regularly reworked, recycled, and simply stole jokes from their rivals. No one thought it was particularly unusual or wrong to do so, and many—no surprise—joked about it. We are not sure what led to the change in views over the merits of copying. Certainly technological changes have made it easier for audiences to notice copying. In the Borscht Belt days, audiences were all live. Today, there are television specials, comedy albums, and of course YouTube. Whatever the precise reason, however, comedians today are far more vigilant against copying underlying ideas and expressions.

Own the Premise, Own the Joke

Jokes are often produced collaboratively. Comics spend a lot of time together in clubs and on the road, and often they work out new material while hanging out with other comics. It is not uncommon for a comedian with a great premise to probe another for punch lines, or to try out new jokes on a friend and replace a punch line with one suggested by a peer. Under the rules of copyright law, the comedian originating the premise and the comedian originating the punch line would be joint authors and co-owners of the resulting joke. Comedians, however, adhere to a different rule: *the comedian who came up with the premise owns the joke.* The comedian who offered the punch line would know that she has in effect donated her services.

Why do comedians reject the legal rules governing joint authorship? Because they are incompatible with effective enforcement of the norm against copying. If two comedians were true joint authors, both would own equal rights in the joke. But if both told the same joke, fellow comedians and audience members would think one copied the other.

Joint ownership of a joke, in short, would frustrate enforcement of the cardinal anti-copying norm. Today, all that one needs to enforce the norm is to witness two comedians telling a similar joke. However, under a norms system that recognized joint authorship, detection of stealing would be more difficult, because two comedians telling the same joke can indicate either theft or co-ownership. With the signals muddied in this way, the norm system might well break down.

The same basic concern drives a separate norm governing how comedians buy and sell jokes. Copyright law says that to license or purchase a work, the buyer must have a signed, written agreement. But again, comedians follow their own rule. Jokes are usually sold with a handshake. And whatever the law may say, it is clear to comedians that an oral deal is binding and that the seller has transferred all of his rights in the joke. The transfer of rights in the joke is so complete that the originator cannot even identify himself publicly as the joke's writer. As one comedian explained: "[When I buy a joke,] it's mine, lock, stock and barrel. [My] oral agreement with my writers is you can't even tell anybody that you wrote the joke. You can say on a resume that you write for me but you cannot say specifically what jokes you have written for me."

Who's on First?

In copyright law, "firstness," or "priority" of authorship, has little relevance to the validity of a copyright. If a second author happened to *independently* create a work that is identical to a previous work, the second creator still has a valid copyright. But comedians' norms system favors those who get there first. Also, comedians agree that as a practical matter, when two comedians have been performing a similar joke, the first to perform the joke on television owns it exclusively. The act of doing a joke or routine on TV is, in many senses, a bit like filing for patent protection: it grants exclusive title to a joke publicly.

Firstness also has a role in determining who owns jokes submitted to late-night talk shows. Hosts like Jay Leno and David Letterman maintain email addresses (initially these were fax lines) that comedians use to submit material for the nightly monologue. If the jokes are aired, the lucky writer gets a check in the mail. It sometimes happens, however, that two comedians send in the same basic joke; many are topical and regard the events of the day. If that happens, the first to email gets paid, and the comedian who saw his jokes aired but did not see a check following knows that she was simply too late.

Enforcement

A central issue with all social norms is how to enforce them. Comedians say that despite feuds like those between Joe Rogan and Carlos Mencia, copying is not very prevalent today. That makes intuitive sense: there are thousands of comics performing regularly, and each show might contain several routines, plus various scattered funny asides. Given this volume, copying does seem infrequent. But it happens. And when a comedian believes she has been copied, she's likely to confront the suspected offender. These confrontations are, for the most part, brief, civil, and effective. Persistent copying is limited to a few bad actors who are identified as such in the community.

To make the norms system work, though, comedians must have a reliable way to detect copying. And they do: detection is, for stand-up comedians, a community project. On the typical bill in a stand-up club there are usually several (sometimes as many as eight or ten) comedians. These comedians are often performing several nights a week, and watching other comedians. Given such wide exposure to their peers' material, comedians are well placed to detect imitation. As one comedian put it,

> They police each other. That's how it works. It's tribal. If you get a rep as a thief or a hack (as they call it), it can hurt your career. You're not going to work. They just cast you out.

So what happens when a comedian thinks a rival has taken one of his jokes? The first step is to try to get a settlement. An aggrieved comic may confront the suspect, detail the similarities, and describe how long he has performed the joke. He might also state where the joke was performed and name witnesses. Sometimes the accused comedian admits fault and promises to stop doing the bit in question. This may happen, for example, in cases where the accused recognizes that he has borrowed from a rival without realizing it— something that the copyright law refers to as "subconscious appropriation."

Or the two comics may conclude that they had each come up with the joke independently. If so, the comics might agree that they will simply not perform the same joke on the same bill, or that they will each tell it in different ways or in different parts of the country. One might volunteer to drop the joke as a courtesy. Maybe the joke fits one of the comedians' acts better, or one of them is more passionate about the joke, "needs" the joke more, or simply tells it better.[19]

If an aggrieved comedian does not successfully settle a dispute and decides to pursue the matter, in most cases he will seek to impose two types of sanctions: *attacks on reputation* and *refusals to deal*. Two comedians described the process and the consequences:

> The guy [who thinks he's been copied] is going to try to get the [other comedian] banned from clubs. He's gonna bad mouth him. He is gonna turn other comics against him. The [other comedian] will be shunned.
>
> If you steal jokes, [other comedians] will treat you like a leper, and they will also make phone calls to people who might give you work. You want to get a good rep coming up so that people will talk about you to the bookers for the TV shows and club dates. Comics help other comics get work on the road.

Although these sanctions are informal, they are powerful. Credible allegations may impair or destroy a comic's reputation among his peers, an asset that most comedians prize. Many comedians indicated that appreciation by their peers is very important. There are perhaps 3,000 working comedians in the United States. Still, many interviewees referred to stand-ups as members of a "tribe." In this context, a reputation for imitation can be a barrier to career success[*]:

---

[*] Robin Williams, who has faced long-standing and repeated allegations of joke stealing, described the experience in an interview in *Playboy* magazine in 1992: "Yeah, I hung out in clubs eight hours a night, improvising with people, playing with them, doing routines. And I heard some lines once in a while and I used some lines on talk shows accidentally. That's what got me that reputation and that's why I'm fucking fed up with it. . . . To say that I go out and look for people's material is bullshit and fucked. And I'm tired of taking the rap for it. . . . I avoid anything to do with clubs. People keep saying, "Why don't you do The Comedy Store?" I don't want to go back and get that rap again from anybody. . . . I got tired of [other comics] giving me looks, like, what the fuck are you doing here?"

It's a pretty small fraternity of people who make their living telling jokes. And so we kind of run into each other and see each other on TV and pass each other in clubs and hang out in New York together and you know, so there's nothing more taboo in the comedy world, there's no worse claim to make against somebody than "oh, he's a fucking thief."

You know, there are a handful of guys [who] just have a reputation for being thieves and for the most part it's amazing to me, actually if you think about it, how rarely it happens, because it's so professionally useful. A joke is such—it's hard to really explain this—but, it's a series of words that makes a room full of strangers laugh out loud consistently: it's such a beautiful little gem. It comes along so rarely and it hopefully reveals something and it connects with them and it fits the voice and it's short and concise and relatable and gut-laugh funny and it has to be a lot of different things at the same time.

So the development of those little phrases is a lot of work and when someone comes along and sort of lifts that idea from you and uses it, it's aggravating—it can't be described how aggravating it is. The thing that's amazing to me about it is it doesn't happen more often. Because the fraternity of comedy and the people who book comedy, they feel like a vested interest and so they also don't want to book someone who would steal jokes. Even once you're already really famous you really can't successfully run around and steal jokes and have a career. It's amazing that there's enough sort of self-policing within the system.

If shunning and bad-mouthing fail to work, there is a second level of sanction. Comedians can make clear to booking agents that they will not appear in the same night's lineup with someone they believe is a copyist. Intermediaries—club owners, booking agents, agents, and managers—may also refuse to deal with copyists. In particular, at least some booking agents, many of them former comedians themselves, disdain those who copy:

The guys who book clubs, with a few exceptions . . . they don't want to book a guy who has stolen a joke. Very often, people associated with the comedy business either used to be comics or they think of themselves as funny people and they like the business. . . . And so for the most part those people do it for the love of the craft. And so again, there's sort of a built in network of folks who are trying to do the right thing. I mean if it's a clear reputation [as a thief] and he's trying to book himself as the middle at the Funny Bone in Omaha, [the agent] who books the Funny Bone in Omaha is likely to have heard of this and not take his calls. It could very directly hurt his career. It might end his career if he's famous enough for doing it. It certainly will keep him down below the middle at Funny Bone level. Then he's going to end up telling jokes at [low-class] bars and one-nighters who have a comedy night on a Tuesday, you know. And then it's karaoke and the next night it's trivia night. Some guys wind up in that sort of a circuit.

Reputational sanctions and refusals to deal are the most common retaliatory strategies. But if nothing else works, aggrieved comedians may retaliate with violence. As one comedian recounted, a comic may go up to another, who he thinks lifted a joke, and say "'Hey, that's my material, and here's the freshness date—when I wrote it. I've been doing it for years and suddenly it's in your act and it has to be removed.' About 90% of the comics will say, 'OK, fine.' But there is 10% out there who will say, 'Oh yeah? Well, it's mine now.' And then the only copyright protection you have is a quick upper cut."[20]

This kind of violence is rare. Yet many comedians support or at least refuse to condemn violent retribution. George Lopez did not try to hide the fact that he punched Carlos Mencia—in fact, he boasted about it on *The Howard Stern Show*. An article on the attack on Boston comedian Dan Kinno at the hands of several rival comedians hints at the identities of some of the attackers, who seem to have contributed to bringing the story to print.[21] Kinno's reaction is also telling: the accused comic is apologetic regarding the use of others' material and at no point suggests that the violent "intervention" was out of bounds. Perhaps most important, the comedy community seemed to accept it. A comedy blog commenting on the Kinno incident suggested that "it's refreshing to see the boys in Boston stand up for their intellectual property. . . . It's admirable that they look out for each other and it's entirely appropriate that they brought the hammer down on someone who so blatantly ignored the unwritten laws."[22]

Social norms are certainly not a perfect means of controlling copying. For one, many comedians say that enforcement is difficult when the imitator is significantly more well known than the originator. Attempting to enforce the norms by refusing to appear on a club bill is not likely to work. Also, intermediaries are less likely to enforce the norms or refuse to deal when the imitator is a famous comedian. Fame, in short, is at least a partial escape from the norms system.

There is another limit to the effectiveness of the anti-copying norm: it is not widely shared by the general public. Like consumers who don't hesitate to purchase a cheap knockoff of an expensive dress, many comedians say that audience members do not care about originality or copying; the audience is there to drink, laugh, and have a good time. Not all comedians agree, though, and some suggest that a small slice of the audience is composed of aficionados who care about originality. Several comedians noted that these aficionados can be useful in enforcing the norm against joke stealing. Running afoul of them can hurt: fans talk, especially online, and a reputation for copying can spread to the more casual consumer of stand-up. And of course there are the comic "shaming" videos on YouTube, such as the video of Joe Rogan shaming Carlos Mencia that we began this chapter with, that work to spread accusations far and wide. In short, social norms are not always effective regulators. But of course legal protection is not always effective either.[*]

Anti-Copying Norms and Innovation in Comedy

That comedians have developed their own private, extra-legal system of social norms about copying is fascinating. But this norms system also sheds light on the central question of this book: how does imitation influence innovation? Three points jump out.

First, the comedy world illustrates that, at least in some instances, social norms can be an effective stand-in for legal rights. The behavior of chefs we described in our chapter on cuisine is certainly guided, to some extent, by social norms, yet with the exception of the high-end Parisian chefs studied by von Hippel and Fauchart, the norms among chefs about copying and ownership are relatively weak and loose. In comedy, by contrast, the norms are much stronger and more widely shared. Social norms about copying appear to be weakest of all in the fashion world.

We suspect this may reflect something about the organization of creativity in these three fields. Comedians are essentially sole proprietors, typically working alone; chefs work as part of small teams; and fashion

---

[*] Just ask the music industry—the topic of this book's Epilogue.

designers are (usually) embedded in firms that range from a dozen people to hundreds or even thousands of employees. Social norms about creativity probably work best, and are most likely to take root, in contexts that are most social—that is, where individuals are the key actors and where they rub up against each other frequently. This notion is at least consistent with the pattern we observe in the three fields we have explored so far in this book.

The success of social norms in comedy does not mean that intellectual property rules are unnecessary to stem copying in other creative arenas. Yet it does show that these rules are not necessary in *all* creative arenas. Like fashion and food, legal rules on copying are, as a practical matter, absent in comedy. Yet creativity is thriving.

Second, the fact that comedians have created their own—and often quite different—system of rules suggests that even if the practical barriers to litigation over jokes could be overcome, the existing rules of copyright are not so attractive to comedians. Earlier we detailed several areas where the norms of comedy deviate substantially from the basic structure of copyright. We think this underscores a broader point about good policy: existing IP law is a one-size-fits-all system, and a more focused, industry-specific set of rules might be more effective.

Indeed, we will go one step further: some industries, like fashion and food, do very well with no real rules about copying. We will describe more such industries later on in this book. And that is one reason these industries have neither developed powerful norms system nor successfully convinced Congress to change the law to bar copying. (As we noted in Chapter 1, however, there have several such efforts over the years with regard to fashion—none successful.)

Third, comedians' norms suggest that rules about ownership often have an important effect on *what kind* of creativity is produced, as well as on *how much* is produced. In other words, the rules don't just regulate copying; they shape the kinds of works that get created. These observations raise not just economic but cultural questions.

Consider the history of stand-up recounted in this chapter. During the postwar heyday of the one-liner, there was no strong norm against imitating another comedian. In fact, comedians copied one another shamelessly, joking about it as they did so. And the type of comedy prevalent then permitted and even encouraged this practice. Comedians were telling largely interchangeable generic jokes that a wide audience could appreciate. Comics differentiated themselves by their performance style: who delivered the joke better, timed the audience better, was able to compile and assemble from a repository of jokes a subset that fitted the particular audience. Many comedians based their acts on a blend of stock jokes, purchased jokes, and copied jokes. There was not much investment in the kind of personalized material that dominates today. Given the system at the time, this made sense. One-liners were easy to copy; delivery, however, was relatively more difficult to steal. Post-vaudeville comedians were incentivized to invest in their delivery, not in writing new jokes.

Now compare those comedians with their modern counterparts. Contemporary comics invest far more in original and personal content. The medium is no longer focused on reworking preexisting genres like mother-in-law jokes. Nor is it just about slinging one funny joke after another. Comedy today is more personal, devoted more to storytelling than to one-liners, and more consistent with a real or assumed stage persona. In short, comedians in the post–Lenny-Bruce era invest in a personality. They create a comedic brand of sorts. And to protect that investment and that brand, they have developed a system of social norms that punishes copying. At the same time, comedians invest less in some of the performative aspects of their work: many today stand at a microphone, dress simply, and move around very little, with none of the more elaborate costuming, mimicry, musicianship, and play-acting that characterized the post-vaudeville comics.

The way in which comedy is produced has also changed. Fewer present-day comedians purchase jokes than in the past. This also makes sense, because the risk inherent in buying and selling has likely gone up. From the comedian's perspective, she has to look for writers who can write well for her unique persona. There are fewer writers who can do that than can write generic jokes. And from the writer's perspective, he must now spend time to get to know his client's act before writing for her (which also raises cost) and has a much lower chance of recouping his investment if the deal falls through (since few other comedians are likely to be interested in a joke tailor-written for another).

It is important to pause here to clarify that we think it is probably impossible to prove that the shift to personal, narrative stand-up comedy *caused* the rise of the norms system (or for that matter whether the causal arrow points in the other direction). But this does not mean that the changing style of comedy and the rise of norms about copying are not linked. The norms system emerged and won increasing adherence alongside the growing transformation of comedy toward personal, point-of-view driven humor. Each probably contributed to the evolution of the other.

One comedian captured this in a way that illustrates a view many others espoused in interviews:

> Yes, I must say I got at least three occurrences where I've seen people do one of my jokes and it happens less frequently now because I've become a comedian who's hard to copy. As I've grown as a comedian myself I have become more and more original. So if someone were to steal it nowadays it would be more obvious . . . The number one reason that I think I did it was, well, maybe two reasons, was to be unique. Because in order to be successful in standup comedy when you're fighting against a thousand other guys . . . I needed to start talking about things that not everyone was talking about. And as a side effect that also makes it more difficult for people to steal from me, and made it more difficult for someone to accuse me of stealing some topic.
>
> [N]ow my jokes are longer too. . . . They generally are two or three minutes long and made up of several paragraphs and so if someone were to steal it word for word it would be quite obvious. It would be incredibly obvious that they had stolen three paragraphs out of my act.

The more entrenched the norms system becomes, the more it makes sense for comedians to do this. And the more unique their material is, the easier it is to enforce and maintain a norms system.

Now, it may be that in the past creativity in jokes was more limited, but comedy was also more accessible and communal. Mother-in-law jokes, one-liners, and puns were the types of jokes that all kinds of listeners found easy to appreciate and retell to others. This kind of comedy may have been less personal and inventive, but it was more social. Today, stand-up is more innovative and personalized, but it is also less inclusive and not as easy to recount at your cocktail party.

In short, rules about copying are not just about promoting more or less innovation; they also shape *what kind of innovation* occurs. And this suggests that when we think about the rules governing creativity, we also have to think about what sort of innovation we really want.

Conclusion: The Magic of Norms

Comedians copying jokes are not the only group of creative performers to worry about rivals imitating their routines. Nor are they the only ones to develop norms to regulate them. There is another group of performers—one that's been around much longer than stand-up comedians—that relies heavily on norms as a way of protecting their creativity. A study by a young lawyer, Jacob Loshin, reveals how *magicians* use social norms to help keep the secrets behind their tricks from being disclosed.[23]

The story of magicians is different from that of comedians. Magicians worry less than do comedians about borrowing: they are, on the whole, much more willing to share their secrets with other magicians, whom they view more as colleagues than rivals. Indeed, magicians often publish instructions for performing specific tricks in trade journals such as *Genii*, *Magic*, and *The Linking Ring*, and magicians who invent and share tricks enjoy a special cachet within the fraternity. And because their needs are different, their norms are also different.

Perhaps not surprisingly, given how long magicians have been developing their craft, a lot of creativity in magic is of the tweaking variety—some of the most skilled and inventive magicians gained fame by refining the execution of tricks that have been known for decades, or sometimes centuries.[24] Nevil Maskelyne, one of magic's old masters, claimed that "the difficulty of producing a new magical effect is about equivalent to that of inventing a new proposition in Euclid."[25] Whether it's because there's little that's completely new, or for some other reason, magicians seem to worry less than comedians do about imitation.

They do, however, worry a lot about *traitors*—those magicians who expose the secrets behind a trick to the public. Once a trick is exposed in this way, its value as "magic" is destroyed, and this harms everyone in the industry. For this reason, magicians' norms are focused mostly on punishing magicians who expose tricks to the public—even if the trick is the exposer's own invention.

Exposure is certainly harmful to the world of magic, though normally we think of the exposure and spread of ideas as a good thing. Indeed, usually the law tries to encourage it. A good example is patent, where part of the bargain in obtaining a patent is revealing the "secret" that makes the invention work. With magic tricks, however, exposure can destroy the secret and reduce or even eliminate the value of the trick. Tricks must be mysterious to work as magic.

So why don't magicians use the law to prevent exposure of their tricks? The answer is simple: as a practical matter, IP law is no friendlier to magicians than it is to comedians. The procedure describing the way a trick or illusion is performed is simply not copyrightable. Like the recipe for crème brulee, the recipe for making a lady disappear is a set of facts and processes. Both are excluded from copyright protection under copyright's distinction between unprotectable ideas and protectable creative expression. A few creative magicians have tried to sue for copyright infringement, but so far without success. In 2003, a federal court rejected a suit brought by a magician who claimed that a television program infringed his act by revealing the secret behind his magic trick.[26] Very recently Teller, of the famous magical duo Penn and Teller, broke his longtime silence to file a copyright suit in Nevada. Teller's suit seeks damages against an Australian magician who posted a video on YouTube imitating a Penn and Teller trick, and who offered to sell the secret behind the trick for just over $3000.[27] While Teller's suit is pending as of this writing, it aptly illustrates the limit of copyright protection for magic. Teller is not actually claiming copyright in the way the trick works; he is asserting a copyright in the elaborate (and unusual) pantomime that accompanies the trick. Most magic tricks do not require an elaborate pantomime, and so the suit, even if ultimately successful, has little relevance to the community of magicians.[28]

Patent offers no help either. In theory a magic trick may, if it is novel and nonobvious, be patentable. But given that most magic tricks are tweaks of well-established routines, few are likely to meet that high threshold. Even for those that do, there is an overwhelming problem. Patent protection is granted only where the patentee adequately *discloses* the idea to the public—and that's exactly what magicians don't want.

There is another form of IP—trade secret—which provides some limited protection to carefully guarded tricks. Trade secret law was once useful to magicians. For example, magician Horace Goldin used a trade secret lawsuit in 1922 to block a film company from exposing his "sawing a lady in half" illusion.[29] However, cases like Goldin's have little continuing relevance, because modern trade secret law is much narrower than it was in the early 20th century.

This is true for two reasons. First, the law today is effective only in cases where the secret is revealed by "improper" means, such as theft or breach of a contract. Thus the law can still provide remedies to a magician for disclosure by a former assistant, but it does not reach the most common form of disclosure—reverse engineering by a rival magician or audience member. In other words, anyone witnessing a trick can legitimately recreate it, if they can deduce how it works. Second, and perhaps most important, modern trade secret law requires that the holder of a secret make reasonable efforts to prevent its disclosure. But magicians operate in a culture of sharing among one another, and in many cases disclosure—even just to other magicians— is likely to eliminate protection. In sum, trade secret law is a weak tool for magicians.

As with comedians, when the law fails magicians, their norms step in. The exposure of tricks doesn't occur often. But when it happens, the magic community retaliates. In the 1997–98 television season, Fox broadcast a four-part show titled *Breaking the Magician's Code: Magic's Biggest Secrets Finally Revealed*. In the show a character identified only as the "Masked Magician" performed a series of small tricks and large-scale illusions before revealing the secrets that made them possible. The turncoat magician was ultimately revealed to be a relatively obscure Las Vegas performer named Val Valentino.

The magic community's response was swift and pitiless. Valentino was branded a traitor and shunned by magicians everywhere. "I'm sort of excommunicated now from the magic fraternity's world," Valentino admitted.[30] Largely shut out of work in the United States, Valentino spent a lot of time performing abroad. In subsequent years, he helped to produce a reprise of *Breaking the Magician's Code*, which aired in the United Kingdom and on US TV stations connected with Fox affiliate MyNetworkTV.

It's been more than a decade since the first appearance of the Masked Magician, but the magic community's dislike of Valentino persists. In the fall of 2010, well-known magician Criss Angel spotted Valentino in a Las Vegas casino and had him removed by security. Valentino told the press that Angel "looked at me and yelled, 'Get that piece of [expletive] out of here.' It was bizarre, so unprofessional. I was so disappointed in him." When Valentino and his companion went to a different lounge in the casino, Angel found them and had them removed again.[31]

What can we learn from stories such as these? Magicians need protection, but not the sort that legal rules against copying are likely to provide. Magicians' social norms provide a sort of "super-trade-secret" protection, where magicians are subject to community sanction for disclosing secrets in situations that the formal law would ignore. Exposing tricks is rarely against the law, yet the norms system punishes those who do so. And while the law does not distinguish between sharing with fellow magicians and with ordinary people, the norms system treats the two as entirely different.

And like comedy, the world of magic offers some important lessons about innovation. Social norms can serve as an alternative or supplement to legal protection, especially when legal rules are costly or cumbersome to use. And these norms can evolve, as the story of comedy shows. Is a private, norms-based system preferable to a legal system of copyright, patent, and trade secret rules? This question is impossible to answer as a general matter. Each system comes with its own costs and benefits. On the one hand, the norms system is cheap to enforce and appears to incentivize plenty of innovation. We don't lack for comedy or magic today, either in terms of quantity or variety. But on the other hand, the system presents the danger of mob justice (including gossip and the inability to appeal), does not recognize the full range of forms of ownership and transfer found in the formal law, and lacks a clear fair use standard and reasonable time limitations on the right of ownership.

Of course, all weaknesses are relative. Ordinary IP law offers comedians and magicians little help, and it is unclear whether rewriting legal rules would be possible. More to the point, it does not seem necessary to rewrite the legal rules to better serve comedians and magicians: they are thriving without it.

4

FOOTBALL, FONTS,
FINANCE, AND *FEIST*

In 1950, 20-year-old John Bogle was working late in the Princeton University library researching his senior thesis in economics. Bogle was interested in the growing investment management industry. In particular, he wanted to understand whether people who trusted their money to mutual funds run by professional fund managers were making a good decision. Mutual fund managers charged high fees for their investment funds. Were they worth it? Bogle wondered.

To find the answer, he combed through price reports for hundreds of funds. What Bogle found surprised him. It wasn't just that actively managed mutual funds were failing to beat the market by enough to justify their managers' high fees. They were failing, on average, to beat the market *at all*. Investors would be better off, Bogle argued in his thesis, titled *Mutual Funds Can Make No Claim to Superiority over the Market Averages*, if they could find a low-cost way simply to mimic the market's return.

Bogle's interest in investing, and his skepticism about Wall Street, started in his youth. His father was ruined in the stock market crash of 1929 and was forced to sell the family home. Bogle has said that this experience made him a financial conservative, a perspective that fueled his skepticism about whether actively managed mutual funds delivered for their investors.

Bogle's senior thesis earned him an A+. It also caught the attention of Walter Morgan, the head of the Philadelphia-based Wellington Management Corporation, then, as now, a leading investment management company. Morgan hired Bogle right out of Princeton in 1951. Bogle rose through the ranks and eventually was made head of the firm, but was fired in 1974 following a number of years of below-par performance at Wellington's actively managed funds and a trouble-plagued merger with a Boston-based rival.

Finding himself out of a job in his mid-40s, Bogle picked up where he'd left off as a Princeton senior. He decided to put the ideas in his senior thesis into practice. Immediately after his firing from Wellington in 1974, Bogle founded The Vanguard Group. Vanguard's initial business was providing administrative services to Bogle's old firm, Wellington. But by 1976, Vanguard had introduced its first index fund, the Standard and Poor's 500 stock index.

Veteran investors scoffed, calling the fund "Bogle's folly" and refusing to believe that Americans could be happy with investment returns that were purposefully aimed to achieve the market's average return. They were quickly proven wrong. The Vanguard Group, which started with a paltry $11 million in investment, grew explosively on the wide appeal of its low-cost index funds. Vanguard's flagship 500 Index fund crossed the $100 billion milestone in November 1999, and surpassed the actively managed Magellan fund in 2000 to become the largest mutual fund in existence.[1]

Vanguard itself is now the largest mutual fund company in the United States. And the firm is not just big and rich, it is also innovative. Vanguard was the first firm to introduce bond market index funds, and the first to offer stock market index funds aimed at stocks of particular market capitalization (i.e., small-cap or large-cap stocks), and particular profiles (i.e., value stocks vs. growth stocks). Today these are commonplace ways of structuring mutual funds that investors take for granted. When the new index funds were introduced, however, there was widespread criticism from Wall Street experts. Yet in each case there turned out to be a sizable market for Vanguard's innovations.

John Bogle never tried to patent the idea of the index fund. Even if he had tried, he almost certainly would have failed: at the time the index fund was invented, most courts held that new methods of running a business were not patentable. The idea of a mutual fund that holds a representative index of stocks on behalf of investors would have been treated as an unpatentable business method.

In the years since, business methods have become patentable. At the time Bogle introduced the index fund, however, competitors were perfectly free to copy his idea. They didn't do so right away. Vanguard's first index fund competitor, the Wells Fargo Stagecoach Corporate Stock Fund, arrived only seven years later.

Why did Wall Street not copy Bogle's innovation, even as Vanguard's business boomed? Perhaps because the investment managers who run actively managed mutual funds saw little upside. Index funds don't require much management—that's the whole point—and therefore they limit the amount of money that can be made from investors in the form of management fees. (Unless of course the fund grows to be enormous, as Vanguard's ultimately did.) As clients flocked to Vanguard's funds, though, Wall Street's resistance broke down. In the 1980s, fund giant Fidelity introduced index funds, and by 1990, a number of smaller competitors had followed suit. By the end of the '90s, there were more than 270 index funds competing in the market, 40 of which were benchmarked to the S&P 500, exactly as Bogle's had been almost 30 years earlier. By 2001, over 400 index funds were in existence, and today, there are more than a thousand.

So John Bogle invented the index fund, but the absence of patents meant that Vanguard's rivals were free to copy Bogle's innovation. And eventually they did. This was a smart move for Vanguard's rivals, who got to market their own version of an investment product that people wanted. This was also a great development for consumers. Many people are locked into employer-administered retirement accounts that force them to use funds from companies other than Vanguard. Only after the widespread imitation of index funds were these people able to get the same access to low-cost index funds that Vanguard had been alone in providing for years.

And yet, here's the puzzle: even though any firm is free to market index funds, and many dozens do, *Vanguard is today still by far the biggest provider of index funds.* The firm has done very well from its innovation. And even in the face of widespread copying of its central innovation, it has managed to stay on top.

Vanguard is not an isolated example. Like fashion, food, and stand-up comedy, finance is an innovative industry that operates with a surprisingly limited focus on intellectual property protection. In this chapter, we briefly look at finance, and we also present a number of snapshots of other creative endeavors in which copying is common and, for the most part, legal. Each has its own story, its own creative culture, and its own way of maintaining that creativity despite copying. We will sketch out the basics of these industries and show how they add to our understanding of innovation. Along the way, we will explore the importance of a key aspect of the creativity-copying relationship: tweaking, or the freedom to rework and refine an innovation into something bigger and better.

We will start with *football*, which has a rich history of innovation without the use of patents, copyrights, or any other form of legal protection. We'll then move on to the very different world of typefaces—or, in more modern argot, *fonts*. The shapes of letters are not copyrightable, and for that reason, font designers cannot prevent rivals from copying their work. And yet production of new fonts has boomed. We'll then return to where we started—with innovation in the *financial services industry*. As it turns out, John Bogle's story is not unique. The financial services industry has a long record of innovating despite imitation. We'll examine how. We finish with a quick look at *databases*. In a landmark case called *Feist*, the Supreme Court held that facts, including facts collected in databases, could be freely copied. Immediately thereafter, the European Union went the other way and banned the copying of databases. And yet since the European rule went in effect almost two decades ago, the United States has *increased* its lead over Europe in the number and value of databases produced. How did this happen?

Each of these industries is different from the others. Finance is an economic powerhouse; databases are big and growing; football is smaller but still quite significant economically, and fonts are a tiny market. The four differ in many other (and obvious) ways. But each tells us something about the variety of ways in which creative cultures can be organized to help innovation co-exist with and even benefit from imitation.

FOOTBALL: INNOVATION AND THE I-BONE

Football in the late 19th and early 20th centuries was a pure running game—big running backs bashing their way through a scrum of defensive linemen. And in an era where players wore little protective equipment, the results were not pretty. As we noted in the Introduction to this book, 18 college football players were killed in 1905, and many more seriously injured. (Football was predominantly a college game in those days, and of course college football remains hugely important today.) The national out-cry over gridiron carnage led the White House to intervene, resulting in the formation of a college cartel that would eventually become the National Collegiate Athletic Association, or NCAA.[*] Perhaps of equal importance, however, the outcry led to a rethinking of the rules of football. The most noteworthy change was the introduction of the forward pass.

The great allure of the pass was that it was thought to be less dangerous to players than the run. Yet it had an effect on the game that went far beyond safety. The pass catalyzed a process of change that continues today. It made football a much more complex and interesting game, with an enormous variety of new plays and formations. And over time the importance of passing has only grown, to the point that few teams succeed without a strong passing game.

Some stats from the first 11 games of the 2011 National Football League (NFL) season make the point. During that period, the Jacksonville Jaguars went an unimpressive 3–8. The Jaguars were simultaneously the worst passing team in football and one of the better teams at the run (number 12 of 32). Yet they gained *more* yardage passing (1,444) than running (1,306). And those figures underplay the value of the pass to even teams with a very weak passing offense. The Jaguars gained 5.2 yards per passing attempt (pretty anemic actually—good passing teams average over 7 yards) versus only 3.8 for the run. In a game of inches, that's a big difference. The funda-mental problem that keeps the Jaguars from scoring more points is that they are so bad at passing the ball.[*]

Passing is critical today, and has been for a long time. As football shifted its offensive focus from running to passing, teams developed an array of new plays and formations. In turn, defenses mutated to counter the aerial game. The result was a long-standing dynamic of innovative offensive strategies and defensive counterstrategies that has continually renewed the game. No other

---

[*] Then-president Teddy Roosevelt, famously obsessed with manliness, saw football as a game that instilled, he said in a 1907 speech, "the courage that dares as well as the courage that endures." But TR didn't hesitate to summon Yale coach and football pioneer Walter Camp to the White House in 1905 to discuss cleaning up the game—especially since TR's son, TR Jr. was now a freshman on the Harvard squad.

[*] It's true that passing causes more turnovers (in the form of interceptions) than does running (in the form of fumbles). And yet the football statistic with the highest correlation to wins is the number of yards gained per passing attempt, which is a measure of the efficiency of a team's passing offense. Even with the relatively higher rate of turnovers that a pass-based offense tends to create, a good passing game is still more important to winning than the run. And a team built to pass while keeping interceptions relatively low has, in general, the best chance of winning football games. See Advanced NFL Stats, "What Makes Teams Win?" www.advancednflstats.com/2007/07/what-makes-teams-win-part-1.html.

major sport has changed as profoundly or frequently as has football. The closest baseball comes is the designated hitter rule; in basketball, the shot clock and the three-point shot. These are important innovations and certainly controversial in some quarters. But none transformed their respective games as much as passing transformed football. Forward passing added a range of complexities to the gridiron. The result has been a continuous wave of innovation aimed at effectively deploying, and countering, the ability to pass the ball.

In this chapter we are interested in how this innovation occurs, but also in how it survives the inevitable copying that ensues. Football plays and formations, like most everything in this book, are not covered by copyright or patent law. Not that some haven't tried: in the 1980s James R. Smith applied for a copyright on his "I-bone" offensive formation. We can find no record of a Copyright Office registration (although they did grant a copyright to a book describing the I-bone). While, as we will explain in a moment, it might be possible in theory to copyright a formation, as a practical matter copying is free and easy in football. Nothing stops another coach or team from imitating a great innovation on the field. But at the same time, that prospect doesn't stop great innovations from being introduced.

Let's take a quick look at a few of the more famous examples:

The West Coast Offense. The West Coast Offense, which relied on quick, short passes to control the ball and gain incremental yardage, was the brainchild of Bill Walsh, a three-time Super Bowl winner as head coach of the San Francisco 49ers and a man players referred to as "The Genius." Walsh formulated the West Coast offense when he was offensive coordinator for the Cincinnati Bengals, which, in the late 1960s, were a recently formed and hapless NFL expansion team. He was one of the first to really understand how the short passing strategy could reshape the game.

In an interview given to *Football Digest* not long before being diagnosed with the leukemia that would eventually end his life, Walsh described how the West Coast Offense was born. The Bengals, he said, were an

> expansion franchise that just didn't have near the talent to compete. That was probably the worst-stocked franchise in the history of the NFL. So in putting the team together, I personally was trying to find a way we could compete. The best possible way . . . would be a team that could make as many first downs as possible in a contest and control the football. We couldn't control the football with the run; teams were just too strong. So it

had to be the forward pass, and obviously it had to be a high-percentage, short, controlled passing game. So through a series of formation-changing and timed passes—using all eligible receivers, especially the fullback—we were able to put together an offense and develop it over a period of time. In the process, we managed to win our share.[2]

Walsh's new approach did more than win a reasonable share; when used by the 49ers and Joe Montana it led to three Super Bowl victories. Still, the West Coast Offense was not universally lauded; football traditionalists saw it as a cheap trick. As Walsh told *Football Digest*, "The old-line NFL people called it a nickel-and-dime offense. They, in a sense, had disregard and contempt for it, but whenever they played us, they had to deal with it."[3] Eventually, the West Coast's advantages were recognized—and imitated—by Mike Holmgren and the Green Bay Packers, Jon Gruden and the Philadelphia Eagles, and many others.

The Zone Blitz. Once the West Coast Offense proved its mettle on the field, it began to spread around the NFL. Defenses, accustomed to seeing offenses that relied on the run most of the time, were ill-prepared to deal with an attack based mostly in short passes. They had to adapt. One particularly successful adaptation was the Zone Blitz—a defensive innovation perfected by Dick LeBeau during his mid-80s stint as defensive coordinator of the same Cincinnati Bengals franchise that had been the platform for Walsh's offensive ideas, and originated by the early '70s Miami Dolphins under Bill Arnsbarger.

LeBeau's aim was to disrupt the quick, short passes of the West Coast Offense by increasing pressure on the quarterback while still covering receivers. He did this by focusing on cornerbacks capable of fulfilling demanding man-to-man coverage assignments, and by using a defensive lineman or a linebacker to play a shallow zone defense. He would then send a fast defensive player after the quarterback. The problem for the offense was picking up where the blitz was coming from. The result was a potent counterstrategy to the West Coast attack.

The No-Huddle Offense. As we noted in the introduction, in 1989, Sam Wyche, then head coach of the Cincinnati Bengals (the Bengals again!) pioneered the use of the "hurry-up" offense during the entire game. Known as the "No Huddle," it worked exactly as it sounds—Wyche's Bengals rapidly ran plays, confusing and tiring the larger, less mobile players on the opposing defense. The strategy was very effective, but equally controversial. It was first denounced as cheating by Buffalo Bills coach Marv Levy, among others. But Levy's Bills soon saw the light and ran the no-huddle offense themselves—and went on to play in four straight Super Bowls.

The Spread Offense. Until he lost his job in a scandal involving mistreatment of an injured player, Mike Leach of the Texas Tech Red Raiders ran perhaps the most consistently innovative offense in college football. Leach's principal innovation was the spread—an offensive system that throws (both short passes and long) on almost every down, that uses every eligible receiver, and that implements a limited number of plays run out of a variety of formations in which the offensive linemen spread out across the field. The result is a defense that is both confused (so many receivers!) and tired from covering an offense spread over the entire field. Leach's Texas Tech teams, long treated as also-rans in a conference dominated by powerhouses like Texas, Oklahoma, and Texas A&M, won a disproportionate number of games despite their inability to compete with better known rivals for the most talented players.

The initial reaction to Leach's spread offense was, as with Walsh's West Coast Offense, contempt. The second reaction, just as inevitably, was imitation. Teams on both the college and pro levels adopted various forms of the spread—Rich Rodriguez developed a "spread-option" offense at West Virginia and Michigan, and in 2007 the New England Patriots used the spread and compiled a perfect 16–0 regular season.

There are many other variations and plays we could recount. But we think the basic point is clear: football is a very innovative sport. And rules about copying have played almost no role in shaping that innovation. It is not as if the NFL is unaware of intellectual property. The league and team owners employ some very expensive lawyers, and they are highly attuned to the value of things like trademarks. But to our knowledge no football play or formation has ever been patented, or successfully claimed to be copyrighted.

And this is not because there is an insuperable legal barrier. Crazy as it seems, a football formation might be copyrighted as a sort of dance. In fact, that is exactly what James R. Smith tried with his I-bone (though his effort apparently failed). Choreographic works are specifically mentioned in the US copyright statute as protectable. And formations and plays are, broadly, a way to choreograph the movements of a group of athletes. If an innovative

coach or player could successfully copyright a formation as a piece of chore-
ography, rival teams could not copy it.* But no such claim has ever been
upheld or even seriously attempted, to our knowledge. It is also possible that
patent law might protect these innovations. Patent protection extends to
new and useful "systems," and a formation or play might be characterized
this way. It might also be characterized as a "method of doing business,"
which is also patentable, with some restrictions, under American law. (Football is nothing if not a business.) In sum, IP law might conceivably protect
gridiron innovations. But it never has.

Why then do football coaches continue to innovate, even when they
know their rivals will study their innovations, copy them, and even use these
innovations against them? We think there are several reasons.

First, as the previous stories suggest, innovations in football often involve
coaches who are struggling to find a way to win with players of inferior
talent. An effective innovation may be the only way to level the playing field,
at least temporarily. So competition spurs teams to innovate, even if in the
long run these innovations will be adopted by opponents. This dynamic of
innovation by competitive underdogs is by no means limited to sports, of
course. But football, with its intensive rivalries and big money riding on winning seasons, highlights how important competition can be to spurring
innovation.

Second, and related, all football coaches are short-term thinkers. The
rewards of winning a game can be immense—one Super Bowl victory makes
a career—and this means that they are focused on winning *now*, and less
deterred by the prospect of losing their edge over the long term. An innovation that gives any advantage—even a temporary one—is worth pursuing
no matter what will happen next week, or next season.

Third—and perhaps most important—even though there are no protections against copying a successful play in the long term, there are practical
barriers that prevent immediate copying. These barriers ensure a brief

---

* It's possible that if a team were to apply for and receive a copyright or patent on a particular play or
formation, the National Football League would react either by banning the use of IP to protect the
innovation, or by mandating that any patent or copyright be licensed to rival teams. Such a move by the
NFL might, however, raise antitrust issues. The Supreme Court recently ruled, in the *American Needle v.
NFL* case, that the NFL's teams are economic competitors, and that they and the league itself are not one
entity. As a result, NFL rules that unnecessarily restrict competition—and a ban on obtaining IP rights
might be perceived as such—would be subject to federal antitrust review.

window during which the innovator can't effectively be imitated. Innovative offenses and defenses must be understood to be copied. The first time a formation or play is used, it can create a big element of surprise that really favors the innovating team. Once the innovation is deployed on the field, however, reverse engineering is relatively quick. More difficult—or at least, more time-consuming—is the process of rebuilding a team to take full advantage of the innovation once it is understood. Employing any complex offense or defense requires players to be retrained in that system. It also may require a different type of player—for example, the spread offense favors smaller, speedier, and more highly conditioned offensive players and places less emphasis on enormous offensive linemen.

Economists refer to this brief window as *first-mover advantage*—the period of de facto exclusivity that innovators often enjoy, even in the absence of any legal protection for their innovations, due to the practical difficulties of copying. If the first-mover advantage is substantial enough, it might offer a sufficient incentive to engage in innovation even if copying is inevitable. In football, where the potential rewards of a successful innovation are large, the time until the reward short, and the period required for successful imitation not inconsiderable, first-mover advantage may be enough to incentivize innovations.

Pioneers versus Tweakers

Football highlights another important facet of innovation that deserves more attention. Innovators, like innovations, come in different varieties. Consider one major distinction among innovators. Some innovators come up with something radically different from anything that has been done before. These people—the Thomas Edisons of the world—are the kind that we're likely to call to mind when we think about innovation.* We will call them "Pioneers." But the Pioneers aren't alone. There are many innovators who improve ideas and products by refining or reconceptualizing what others have done. This type of innovator adds something new to a familiar way of doing things, improving and refining it. We will call these people "Tweakers."[4]

---

* The irony is that Edison did not really invent the light bulb. As Mark Lemley of Stanford Law School has noted, Edison simply found a bamboo fiber that worked better as a filament in the light bulb developed by Sawyer and Man, who in turn built on lighting work done by others. This kind of innovation—incremental, tweaking—is precisely our topic in this section.

Tweakers do not get nearly the attention that Pioneers do. In particular, legal rules about copying are generally focused on the interests of Pioneers. As many observers have noted, IP law often reflects a romantic notion of the lonely Pioneer, toiling away in obscurity while creating a new and great invention. Tweakers, on the other hand, are mostly an afterthought. Yet as football illustrates, Tweakers can be very important to the development of successful, effective innovations.

Consider one of many examples from the offensive side of football. Traditionally, football offenses were run out of "power" formations like the wishbone. In this formation, the quarterback took the snap directly behind the center, a fullback was behind him, and offset from behind the fullback were two halfbacks. The positions of the backs formed an extended V, in the shape of a wishbone, as shown in the following diagram.

```
TE  LT  LG  C  RG  RT  WR
        QB
        FB
     HB  HB
```

The wishbone was adapted for a game that focused on running, and it became progressively less effective as the pass became the dominant offensive weapon. The game's shift toward passing prompted a major rethinking of offensive philosophy, one outcome of which was the spread offense.

Mike Leach of Texas Tech, as we noted earlier, is typically thought of as the Pioneer who brought us the spread. But perhaps Leach was really a Tweaker. The deep origins of the spread are disputed, but a lot of fans think that the principal Pioneer was Darrel "Mouse" Davis,[*] who, during the 1970s, ran an early version of the spread called the "run-and-shoot" as head coach of the Portland State Vikings.[5] Leach tweaked the run-and-shoot by moving the quarterback from behind the center to the shotgun position (about 7 yards behind the center), moving the running

---

[*] Davis himself may have tweaked an earlier version of the run-and-shoot pioneered by a high school coach from Middletown, Ohio, named Glenn "Tiger" Ellison. Davis's version of the run-and-shoot was more pass oriented.

back from behind the quarterback to beside him, and spreading the offensive linemen and receivers farther apart across the field. By doing this, Leach oriented the spread further toward aerial attack—his spread was built around a corps of great wide receivers and threw on virtually every down. The result was an offense that led the NCAA in passing yardage for four consecutive years.

Leach also tweaked the spread by speeding it up. An ordinary offense runs about 70 plays per game. Working often without a huddle, the Red Raiders averaged nearly 90—and the rapidity of the game plus the speed of Leach's receivers caused defensive backs to tire and make more mistakes. Perhaps most important, Leach tweaked the spread by spacing out not just receivers but also offensive linemen, leaving gaps as large as a yard or two just in front of the quarterback. A Leach offensive formation often looked like the next diagram.

WR   WR   LT   LG   C   RG   RT   WR   WR

QB   HB

Leach's approach was on one level deeply counterintuitive—the quarterback looks unprotected and communication at the line of scrimmage is more difficult over the greater distance, which makes last-minute reactions to unexpected defensive alignments more difficult. But it worked, mostly by forcing the defensive ends to start very far from the quarterback. That gave the quarterback an instant longer to read the field or to let a play develop, and it also created more passing lanes.

How are the run-and-shoot and the spread different from the power formations that preceded them? The wide spacing creates multiple openings to exploit, as the defense is forced to spread itself thinly across the field to cover everyone. In the years since Mouse Davis introduced the run-and-shoot, and Mike Leached tweaked it into the spread, various forms of spread offense have proliferated at every level of football, from high school to the NFL.

And it has been repeatedly tweaked. One important tweaker was Rich Rodriquez, formerly head coach at West Virginia and later at Michigan. Rodriguez took the spread and moved it back toward a more balanced attack, mixing more runs with passing. And he did this by mashing up the spread with an older offense, the triple option, to create his signature "spread-option." Like the spread, Rodriguez's spread-option starts out as a shotgun. Rodriguez also used receivers spaced wide, scattering the defense thinly over the field. Unlike the pure spread, however, Rodriguez used two halfbacks, one on each side of the quarterback. Each of these backs could run the ball or catch passes, and the quarterback often ran as well—see the following diagram.

WR   LT   LG   C   RG   RT   WR   WR

HB   QB   HB

Rodriguez's spread-option was successful at West Virginia, but much less so against Michigan's powerful Big 10 rivals. Part of this may be due to something we mentioned earlier—it takes time to adapt a team to fit a new offensive (or defensive) system. Rodriguez's stint as the Wolverines' head coach started in the 2008 season, and he was out by the end of 2010. When Rodriguez started at Michigan, the players he inherited were not recruited with the requirements of the spread-option in mind. Perhaps Rodriguez set out to change that but simply ran out of time. In any event, systems similar to Rodriguez's are run by Urban Meyer, formerly at the University of Florida, and by many other coaches in both college and pro football.

Inevitably, however, the tweaking continues. For example, University of Nevada head coach Chris Ault further tweaked the spread-option by moving the quarterback from the shotgun position to the "pistol"—a position about half as far back from center as the shotgun—with the twin halfbacks slightly farther back (see the next diagram).

WR   LT   LG   C   RG   RT   WR   WR

QB

HB   HB

This tweak produced excellent results for Ault's previously unheralded Wolf Pack in the 2009 season. The pistol puts the ball into the quarterback's hands a split-second earlier than before, allowing him to lift his eyes sooner and see the play start developing. Additionally, because the halfbacks are slightly behind the quarterback, they can run both outside routes (as with the shotgun) and straight ahead (more difficult from the shotgun). Ault noted this advantage in an interview: "I came up with the name because a pistol fires straight ahead; it's one bullet straight ahead," he said. "We still want to run the ball north-south."[6]

Football reminds us that when it comes to innovation, Tweakers can be as important as Pioneers—maybe more so. Pioneers provide big insights that improve the game, but they may be untested or unfocused. Tweakers diversify and improve upon what the Pioneers create, refining the underlying idea into an often-more effective version. And the Tweakers are an important part of football's continuous creative renewal. By pushing foundational innovations to their limits, Tweakers open up the next round of creativity. What comes after the spread? We'll know once the Tweakers have finished exploring the spread's strengths and exposing its weaknesses.

Tweakonomics

We want to stay on this point about Pioneers and Tweakers for a moment because Tweakers play an important role in many forms of creative work other than football. We can see this if we take a quick side trip to examine something about as different from football as can be imagined—that longtime fixture of geek culture, the computer programming contest.

MathWorks, a Natick, Massachusetts, firm that produces software for engineers and scientists, has sponsored a series of online programming contests to promote their MATLAB programming language. In these contests, contestants try to write a program that solves a single difficult math problem in the least amount of time. An example is the classic traveling salesman problem, in which contestants compete to find the shortest possible round trip a salesman can make through a given list of cities. Contestants write computer code to calculate the shortest trip, and then submit the code to the Math-Works contest Web site. Their code is graded not only for how closely it approaches the optimal route but also for how quickly it produces the answer.[*]

---

[*] Other MathWorks contests have asked contestants to design a formula to map the surface of Mars, find the most efficient way to fold a complex protein molecule, and tackle a difficult positional problem in the classic Mastermind game.

Contestants can submit as many entries via the MathWorks Web site as they like over a period of several days. Each is scored and the rankings made continually visible to all. At the end of the contest, the winner receives a MathWorks T-shirt and public acknowledgment of his or her victory. That's it. And for this, quite a few highly skilled people will spend a lot of time—sometimes more than a hundred hours—writing code. A chance at glory within the programming community means a lot.

Yet here's an even more surprising twist: after a short initial period of "darkness," where the submitted code is hidden from other participants, the contest is played out in "daylight"—all of the contestants get to see each others' code. And they not only get to see—*they are allowed, indeed encouraged, to take and tweak what they see.*

These rules lead to an innovation environment similar to what we see in football. Some contestants are Pioneers—they work out a fundamental insight that helps address the problem and submit code embodying it. Others are Tweakers: they take code from their Pioneer rivals, improve it, and resubmit it.

As more and more Tweakers wring the flaws out of a Pioneer's code, the solutions to the problem get better and better. More subtly, as the Tweakers push any particular Pioneer's solution toward its best implementation, the limitations of the Pioneer's original insight become apparent. In this way, the Tweakers help to prepare the ground for the next Pioneer—someone who comes in with radically different code that avoids the bottleneck that limited the performance of the previous best solution.

OK, you say, so the Tweakers create some value. But doesn't any set of rules that promotes tweaking crush the incentive to be a Pioneer? Why would anyone want to work out a pioneering approach to a math contest problem if a Tweaker can simply take it, fiddle with it a bit, and leap ahead in the contest?

Ned Gulley, the MathWorks guru in charge of the contests, has suggested an answer:

We find that tweaking is the thing our contestants most often complain about, and at the same time it is the feature that keeps them coming back for more. Our discussion boards swirl with questions like this:

- Who deserves the most credit for this code?
- Who is a big contributor and who is "just a tweaker"?
- What is the difference between a significant change and a tweak?

These kinds of questions bedevil real-world software projects. There seems to be a cultural predisposition to find and glorify the (often mythical) breakthroughs of a lone genius. Since this model doesn't always match reality, these questions don't have satisfying answers. Happily, the contest framework acts as a solvent that minimizes this kind of I-did-more-than-you-did bickering and maximizes fruitful collaboration among many parties. . . . *Part of this successful formula is the fact that we don't offer valuable prizes to the winners of our contest.* The primary reward is social. [B]y way of analogy, suppose Wikipedia contributors were paid large sums of money based on how many of their words persisted in the articles they touched. You can imagine the noise that would result. An enterprise held together by reputation is easily damaged by cash.

The MathWorks experience shows that there is nothing inherently incentive-destroying about tweaking. Instead, it suggests that people view imitation differently in different contexts, depending on their expectations and the norms of that particular world. Although participants in the Mathworks contests may complain about tweaking, they by and large accept it when they know in advance that it is part of the rules.

Ned Gulley believes that part of the reason Tweakers are accepted in the MathWorks contests is because no real money is at stake. But in football, where big money rides on every game, we also see lots of tweaking. And we also see a surprising amount of information sharing that leads to tweaking. Rich Rodriguez, for example, for many years ran summer camps where coaches came to learn his spread-option. And as the *New York Times* described in 2010, New York Jets head coach Rex Ryan's off-season training camps have become a Mecca for coaches seeking inspiration:

This is all why, throughout this off-season, springing up like gladiolus along the sidelines of Florham Park, [New Jersey—the Jets' practice facility], were dozens of coaches in polo shirts and twill slacks, with return airline tickets to Indiana or Hawaii on their hotel bureaus. One week, Jon Gruden, the broadcaster and former Raiders coach, came up from Florida to take the Ryan cure. Then it was Nick Saban of the University of Alabama, college football's defending national champion, reviewing blitzes. "We're all copycats," Saban says. "I haven't invented anything in this business. I've always watched what Rex does."[7]

Coaches are free to copy in football. Many do, and copying is considered neither illegal nor immoral. As a consequence, we see hardly any handwringing about it, because it is part of the background culture and people expect great ideas to get imitated. In this way, we see that sometimes the rules don't follow morality, but rather that morality follows the rules. What is normal becomes moral.

There is another example of tweaking so commonplace that we hardly notice it, yet it is central to one of our most vibrant art forms. American copyright law normally forbids the tweaking of creative works unless the creator gives permission. For the last century, however, there has been a different rule for songs—actually, to be precise, for *musical compositions*, as opposed to *recordings* of those compositions. This special rule for musical compositions gave birth to what today we know as the cover song. The cover artist must pay something to the original songwriter if she sells recordings of the song. But she doesn't have to ask permission to cover the song and reinterpret, and tweak it, as she sees fit.

Why does American law contain this unusual exception for cover songs? The story concerns an interesting historical accident. In the early days of copyright, the rules about music were straightforward for a simple reason: at the time, there was no way to record music or to mechanically reproduce it. Music existed on paper (in the form of sheet music) and in the air during live performances. Copyright law prevented—at least in theory—the unauthorized copying of sheet music, which was the only copying possible.

That all changed after the Civil War, with the invention of the player piano. By the 1890s player pianos were widely distributed in the United States. (The phonograph was invented at about the same time and it too was everywhere by early 20th century.) The player piano deeply troubled popular music composers such as John Philip Sousa. Sousa worried that the pianos would kill the public's demand for sheet music, and sheet music was the source of composers' copyright royalties. To make matters worse, the player piano companies refused to pay royalties to composers for the songs they put on player piano rolls. These rolls were scrolls of paper with holes punched out in patterns that instructed the piano how to play a particular song. The rolls, argued the player piano companies, did not "copy" the composers' musical compositions. As a result, they were perfectly legal.

As Sousa knew, that argument was more than a little disingenuous. Sheet music "copies" a song by rendering it into musical notation—symbols on paper that tell a musician how to reproduce the song. In a similar fashion, a player piano roll "copies" a musical composition by rendering it into a different sort of musical notation—holes punched into paper that tell a machine how to reproduce the song. Sheet music and player piano rolls are essentially the same instructions, just written in different languages. Nonetheless, the Supreme Court, in its 1908 opinion in *White-Smith Music Publishing Co. v. Apollo Co.*,[8] sided with the player piano companies. The Court held that because humans could not read player piano rolls, they were not in fact copies of the musical compositions they encoded.

The result in *White-Smith* lasted but a year before it was overturned by Congress. The Copyright Act of 1909 extended the law to cover all "mechanical" reproductions of musical compositions, whether they could be read by human beings or not.* With this action, however, Congress mandated that all musical compositions would be subject to what is called a "compulsory license." In short, since 1909 the copyright law has allowed musicians to copy others' songs without asking permission, so long as they paid a specified fee to the original songwriter.*

Why did Congress create this system of copying? Because they feared the power of the Aeolian Company.

---

* John Philip Sousa was among those who testified in Congress in support of this expansion of copyright. Sousa, however, was deeply ambivalent about the advent of mechanically reproduced music, and in 1906 he published a vitriolic essay, "The Menace of Mechanical Music," attacking the new technologies. Sousa believed deeply in the importance of music as a democratic activity:

> There are more pianos, violins, guitars, mandolins, and banjos among the working classes of America than in all the rest of the world, and the presence of these instruments in the homes has given employment to enormous numbers of teachers who have patiently taught the children and inculcated a love for music throughout the various communities.
> Right here is the menace of machine-made music! . . . [I]nstruments . . . are no longer being purchased as formerly, and all because the automatic music devices are usurping their places. And what is the result? The child becomes indifferent to practice, for when music can be heard in the homes without the labor of study and close application, and without the slow process of acquiring a technic, . . . the tide of amateurism cannot but recede, until there will be left only the mechanical device and the professional executants. (John Philip Sousa, "The Menace of Mechanical Music," *Appleton's Magazine* 8 [1906]: 278)

Sousa's worries have, of course, come to pass—far fewer Americans learn to play musical instruments than during Sousa's time, and amateur musicianship long ago receded from American life.

* The fee was initially set at $0.02 per copy, or about 48 cents in 2011 dollars. It is now just over $0.09 per copy for most songs. In other words, the cost of covering a song has been slashed by about 85% since the 1909 act was passed.

Who? Aeolian is a long-vanished manufacturer of pianos, player pianos, and organs. (Aeolian declared bankruptcy and disappeared in 1985.) But back in the first decade of the 20th century, when player pianos were the hot new technology, Aeolian was a dominant firm—the Microsoft (or perhaps Google) of its day. Anticipating that Congress was about to overturn *White-Smith*, Aeolian moved swiftly to buy up song rights from musicians and publishing companies so it could copy them onto player piano rolls. Aeolian's competitors quickly complained to Congress about Aeolian's attempt to corner the music market. Congress responded with the invention of the cover song rule.

The immediate result was that Aeolian's competitors gained the right to make their own player piano rolls, so long as they paid the fee. That was Congress's intent: to keep the Aeolian Company from having a monopoly on the then-crucial player piano roll market. The longer term result was much more significant: because of Aeolian's dominance of a now-defunct technology, we have a musical culture in America in which musicians are free to tweak songs they like—and they do so with great enthusiasm. Bob Dylan wrote "All Along the Watchtower"; Jimi Hendrix tweaked it into something quite different and, arguably, made a great song even greater. Another 1960's classic, Van Morrison's "Gloria," has been covered by performers including Jimi Hendrix, the Doors, David Bowie, Tom Petty, Bruce Springsteen, Rickie Lee Jones, AC/DC, and Patti Smith, in perhaps the song's most memorable and inventive reinterpretation. "Gloria" is an enduring song in part because so many legendary musicians have tweaked it. Cat Power, John Lennon, Willie Nelson, Paul Anka, and many other famous artists have issued albums of nothing but cover songs. All this (legal) tweaking has made our musical culture immeasurably richer.

But has the freedom to tweak others' songs, in exchange for a very low fee that the original songwriter has no power to override, suppressed the incentive to write new songs? There's no evidence of that. Indeed, every day we see a continual outpouring of new musical compositions. Tweakers and pioneers co-exist comfortably in the world of music. It is sometimes hard to tell them apart, in fact. Think for a moment about jazz greats like Charlie Parker and John Coltrane. On one level, they are tweakers—Coltrane's version of the Rogers and Hammerstein standard "My Favorite Things" recognizably appropriates that song's famous melody. But if Coltrane starts there, it's certainly not where he ends up. By the song's end more than 13 minutes later, Coltrane has tweaked the original melody and taken it in a much darker, more contemplative direction. At some point in the song, Coltrane crosses the uncertain border that separates Tweakers from Pioneers.

In sum, tweaking is not just something done by football coaches or software engineers. Tweaking is present in all inventive fields, and in some—like music—is a very prominent part of the creative process. Perhaps the most important point about tweaking is this: tweaking does not appear to suppress pioneering innovation very much. If anything, it may often encourage it. Many of the most significant and enduring innovations rest on tweaking. As Malcolm Gladwell has argued, the late Steve Jobs of Apple—an icon of our innovation economy if there ever was one, and the man behind the iPhone and iPad—"was repeatedly referred to as a large-scale visionary and inventor." But in fact, "he was much more a tweaker."

Steve Jobs, Gladwell goes on to argue, was "the greatest tweaker of his generation."[9] Even the iPad, Jobs' last great success, was a tweak of an idea out of Microsoft. And Gladwell rightly points out that the significance of tweaking to technological innovation is by no means just a New-Economy thing: economists debating the origins of the industrial revolution have claimed that the key reason Britain, and not France or Germany, was the first home of the industrial age was tweaking. As Gladwell describes their argument, Britain was not necessarily the home of pathbreaking Pioneers who created the foundational building blocks of the industrial revolution. Rather,

> Britain dominated the industrial revolution because it had a far larger population of skilled engineers and artisans than its competitors: resourceful and creative men who took the signature inventions of the industrial age and *tweaked* them—refined and perfected them, and made them work.[10]

The Law of Tweaking

Let's turn back now to the actual structure of intellectual property rights; specifically, to patent and copyright, and how they influence tweaking. How good a job does our legal system do at creating an environment where both Pioneers and Tweakers can thrive? The answer, unfortunately, is that both patent and copyright (outside the context of music) come up short.

Patent law is the better of the two, but it is only ambivalent on the subject of tweaking. On the one hand, it allows Tweakers to gain rights in their improvements to others' inventions. So if you invent a patentable machine, and we come up with a new and useful tweak, you can get a patent on the machine and we can get one on the tweak. We can't sell our tweaked version of your machine because doing so would violate your patent rights on the machine. But you can't use our tweak without violating *our* patent rights. The patent system expects that we will negotiate a deal to sell the improved, more valuable machine.

So far so good—patent law gives rights to both Pioneers and Tweakers, and leaves it to private negotiations to sort things out from there. But there's a catch. A patent holder owns exclusive rights to make, use, and sell her patented technology. Return now to our prior example. If we want to tweak your patented machine, often we'll have to use it to understand better how it works, or even make an entirely new one. But we don't have the right to do this, and you may be reluctant to give us those rights if you don't want us to tweak in the first place—maybe because you think we will become (or already are) competitors in the same market. There used to be a broad exception in patent law for such "experimental use." That ended in a 2002 case called *Madey v. Duke University*, and in many instances today Tweakers must get permission from the relevant Pioneer.[11]

That said, compared to copyright, patent's treatment of Tweakers is terrific—not least because even patent's weaker restrictions on tweaking last only 20 years. Copyright owners have the exclusive right to copy, distribute, and perform their works for a very long time—over a century in many cases. And they (again, except for the case of musical compositions) have the exclusive right to make what lawyers call "derivative works"—what we have referred to here as tweaks. So if you write a novel, we can't tweak it by transporting the characters into a different time or place. We can't rewrite an episode of Star Trek, for example, to explore the romantic possibilities between Commander William Riker and Counselor Deanna Troi.[*]

There are only two exceptions to this rule: if the Tweaker gets permission first, usually by buying a license, or if the Tweaker successfully can claim that

---

[*] Which may be a good thing—though in practice there is a huge (and almost all copyright-infringing) world of "fan fiction," in which fans rework, sometimes in X-rated fashion, characters and plots drawn from their favorite books and films. Unsurprisingly, there are several Star Trek fan fiction archives on the Internet.

his or her revision is a "fair use" of the original work. In Chapter 2 we mentioned Alice Randall's creative reworking of *Gone With the Wind* from the point of view of a slave. After *The Wind Done Gone* was published, the estate of Margaret Mitchell sued for copyright infringement. Randall escaped, however, on the grounds that she had (supposedly) written a parody of the original book, and so she was covered under the fair use rule.

The Randall case shows that it is possible to tweak without permission. But it is also the exception that proves the rule: the number of successful fair use cases is small, and regardless, to win one you have to fight the lawsuit. And that is often very expensive. It is much easier to just not tweak a copyrighted work in the first place, or to try to get the Pioneer to license the new, tweaked version.[12]

Unfortunately, however, copyright law has made it increasingly difficult to do this. First, the copyright term keeps expanding. Works are now protected for the life of the author plus 70 years—that's well over a century for most. So Tweakers must obtain permission even to use very old works, and of course as authors die and copyrights pass to heirs, it is often much more difficult to figure out whom to contact for permission. This is particularly true for books that are out of print but technically remain under copyright— a problem known as "orphan works." One of the purported benefits of the massive (and controversial) "Google Books" book scanning project[*] is that it would help bring these books back to life—though it would not necessarily make it easier to find the copyright holder to gain permission for a rewrite.

As this suggests, part of the reason it can be so maddening for a Tweaker to even obtain a license to tweak is that the copyright system provides very little information that Tweakers can use to find rights holders. Unlike in the case of patent, there is no master registry of copyrighted works. In fact, there is not even a need to put the © symbol on your next poem to copyright it— it was covered by copyright from the moment you wrote it down.

While this approach makes copyright very easy to obtain, it can be a major obstacle for Tweakers. American law has actually gone backward in

---

[*] Google Books allows users to search an enormous database of books—Google has digitized over 15 million, and its ambition is to reach all the books ever printed. Google does not allow access to copyrighted books unless it has an agreement with a book's publisher. Instead, users receive a list of books that include their search term. Click on a book, and Google shows as much as its publisher has authorized, or, if there is no agreement with the publisher, Google shows only a few lines of text containing the relevant terms. Google Books also provides, for the first time, access to millions of orphaned books.

this respect. For much of history, those who wished to copyright a work had to register with the copyright office, or, later, provide notice of copyright on all published copies of their works (that © symbol). And they had to reregister their copyright periodically. The result was a public record of who owned what and how they could be contacted.

That system of "formalities" was changed in 1992. Today there is no need to register or renew copyrights or to give notice of copyright claims. Reviving formalities would certainly encourage tweaking. But more fundamentally, if copyright's rules were more like those in patent, tweaking would be far easier. If you improve this book—say by reworking it into an appealing screenplay*—then you should be able to publish what you've done, so long as your changes are substantial. But we should also get paid for what we've contributed. In short, we should have a system, as we already do for patents and for cover songs, where tweaking is made easier—and the benefits shared between Tweakers and Pioneers.

FONTS

For centuries, books were handwritten affairs, each copy the product of hundreds or even thousands of hours of intensive labor by a scribe. That made books expensive and rare. The invention of the printing press by Johannes Gutenberg in 1440 ushered in the era of much cheaper books. But it also soon brought cheap *pirated* books.

It was the threat from cheap but unauthorized copies of books that eventually brought us what we now know as copyright law. By the 1500s English publishers, acting through the guild known as the Stationers' Company, were granted a monopoly on printing by the English crown. In 1709, that monopoly was replaced by the first modern copyright law, known as the Statute of Anne. The statute granted rights to authors rather than publishers and made those rights temporary, ultimately wiping out the perpetual rights that publishers had claimed under the common law. The United States followed suit in 1790, when the first Congress passed a copyright law based closely on the English model.

---

* Not quite as far-fetched as it may seem; the nonfiction book *Freakonomics* (Steven D. Levitt and Stephen J. Dubner, *Freakonomics: A Rogue Economist Explores the Hidden Side of Everything* [William Morrow, 2005]) spawned not only a blog (to which we are contributors), but a motion picture documentary and a radio show.

By making books cheap, and pirated copies even cheaper, the invention of the printing press created the economic realities that led to modern copyright law. But Gutenberg's printing press also brought another important change. Handwriting was inherently variable. The invention of printing was accompanied by the invention of movable type, and that meant that the visual expression of language was increasingly regularized by the use of *typefaces*—the name given to the letter forms carved into wood or metal blocks that early presses used to imprint ink on paper.

The technology of typefaces has of course changed dramatically as printing moved from mechanical to electronic. Typefaces now exist mostly as bits of computer code. And in today's computerized world, most people refer to typefaces as "fonts" (except for typographers and graphic designers, who recognize a technical distinction between the two). We'll use the more common term.

The significance of the change in our visual environment and culture from the advent of fonts is not trivial. Fonts enrich language by allowing us to convey subtle messages not carried in the text itself.[13] Fonts can be restrained or florid, cool or warm, reassuring or arresting, and they shade the meaning of the text in which they are set. That is one reason so much effort has been poured into font design, and why so much attention is directed to choosing the right font for wedding invitations, corporate logos, and store catalogs. Fonts are valuable because they shape they way we communicate.

The earliest fonts imitated then-current styles of handwriting.* They had pronounced serifs (flourishes at the end of strokes) and marked differences between thin and thick sections of the letters, a calligraphic style that proceeded naturally from the dominant writing technology of the time, the quill pen. Over time, fonts moved away from mimicry of handwriting. Fonts diversified into many thousands of varieties, some optimized for legibility in reading (such as for books and newspapers), and others for distinctiveness as display type (such as for use in signs).

By the mid-20th century the reigning aesthetic dictated that fonts have clean lines and no serifs. A very famous font from this period—and probably the only one to be the subject of its own documentary—is Helvetica, a sans-serif type developed in 1957 by Swiss typographer Max Miedlinger.[14] Helvetica may be the most widely used font in the world and is emblematic

---

* The first font was the "Donatus-Kalendar" letter style designed by Peter Schoeffer, the scribe that Gutenberg enlisted to design the first typeface for his new invention. Schoeffer's font mimicked ornate 13th-century German handwriting.

of typographic modernism. It's no surprise to see a variant of Helvetica—Helvetica Neue Light—in use on Apple's iPod, for example. The font fits the marketing message that Apple wants to send: clean and cool.

Helvetica has been widely imitated, perhaps most famously by Microsoft, which knocked off Helvetica to avoid paying licensing fees for its early word processing software. The result, Arial, has become a famous font in its own right. Arial imitates Helvetica very closely. In the following illustration, the black letters show the two fonts superimposed.

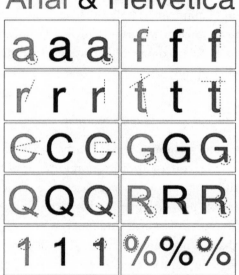

FIGURE 4.1 Helvetica vs. Arial

As this shows, Helvetica and Arial are not identical. They are certainly alike enough, however, that if the general rules of copyright applied, Arial would almost certainly be judged "substantially similar" to Helvetica—and therefore illegal. But copyright does not apply in the world of fonts. Its absence has allowed the wide proliferation of subtle variations on popular fonts. The ordinary consumer may overlook these variations, but for the graphic designer looking for just the right font for a particular job, they are invaluable.

Another familiar, yet very different, font is Times New Roman.[*] Times New Roman was designed to be highly legible using the crude newspaper

---

[*] Times New Roman is called "Times" because it was commissioned by the *Times of London* in 1931, and was created by Cameron Latham of the UK firm Monotype.

printing techniques prevalent in the early 20th century, and to take up less space than comparably legible fonts.

Here is a sentence set in Times New Roman.

The impression this font gives is entirely different from Helvetica's. Where Helvetica is clean and modern, Times New Roman is stately and suggests solidity and credibility—exactly the impression that a "newspaper of record" wishes to make. It is not surprising, then, that there are many variations on Times New Roman. A popular example is Georgia, a design commissioned in 1993 by Microsoft. Georgia is adapted from Times New Roman but with wider serifs. Again, Georgia is similar enough that it would almost certainly break the law if copyright law applied to fonts. The absence of copyright, however, allows designers to imitate fonts like Times New Roman and create subtly different, but overall very similar, families of fonts.

Fonts and Copyright

Fonts, like recipes, and fashion designs, can be freely and legally copied. They are excluded from copyright protection for a lot of the same reasons fashion designs and recipes are. For purposes of copyright law, fonts fall within the category of "pictorial, graphical, or sculptural works." These are not protected if they are "functional," and fonts are considered functional in the simple (or perhaps simpleminded) sense that they are used to construct words and sentences. But for fonts, there would be no books.

Though fonts are clearly functional in this narrow sense, they may still be protectable by copyright if their aesthetic appeal is "separable" in some way from their utilitarian purpose—much like the jewelry designs we discussed in Chapter 1. But given that fonts, to perform their function, must be legible, the utility of fonts is pretty much unavoidable. When Congress passed the current copyright law, the accompanying report from the House of Representatives recognized this basic fact, stating that the relevant committee "does not regard the design of a font . . . to be a copyrightable 'pictorial, graphic, or sculptural work' within the meaning of this bill and the application of the [separability] dividing line."[15] In the years since, the United States Copyright Office has refused to register font designs. The few cases that have considered the issue have followed suit, ruling that fonts are uncopyrightable.[16]

So fonts are unprotected by copyright law.* Is there any law that does protect them against copying? In theory, a truly original font could be protected by a design patent, but for practical reasons patent has only marginal relevance. Patent's novelty requirement would limit protection only to the most unusual fonts. But the most valuable have almost all been attractive but subtle variations on well-known designs. And a very unusual font would most likely be very hard to read.

Trademark law has even less relevance.[17] While the *names* of fonts can be trademarked, fonts themselves cannot. Few consumers can even identify a single font by name, much less associate one with a particular producer. The absence of any consumer association between a font and its producer— what is known as "secondary meaning" or "acquired distinctiveness"— essentially eliminates the possibility of using trademark to protect fonts from copyists.

Font Technology and the Ease of Copying

For hundreds of years the inapplicability of copyright law to fonts didn't really matter, because the technology of printing made fonts very hard to copy. Originally, type was produced in the form of wood blocks and then metal letter shapes. And from the invention of movable type in the 15th century until the early 19th century, the effort involved in designing a font was only a small fraction of the total effort involved in producing print-ready type. Fashioning the metal letterforms would take a punchcutter—a lost art that combined sculpture, metallurgy, and smithery—nearly 800 hours of full-time work.[18] Under these conditions, plagiarizing made little sense, because the work necessary to reproduce the print-ready type meant that copyists and originators faced roughly equivalent costs in producing the finished product.

This changed only at the end of the 19th century with the introduction of photography and something called the pantograph. These technologies, used in combination, allowed easier reproduction of fonts by relatively unskilled workers. But the potential for really cheap font copying arose only

---

* There is one small qualification: once a font is rendered in computer code—which is the form in which modern fonts are employed by almost all users—the code itself can be copyrighted. In practical terms, however, this does not amount to much. Just as a funny idea can be expressed in many different ways, any particular letter shape can be described in many ways in computer code.

in the early 20th century with the spread of the photogravure method of typesetting—or "phototype." Using this technique a copyist could photograph a letter form and then chemically etch that image into a metal plate. The process reduced the cost of copying a font by 90% or more.

So from the early 20th century on, fonts have been relatively easy and cheap to copy. And in the late 20th century, copying became easier and cheaper still. As publishing shifted from mechanical to electronic technologies, fonts also shifted from the physical to the virtual. Fonts exist today not on metal blocks, but as computer code. Once fonts became digital, copying involved a few keystrokes—or, at most, a bit of work with widely available software.

And yet despite the ease of copying fonts—and many individuals do copy them enthusiastically—creativity in fonts continues to thrive. The number of fonts is difficult to count accurately. But the several attempts that do exist reveal a thriving creative environment. A 1974 estimate pegged the number of fonts at 3,621.[19] A 1990 survey identifies 44,000 fonts;[20] a 1996 estimate ranges between 50,000 and 60,000;[21] and in 2002 that number was revised to 100,000.[22] Some current estimates are as high as a quarter million.[23] A quick Google search suggests that even only counting fonts that have been digitized, the growth rate has been substantial. As of April 2012, the Web site fonts.com lists 170,232 computer fonts for sale. That number does not necessarily correspond to the number of *distinct* fonts; as that term is used on fonts.com, it typically refers to a single typesize or weight of a font "family." Nevertheless, the number of distinct fonts is quite large. The Web site dafont.com lists more than 11,500 *free* fonts.

In any event, it is clear that while fonts are easy to copy, and the law does not prevent copying, there is still significant creative effort invested in the design of new fonts. If the 1974 estimate is at all accurate, and if 100,000 serves as a conservative figure for the current number of fonts, then there has been an increase of more than 2,700% in the last 35 years. Moreover, the rate of increase in the production of new fonts seems to be growing, not slowing.

How can it be that innovation in font design is booming in the face of cheap and virtually uncontrolled copying? The digitization of fonts makes copying far easier. The law does not impose any meaningful deterrent to copying. The monopoly theory of IP says that easy and legal copying destroys the incentive to create. And yet the numbers suggest that more fonts have been designed since the rise of the Internet than in the previous five centuries.

A fascinating study by Blake Fry (written when Fry was still a law student) offers several interesting takes on this question, many of which track arguments we make in this book.[24] Fry notes that fonts are in some ways like fashion design. Font trends rise and fall. Fonts are also like food: they come bundled with another product that is harder to copy. In the case of food, particular dishes come bundled with the preparation and ambience of a restaurant. With fonts, particular font designs often come bundled with graphic design software. And they're like jokes, in that their production is governed by a set of norms that exist in a particular creative community and that blunt the harmful consequences of copying. Let's briefly consider some of these arguments.

Technology Makes Copying Easier, but It Also Makes Innovation Easier

Creating fonts before the digital revolution required a lot of investment in time and equipment and probably a team of skilled craftsmen. After digitization, font designers can work solo—all that is needed is some design talent, a computer, and inexpensive software. With low capital costs, and distribution via the Internet, the cost of creativity has fallen markedly. And so too have barriers to entry—would-be font designers no longer need specialized equipment to get into the trade. The digital revolution means that barriers to piracy have fallen too. But since the costs to create new fonts have shrunk so much compared to what they were pre-digitization, the price of fonts can still fall—and they have, significantly. Availability of cheaper (and in many cases free) fonts does not eliminate piracy, but it helps to blunt its appeal, just as the growth of affordable music downloads via Apple's iTunes has led some former music file-sharers back to the legal market.

Likewise, we've seen significant growth in the number of font designers. Before digitization, Fry claims that there were perhaps 100 font designers, and, importantly, virtually all were professionals. There are more professional font designers today—perhaps five to ten times as many as before digitization—but the most important change is the entry of many thousands of amateur font designers. Thanks to digital technologies, amateurs have become a significant source of new font designs.

It's often easy to discount amateur innovation, but it might be especially important in a creative arena like font design. Like so many areas in this book, font innovation is more about tweaking than pioneering: most new fonts involve incremental developments based on well-known designs. Amateurs are well placed to engage in incremental innovation because the investment required is relatively low, and small creative insights can be significant in an art form that is itself composed of subtle variations on the same set of fixed letters.

There is another significant shift in the production of fonts, and it too is driven by technological change. Following digitization, font design has increasingly merged into graphic design. During the era of metal type, the punchcutters who produced usable type were very highly skilled. After the digital revolution, all this changed: general graphic design skills and an interest in type are all that is needed to produce attractive fonts. As a result, many graphic designers today undertake font design projects that would not have occurred before digitization. This also means more fonts.

Changes in the Technology of Printing Induce Innovation in Fonts

Technological innovation has made font design easier and cheaper. But it also has more subtle effects. Because fonts are designed to work well with particular printing technologies, the technologies in wide use at any particular time shape the fonts that get produced. And as these technologies change, the fonts designed for them change as well.

For example, during the 19th century the tremendous growth in newspapers spurred a lot of font innovation. Printers needed to produce legible newspapers using mass printing on cheap, coarse paper. The result was fonts that could be easily read under these adverse conditions. Times New Roman is an example of this wave of newspaper-driven font innovation. Later, as offset printing became more refined, more delicate fonts could be legibly reproduced, and this set off another wave of innovation. As phototypesetting grew in the 1970s, still newer designs appeared, some tied to the technology's ability to render fonts with narrower letter spacing.

The process repeated itself as readers moved from paper to screen in the 1980s and 1990s. Early computers couldn't handle richly detailed fonts, so fonts were made from large blocks. Later, processor and memory limitations eased, but screen resolution remained low. The result was more innovation in sans serif fonts, more legible on low-resolution screens. As screens gained resolution, more new serif fonts began to appear. But the technology does not stand still. Smartphones and tablet computers feature smaller screens. And consequently, screen readability has revived as an issue.

The overall point is that technological change induces innovation in fonts. New technologies have made it easier to create fonts. And other innovations, like the huge success of the iPhone and Android phones, have shaped the kinds of fonts people want. Font innovation is thus driven by innovation in the products that people use to consume text. So long as these technologies continue to evolve, incentives to invest in the production of new fonts arise as a sort of fortunate accident.

Fonts Are Not the Product—Something Else Is

The preceding discussion shows that often innovation in fonts is not undertaken for its own sake, but in service of some other aim. This dynamic is not driven only by changes in technology. The ceaseless demands from advertisers for new and interesting ways of selling things has led to many new fonts. And font innovation is also undertaken in order to sell word processing and graphic design software.

The practice of bundling fonts with software is the primary reason that ordinary consumers do not engage in much piracy of font designs. Most of us think we have plenty of fonts to choose from on whatever word processing software we use. There are font files available on peer-to-peer networks like BitTorrent, but only a tiny group of people care enough to go this route.

Graphic designers are the real market for fonts. For this audience, bundling also plays a major role in inducing innovation and blunting the impetus toward piracy. For example, Adobe, the largest producer of fonts in the world, is in the font business principally as a way to help sell their market-leading Creative Suite graphic design software. Adobe gives away more than 100 fonts with Creative Suite. They sell many additional fonts, but these are just a small sideline business. Nevertheless, Adobe continues to invest in the design of new fonts. Adobe's innovation in font design helps to bolster their position in the product that provides virtually all their revenue: their software. Incentives to create new font design are woven into competitive pressures in a related market for software. In the area of fonts, market competition plays a large role in inducing innovation.

Fonts and Fashion Cycles

Incentives to create new fonts also reflect broader cultural changes. Fonts, like fashion, are subject to trends. To be sure, trends in font design last far longer than in the fashion industry, and also are not as overwhelming a factor in the marketplace. But as in fashion, there are classic styles and bold new designs.

Consider Helvetica, the archetypal clean-lined font we described a few pages back. Helvetica and its many imitators are associated strongly with mid-20th century modernism. These designs still have substantial currency, as Apple's adaptation of Helvetica illustrates. But for all its continuing influence, Helvetica is not really the font of the moment. Other styles have risen to prominence that are the antithesis of the modernist Helvetica style. An example can be found, of all places, on the placemats used in Mario Batali and Nancy Silverton's famed Pizzeria Mozza in Los Angeles.

This Pizzeria Mozza placemat, from 2011, uses fonts that look like recreated letterpress type from the mid-19th century. These sorts of fonts are currently in wide use, in part because they are linked to the contemporary design aesthetic of the "steampunk" movement and to a general love of

FIGURE 4.2 Pizzeria Mozza placemat

antiquarian styles—think of the rash of old-timey cocktail bars in major American cities, manned by bartenders in sleeve garters and waistcoats chipping blocks of ice. Steampunk originated in a Jules Verne-esque genre of science fiction, first appearing in the late-1980s, that was set in a world in which things like computers and space travel are reimagined in a Victorian-era context.

In the 2000s, steampunk emerged as a significant trend in art and design. Designers following the steampunk aesthetic reject the sleek and often cold modernism of objects like the iPhone as inauthentic and alienating, and reach back to older technologies for inspiration. Importantly, steampunk pushes back against the "cleanliness" that has long been dominant in industrial design—including, of course, in modern fonts such as Helvetica. Steampunk-inspired designers find typographic models in the fonts common during the Victorian and Edwardian eras, examples of which we see on the Pizzeria Mozza placemat.

In short, font designs respond to broad cultural and artistic trends. Fonts do not change all that swiftly. But aside from the speed of the cycle, the trend cycle in fonts is similar to that in fashion. If a font is popular enough it will be copied. Sometimes this copying will be exact. Often, however, the copyist will add some variations of her own—and what will emerge is a nonidentical font that is nonetheless recognizably of the same style. Because of digitization, designs in the new style can be made and distributed quickly. As copying and close variation spreads, the style becomes ubiquitous. Like fashion trends that are overdone, once-ubiquitous fonts lose their power, either because they have lost their novelty or the ability to convey what they were originally designed to connote. And as in fashion, font designers innovate in response.

FINANCIAL INNOVATIONS

Over the past several decades the financial services industry has become one of America's biggest economic sectors. Measured in terms of financial flows and trading volumes, the industry is enormous. The capitalization of US stock markets grew from $136.0 billion, or 13.1% of US GDP in 1970, to approximately $19 trillion, or 180% percent of GDP in 2000. Even after the 2008 financial crisis, stock market capitalization is still roughly equivalent to GDP.[25] And as the value and amount of trading in financial markets have grown, so have profits. Profits in the financial industry have more than tripled in size relative to the overall economy since the end of the Second World War.

The financial sector has not just become very large and hugely profitable, however; over this same period it became increasingly filled with America's best and brightest. In 2007, just before the financial crisis began, nearly half of Harvard College's graduating class went into the financial industry or management consulting. And these smart people, unsurprisingly, are also pretty innovative.*

In the wake of the financial crisis, of course, it is very difficult to tell whether many of the recent financial innovations—new kinds of securities, derivatives, pricing models, methods of investing, and so on—are a blessing or a curse. Some commentators, including luminaries like Nobel prize-winning economist Robert Merton, maintain that the financial services industry has benefited society immeasurably through major innovations such as affordable household financing, countless types of derivatives, and low-cost mutual funds. Others argue that most financial innovations serve only to benefit bankers. Famed investor Warren Buffett called derivatives "financial weapons of mass destruction." Former Fed Chairman Paul Volker opined in 2009 that the only socially beneficial financial innovation of the past 25 years has been the ATM.

Whatever the answer, there is no question that the financial services industry has been innovative—and with surprisingly little reliance on IP. Its creative output has included, among other things, thousands of varieties of derivatives, bonds, currency warrants, credit and currency swaps, collateralized debt obligations, exchange traded funds, investment indexes, and the pricing models and trading strategies associated with these instruments. For a long time, as the story of John Bogle and his Vanguard index funds illustrated, the industry produced these innovations with few protections against copying other than, in some cases, secrecy. Considering that the cost of innovation can be substantial—estimates of the investment required to produce most forms of financial innovation range between $500,000 and $5

---

* Maybe too much so. In the fall of 2009, at the depth of the pain on Wall Street, Calvin Trillin wrote in the *New York Times* of meeting a Wall Street veteran who, sitting next to him in a bar, proclaimed he could explain the collapse in one sentence. "Let's hear it," said Trillin. The system collapsed, the man said, because "smart guys had started working on Wall Street." Calvin Trillin, "Wall Street Smarts," *New York Times*, October 14, 2009.

million[26]—this seems surprising. How can the financial services industry's record of innovation be explained?

For much of the industry's history the most plausible form of legal protection, patent, was simply not available for many financial innovations. Nor could innovators rely on trade secrecy law for financial innovations that related to publicly traded securities. Because virtually all the details of a new security become public once the offering is filed with the Securities and Exchange Commission, secrecy is typically impossible. Trade secrecy is more viable for other types of financial investments, such as pricing models, but even in these cases, for reasons we will explain, financial firms often are better off sharing information than keeping it secret.

In 1998, there was a major legal change that made patents much more available to the financial industry. In a case called *State Street Bank and Trust Co. v. Signature Financial Group Inc.,*[27] a federal court established for the first time that novel methods of doing business were patentable. Prior to this ruling, business methods of almost any kind were thought to be unpatentable. (We mentioned business method patents earlier in this chapter, in the context of football plays and formations.) The decision in *State Street* directly involved the financial industry—at the core of the case was a "hub and spoke" method of pooling mutual fund assets.

In the wake of *State Street* bankers began to seek patents for their inventions. In 1997, the year before *State Street*, the Patent and Trademark Office (PTO) granted just 198 patents in the category of "Data Processing: Financial, Business Practice, Management, or Cost/Price Determination." (This category includes most patents relevant to the financial industry, but also a large number which are not.) In 1999, after *State Street*, the PTO granted 833 patents in this category. In 2006, it granted 1,260, and in 2009, 1,956. Yet the raw data on the number of business method patents may be misleading. More than a decade now after *State Street*, the latest data suggests that only about a tenth of the granted business method patents appear to be relevant to the financial industry.[28] That's still hundreds of patents, but less has changed in the industry than even this smaller number suggests.

This is due partly to the actions of the industry itself in the wake of *State Street*. Fearing that they would often end up as defendants in costly patent lawsuits, financial firms worked in concert to secure from Congress a "prior user" defense to accusations of copying.[29] This means that firms that have developed confidential methods of doing business—such as internal business processes—cannot be sued for patent infringement so long as the method of doing business was kept as a trade secret and practiced at least one year before a patent holder brought suit.

This provision made the patents issued after *State Street* less useful as offensive tools against competitors. But it did not shield the industry altogether. A 2006 study unsurprisingly found an increase in patent suits after *State Street*. The defendants in these suits were typically large finance companies.[30] Several suits involved significant sums.[*] A number of useful business method patents have been obtained by outside firms, including, importantly, "non-practicing entities"—that is, firms that collect patents and make their money by licensing and litigating them rather than actually using the inventions covered by the patents they own. These firms are sometimes referred to as "patent trolls": like the troll in the *Three Billy Goats Gruff*, they wait in hiding and demand tribute, in this case, from those who innocently try to use an invention they think is theirs.

So *State Street* has changed some things on Wall Street. But whether the introduction of rules restraining copying led to any significant change in how the industry innovates is less clear. For example, the National Science Foundation, which tracks research and development (R&D) spending across a number of US industries, has measured no significant increase in financial industry R&D investment following the advent of business method patents.[31] A survey of data from the US Bureau of Labor Statistics also revealed no trend in the financial services industry of hiring more R&D workers following the introduction of business method patents, as we might expect if the availability of those patents was making a significant difference in industry resources devoted to innovation.[32]

Perhaps it is not a surprise that we find little evidence to link the advent of financial industry business method patents to an industry innovation boom. Even before *State Street* the financial services industry produced a great deal of important innovation. Often-noted examples include the Black-Scholes option pricing formula, which transformed how Wall Street understood and

---

[*] Recently, Wall Street banks called on New York senator Charles Schumer to provide relief from a particularly nettlesome patent plaintiff, a Texas entrepreneur named Claudio Ballard, who owns patents on a method for processing digital copies of paper checks. Ballard has asserted his patents successfully against many of the biggest banks. In 2011, Schumer inserted a provision into the America Invents Act, signed into law by President Obama on September 16, 2011, that would allow the banks to get Ballard's patents reexamined by the PTO.

priced derivatives, the formation of index mutual funds in the 1970s (as described at the beginning of this chapter), the 1980s-era innovations in the use of high-yield or "junk" bonds as means of financing mergers and acquisitions, and the boom in the 1990s in exchange-traded funds (an evolution of the index fund) and asset securitization (a method of financing that pools various types of debt to sell as a bond). In each instance, significant innovations appeared without the prospect of patent protection.

So how do we explain intellectual production without intellectual property in the financial services industry? Back in 2002, former Harvard Business School professor Peter Tufano (now Dean of Oxford's Saïd Business School) wrote an influential paper that posits a number of interacting reasons. Financial firms innovate to satisfy the unmet needs of particular customers; to lower transaction costs; to avoid taxes and regulation; to take advantage of rating agencies' rules for assessing the quality of debt; and to take advantage of opportunities offered by new technologies.[33] And for many of these kinds of innovations, patent protection would be counterproductive, because sharing with rivals is helpful or even necessary to grow markets to the size at which they become efficient and lucrative.

To understand this point, consider the market for a new type of investment security. In most cases, new securities are likely to be much more lucrative if they trade in markets big enough to become standardized and deeply capitalized. In practice, this typically requires a number of firms to enter the market. Patents, however, can act as a barrier to this. If the innovator patents the new security, potential market participants may hesitate to enter the market for fear that the patent might be used against them. This fear might persist even if the innovator is willing to license the patent to its rivals—especially if those rivals worry that, as a consequence of the license fees, they will face higher costs in marketing the security and will be hobbled in competing with the innovator. The result, Tufano argues, is that as a practical matter patents rarely figure in the development of new securities.[34]

There are some markets in which financial firms are not pursuing standardization—such as the market in over-the-counter, or OTC, derivatives, which includes the now-infamous "credit default swaps" that grew explosively (in many senses) before the 2008 financial crisis. OTC derivatives are basically bets based on the value of some underlying asset, such as stocks, currencies, or interest rates, that are negotiated directly between private parties.

Many markets in OTC derivatives were deliberately structured to not be standardized in order to keep financial firms' margins high. Yet even in these markets, firms tend not to rely on patents to protect their innovations. The reason is that although rival firms are free to imitate new OTC derivatives, it takes time for the details of a private OTC deal to leak out. In part, this is because any successful new OTC derivative requires more than just a clever idea—the innovator must also "de-bug" the transaction by making sure that someone on the other side of the trade can't manipulate the market in his favor. And, importantly, the innovator must also figure out how to *price* the transaction—this tends to be more difficult for OTC derivatives because there is no public market generating thousands or even millions of transactions, and so there is apt to be much less pricing information available.

Once this is done, innovators tend to rely on nondisclosure agreements— that is, contracts—to discourage their counter-parties from disclosing the details of the deal. As the innovator markets the deal more widely, information leaks out, and as rivals learn more, they are almost always able eventually to reverse engineer the deal. Still, this takes time, and the delay means that the originators of new OTC derivative transactions enjoy some first-mover advantage.

And this leads to a broader point about why patents are rarely used for financial innovations: they do not seem to matter much to success in the market. Financial firms that introduce a new and unpatented type of security typically retain a dominant market share for several years, even though rival firms rapidly copy the innovation.[35]

Why? It may have something to do with the in-house expertise developed in the process of innovation. Like a football team that has trained and recruited to run a particular offense—and is thereby better able to implement that offense than are its rivals—the innovating firm is more likely (at least until rival firms catch up or hire away key personnel) to have specialized in-house expertise in using the security that will advantage it over rivals.

But perhaps a deeper explanation relates to the market power of large banks. Many of the markets that together comprise "Wall Street" are dominated by an exclusive cohort of US investment giants—firms like Goldman Sachs, Morgan Stanley, and Citigroup—and an equally exclusive group of foreign-based firms, including Deutsche Bank, Credit Suisse and HSBC. These firms control large shares in particular lines of business, and, importantly, their clients can be "sticky." Investment banking is driven by relationships, and many clients have long-term ties to their bankers that span a variety of product areas. As a result, even if innovations can freely be copied, a large bank can capture a lot of the return on its investment in innovation simply by virtue of its control over a large amount of the particular business at issue and its enduring client relationships.[36]

Consistent with this, the leading innovators in most areas of the financial services industry have been the biggest firms. There appears to be a strong link between innovativeness and market share—large firms appear better placed to capture benefits from innovation, even in the face of copying. For that reason, when a relatively small bank innovates, it has a strong incentive to partner with a large bank—the larger institution is able to capture a greater share of the returns from the innovation, which the smaller institution will share. In some instances, banks will be incentivized to sell innovations to the institution that has a leading role in the particular line of business addressed by the innovation.[37]

Financial innovation is a complex topic. But the bottom line is relatively simple. Much of the innovation that we see in the financial services industry has been led by firms responding to *market* incentives, rather than the incentives created by IP rules. As these innovations are introduced, they eventually spread. The prospect that rivals will copy the inventions does not destroy the incentive to create them in the first place, and indeed in some situations copying enhances the value of these innovations by creating a larger market for them. Investment firms locked in a competitive market for clients innovate to serve clients better, and their rivals imitate those innovations to remain competitive.

Robert Merton, the Nobel laureate who formulated the pricing model that helped spark the huge growth in derivatives transactions, described the financial industry in terms of an "innovation spiral" in which one advance begets the next.[38] Merton wasn't thinking explicitly about the role of law. But his point fits well with what we've described here. The financial industry's innovation spiral has proceeded mostly without protection against copying, and this history suggests that innovation in finance may be much more resilient in the age of copying than the standard justification for IP rights suggests. Imitation has not killed innovation in the financial world— and in some instances it may have even spurred it.

DATABASES

Databases are collections of materials organized for easy search and retrieval. Lawyers, for instance, rely heavily on Westlaw and Lexis-Nexis; likewise many scientists conducting research in human genetics use the OMIM (Online Mendelian Inheritance in Man) database maintained by the Johns Hopkins School of Medicine.[39] Many of us use databases on a regular basis, maybe even daily, but do not think about the economics of them much. Yet databases are a surprisingly big business—and one that has interesting things to teach us about innovation.

Databases may not seem all that creative. Yet how to organize the material, and what to include, can make a big difference in how successful a database is. The content in some databases is copyrightable—for example, the huge collections of news articles available via Lexis-Nexis or the DowJones "Factiva" database. But in many other instances, the content of databases is, at least in the United States, uncopyrightable because it is composed of basic facts. This is a contrast with Europe, where factual databases *are* protected against copying. Yet the surprising thing is that the database industry is growing on this side of the Atlantic, and stagnant on the other. The freedom to copy has not killed the American database industry. If anything, it seems to have strengthened it. Let's take a look at why.

That databases can often be legally copied has been true since the Supreme Court decided a case called *Feist Publications v. Rural Telephone Service.*[40] *Feist* involved the familiar telephone white pages. (The white pages are really just a database distributed on paper.) The question in *Feist* was whether others could copy the names and numbers in the white pages. In a manner reminiscent of decisions denying copyright protection to recipes, the Supreme Court held that copyright does not protect mere facts. Original ways of selecting and organizing those facts could be copyrighted, but not the underlying data. And, in the case of the white pages, the Court thought the organizational scheme—an alphabetical listing—was so lacking in originality that it could not be protected by copyright either.

So *Feist* established that anyone is free to copy the white pages. The impact of the decision wasn't confined to the phone book, however. *Feist* overturned a line of earlier cases that had held that even databases composed wholly of facts could be copyrighted. The theory behind these decisions was that it is hard work to collect facts into a useful database. To allow others to copy would be unfair. But the *Feist* Court rejected this "sweat of the brow" theory for databases. The Constitution, held the Court, allows copyright only for "original" works that show some spark of creativity. And there is nothing original or creative about a fact.

In the wake of *Feist* there was a campaign to change American law to grant databases some legal protection against copying. The proponents of database protection made the standard argument that we have referred to often: if we don't grant property rights in facts, people will copy them freely. And free and legal copying will destroy the incentive to spend time and money to collect facts in the first place.

Unsurprisingly, these people predicted that the Supreme Court's decision would doom the US database industry to decline. And soon they were able to bolster their case by pointing to developments in Europe. Following *Feist*, database protection proponents in the European Union warned that weak national copyright laws there posed the same risk of underprotection that *Feist* had created in the United States. And the European Union responded, granting strong protections to fact-based databases.

The EU rule, passed in 1992, establishes protection for an initial period of 15 years, and allows extensions under certain circumstances. Notably, however, the EU law protects only databases whose makers are European or who come from third-party countries that have "comparable protection" to that in Europe. That rule shuts out American database producers. With the new EU rule in place, database protection supporters in the United States warned that the EU database industry, aided by the new protections, would outcompete its American counterpart.

What actually happened? Despite the fact that no law stopped the copying of facts, the American database industry continued to grow. You can find dozens of examples of fact-based databases just by visiting the Web site of information giant Dow Jones (now a subsidiary of multinational media conglomerate News Corporation),[41] which provides databases containing energy and commodities data, real-time market indexes, foreign exchange rates, company reports including revenues and key corporate officers and investors, price information for US Treasury auctions, and a variety of regulatory data including government anticorruption and antimoney laundering sanction lists.

And Dow Jones is only one of many companies competing to provide databases that collect and organize otherwise uncopyrightable facts. Take the example of Fortune 500 firm Dun & Bradstreet. Dun & Bradstreet databases contain detailed information on more than 150 million companies worldwide. Companies like Dow Jones and Dun & Bradstreet invest hundreds of millions of dollars to collect this information, and to keep it accurate and timely. And they do this despite the absence of copyright protection for the facts that make up most of the content of their databases.

The success of the American industry is surprising enough. Even more surprising—at least to those who believe copying inevitably leads to decline—is that European firms have not outcompeted American firms. In fact, the opposite is true.

In 2005, the European Union conducted a study of its 1992 rule granting protection to databases. The study concluded that the economic impact of the new protections was "unproven," and that, although the new rule "was introduced to stimulate the production of databases in Europe, the new instrument has had no proven impact on the production of databases."[42] Things are somewhat worse for the European database industry, moreover, than even the 2005 EU study let on.

By 2004, database production in the European Union had fallen below 1998 levels, which was just before the EU rule took effect across the entire community. In other words, the implementation of the new protection against copying correlated with a decline in production, not an increase. And, perhaps more significant, the European Union's share of the global database market has stagnated. In 1992 about 26% of all online databases were produced by European firms, while about 60% were of North American origin.[43] By 2005, North American production had swelled to approximately 70% of the global total. The European Union's share had barely budged, and, by some measures, had even declined slightly. In essence, while database production in the United States and Canada (which, like the United States, lacks protection for fact-based databases) has continued to grow, database production in the European Union has stayed at best constant, and more likely has slowed a bit.[44]

This is a nice natural experiment in the economics of innovation. And it raises the question of why the production of fact-based databases has continued to thrive in the United States despite the absence of protection. The answer has, as it often does in these instances, a few dimensions:

First, even after *Feist*, some important copyright protection applies to American databases. *Feist* made clear that *original ways of organizing databases* are protected against appropriation, even if rivals are free to copy underlying data. This is a much narrower scope of copyright protection than applies in many other industries. But it is still useful. If the way in which a database is organized is original and valuable, rivals cannot copy that organization. Again, that is a far cry from the full panoply of rights that copyright could provide, but it is significant.

Second, copyright is not the only thing that database producers can rely on to discourage copying. Some of these strategies mimic those we have seen in other low-IP industries. Database makers use contract law to bind users to terms of use that forbid or limit copying. They use encryption and digital rights management tools for the same purpose. They employ ordinary property rights—for example, online auction giant eBay pressed a successful trespass action to prevent Bidders' Edge, an auction "aggregator" site, from acquiring auction data from its servers. And they file lawsuits alleging misappropriation and unfair competition—common law torts that provide some protection against copying that, for example, involves misrepresentation.

These are not fail-safe strategies. Contracts bind only those who agree to them. Encryption and other technical fixes can be circumvented. Data can be recovered from many databases without trespassing on the owner's network (for example, when data are distributed on a DVD, or downloaded onto a third party's server). And unfair competition lawsuits in state courts are narrower and less useful than copyright lawsuits in federal court. But together, the legal tools seem, overall, to provide sufficient shelter from copying to maintain a healthy environment in the United States for the creation of databases.

Third, and perhaps most important, the freedom to copy under American law *reduces the cost of creating new (and better) databases*. That is, the absence of broad database protections means that rivals can reuse existing data in new and creative ways. Think of our discussion of Pioneers and Tweakers. The rule that governs the US database industry gives wide latitude to Tweakers, who use existing data, often gathered at others' expense, to provide new functionality and make users' lives easier. There may be some downsides as well to this system, of course. The EU approach may give individual database producers higher profits, for instance. But it has not *grown the overall industry*, in part because it chokes off the kind of beneficial tweaking and reworking that are here, as in many other instances, so useful to innovation.

A good example of this is the *Los Angeles Times'* tweaking of a database maintained by the L.A. Unified School District. L.A. Unified, the second-largest district in the nation, collected the names of thousands of English and math teachers working in the district and the test scores of their students over several years.[*] The *Times* took the L.A. Unified data and tweaked it by applying statistical tools designed to measure the "value added" by individual teachers—that is, the extent to which the quality of a teacher improved students' progress compared to what they would have been expected to achieve, on average.[45]

The result was published as the *Times'* Los Angeles Teacher Ratings database, and it created a sensation in L.A. It sparked a furious response from teachers' unions and some academics who study education, who complained that the measures of teacher "value-added" were poorly done and their conclusions overbroad. In response to the *Times'* database, L.A. Unified published a value-added database of their own, using different statistical measures and presenting the results in a different way. Ultimately, the database competition resulted in the public receiving much more insight into the quality of the education on offer in L.A. Unified. And if the push-and-pull between the *Los Angeles Times* and the district leads to a better understanding of when and how teachers add value, then the tweaking of this database might even lead to better results for L.A.'s kids.

This episode illustrates a broader point. The monopoly theory tells us that copying kills creativity. But in the world of databases, we see the opposite: copying actually sparks innovation. The US, where copying is allowed, has a much more vibrant database industry than does Europe, where copying is banned. Theory can tell us something about the relationship between imitation and innovation. But to really understand it, we have to get out there and look at how real industries behave. What we found, in all of the cases we've examined, is a lot of imitation. That's not all that surprising. The surprising part is how much innovation is taking place.

---

[*] These data were subject to California public records laws that made them widely available—so even if there were broader copyright protection for data generally, information like this would remain largely free for the taking—but the example is nonetheless illuminating.

CONCLUSION:
COPIES AND CREATIVITY

Well before there were rules about intellectual property, there was the human urge to create. The famed cave paintings in Lascaux, France, are at least 15,000 years old, and there are creative works that may be far older. Some even contend that there is an "art instinct" that drives individuals to produce things of beauty and meaning.[1]

Regardless of its origin, clearly many of us do have an urge to create new things, or at least a preference for it, and we indulge that preference when we can—whether or not our innovations are protected against copying. One writer aptly put it this way: "Edison was born to be an inventor, Barishnikov was born to be a dancer, and no matter what the legal rules, Edison would no more have stopped inventing than Barishnikov would have stopped dancing."[2]

Still, it is widely believed that copying is bad for creativity. And the premise of laws against copying is that humanity's innate or socially determined desire to create is simply not enough in a modern innovation-based economy. To have sustained innovation—and to do so in areas that require significant investments of time and money—it is necessary to have a reliable expectation of economic reward. This is thought to be true both for creators and for the intermediaries—publishers, pharmaceutical companies, and the like—that in a modern economy often fund, organize, and distribute innovative work.

In our legal system, that expectation of reward rests on rules that guarantee a monopoly over a given creation for a period of time and restrain copying by others.[3] The intended result is that the creator, and not the copyist, enjoys whatever profits flow from the innovation. Knowing this, the creator is encouraged to create. We have called this basic approach the *monopoly theory* of innovation.

The monopoly theory is hostile to imitation because imitation, it is thought, inevitably undermines later rewards. As a result, imitation can destroy the incentive to innovate in the first place. This is why so many observers are so fearful of the emergence of technologies, such as the Internet and filesharing, that make copying cheaper and easier.[4] More copying, they believe, must mean less creativity.

But is this really the case? We have examined a wide array of innovative industries that, in one way or another, challenge this basic premise. Fashion, food, fonts, football, financial innovations—in all of these creative areas, and more, copying is free and often legal. Sometimes copying is simply permitted as a matter of practicality. But in all, innovations are open to imitation. By the lights of the monopoly theory, these industries should be only weakly creative. Yet the opposite is true: these industries are vibrantly creative.

Just recognizing this fact is significant, because it demonstrates that copying and creativity *can* co-exist. This does not mean that copying is always good. Nor does it mean that our copyright and patent laws ought to be abolished; they are an important element in our economic and cultural vibrancy.[5] But it does mean that the relationship between imitation and innovation is much more subtle than commonly believed. We do not face a stark choice between the two. In some creative endeavors imitation has little effect on innovation. And in others, imitation can even spark innovation. The really interesting question is when—and why—this is true.

Answering this question is important, because rules against copying come at the expense of another extremely significant source of economic and cultural vibrancy: competition. The basic logic of the monopoly theory is that copies will outcompete originals and, in doing so, destroy the incentive to originate in the first place. (If the copies did not outcompete the original, the original would not need protection against copying.) At the same time, our economic system fundamentally rests on competition. Competition is a powerful force for keeping prices low and quality high. It is also a potent instigator of innovation—as we've seen in contexts like football and financial innovation, competitors locked in battle against powerful rivals innovate just to stay in the game, without heed of intellectual property protections.

So copying and competition are closely linked, and that makes restraints on copying less unambiguously good than they may appear at first glance. Rules against copying carve out special zones on the field of free competition; they declare that some forms of competition—those that rely on certain kinds of copying—are not permissible. Yet not all competition through copying is barred, and not only because the relevant patent or copyright has reached its time limit. In many areas, our social preference for competition trumps concerns over copying. Indeed, in some settings we welcome copying.

To see this, consider a visionary restaurateur who opens a café on a decaying industrial street. If the café really takes off, another entrepreneur might quickly open a similar café, perhaps across the street or on the next block. In time, the street might be transformed as new restaurants and shops open up, transitioning from decrepit industrial zone to effervescent nightlife destination.* Did the second café copy the first simply by installing the same basic concept at the same basic location? Yes. But we typically call that kind of copying free market competition. As long as the two cafés differ enough in their names and décor for a customer to know that they are distinct entities, there is no legal barrier to the second café copying the first. And as a society we are better off: the cafés compete with one another for our dollars and patronage, and the result is better and more affordable coffee and croissants.[6]

This does not mean that the first café owner might not feel the second acted unfairly. A great idea has been adopted by second-comer; one taper, in Thomas Jefferson's words, has been lit by another's flame. And that can burn a little. In an early episode of the HBO series *The Sopranos*, Paulie Walnuts and Big Pussy walk into a coffee shop with a strong resemblance to Starbucks. Paulie gets agitated at the sight of the cashiers ringing up lattes and cappuccinos:

PAULIE: The fuckin' Italian people. How did we miss out on this?
PUSSY: What?

---

* And the originator might not even survive the process that it sparked. In the once-decaying meatpacking district of New York the quirky bistro Florent was a pioneer, but today—in a neighborhood where a handful of meatpacking operations eke out an existence amid an onslaught of restaurants, clubs, hotels, and high-end retail—Florent is a just a memory.

PAULIE: Fuckin' espresso, cappuccino. We invented this shit and all these other cocksuckers are getting' rich off it.

PUSSY: Yeah, isn't it amazing?

PAULIE: And it's not just the money. It's a pride thing. All our food: pizza, calzone, buffalo mozzarell', olive oil. These fucks had nothing. They ate pootsie before we gave them the gift of our cuisine. But this, this is the worst. This espresso shit.

PUSSY: Take it easy.[7]

Our legal system allows this kind of copying because the desire for free and full competition outweighs concerns about imitation. That is good for all of us, even if Italians (let alone Italian-Americans like us) might be better off if they possessed a monopoly on cappuccino.[8] As one court aptly put it, in our system "there exists a fundamental right to compete through imitation of a competitor's product, which right can only be temporarily denied by the patent or copyright laws."[9]

Of course, between two cafés competing on the same gentrifying block and two films, or novels, or cancer-fighting drugs, there is a lot of space: our rules against copying, and what the law calls "unfair competition," exist for good reason. The important point here is simply that copying and competition are two sides of a coin, and that makes the determination of the right set of rules about copying tricky. And when competition and creativity can co-exist with copying, it is best to leave well enough alone. That is a key message of this book: in a surprising number of innovative industries, competition, copying, and creativity all run together, and in this good news story our intellectual property system rightly stays out of the picture.

With this in mind, in this concluding chapter we draw together the various examples in this book to sketch out some broader patterns. What have we learned about the relationship between imitation and innovation? How do we explain the surprising creativity we have found? And are there tools or techniques that might help other industries stay competitive when confronted with copying?

Just because fashion, finance, or font design remain successful in the face of pervasive copying does not mean every creative industry can do so, and we want to acknowledge the variety of innovative fields forthrightly. Innovative industries vary in many ways, but one of the most consequential is in the cost of creation. By "cost" we mean the expenses incurred in dreaming up something new and distributing it to consumers. Think of a blockbuster drug that requires armies of scientists to refine. These drugs can cost as much as $800 million to formulate and produce.[10] Or a blockbuster film, full of special effects and boldface names. James Cameron's 3-D film *Avatar*, for instance, cost nearly $300 million to make and $100–$200 million to market.[11] For both films and pharmaceuticals, the upfront costs of creation can be very high.

Other innovations are quite inexpensive, however. Musicians sometimes say that a lyric or chord change popped into their mind in a flash, and a few hours later they had a full-fledged song.* Marcel Duchamp drew a moustache and beard on a found postcard of the Mona Lisa and, *et voila*, a Dada masterpiece was born. Even with less dramatic (or swift) inspiration, songs, stories, poems, and many artworks are comparatively cheap to produce. There is a continuum of innovation, in other words, that runs from very cheap to very expensive.

The creative industries we have explored in this book mostly fall at the low-cost end of the spectrum. Compared to new drugs, fashion designs are not especially costly to create; neither are new comedy routines, recipes, or football plays.* Whatever lessons we draw from our case studies, consequently, can be applied to high-cost creations only with care. Nonetheless, even for high-cost industries there are useful lessons that can be gleaned. As is probably obvious to everyone reading this, moreover, the cost of innovation can be significantly affected by a vital phenomenon in the contemporary world: technology. (We'll say more about this at the end of this chapter.) The cost of creation is an important factor to consider as we weigh the broader messages that emerge from our cases studies.

The basic point that we began this book with, however, remains: the traditional justification for IP rights—that copying kills creativity—cannot explain the surprisingly vital world of innovation we have detailed. And this has important ramifications elsewhere because, whether we like it or not, in many industries copying is here to stay. The increasing ease of copying has

---

* As we discuss further, creation and distribution are not the same, and music illustrates this well. Creating a new song has always been relatively cheap. But distributing it was, until recently, expensive. Technology has changed that in ways that have important implications for how we think about the threat of copying.

* As it turns out, IP law does not take this wide spectrum of costs into account. Whether a work is cheap or expensive to produce matters not at all to whether, or how long, it is protected by a copyright or patent.

been widely perceived as a crisis. Indeed, the former head of the Motion Picture Association of America (MPAA), Jack Valenti, who once likened the original videocassette recorder (VCR) to a rapist, would surely be turning over in his grave if he could see some of the most recent technologies used to pirate movies.[12] Yet Valenti was wrong about the VCR. Far from killing the industry through copying, the home movie rental business it spawned turned out to be very profitable.

We believe that there are ways to profit from today's copying technologies as well. To do so we have to think about copying in a different light—not as a scourge to be eliminated but as a complex phenomenon that can help as much as harm. Ever-easier copying is only a crisis if our focus is solely to stop copying. If instead we focus—as we should—*on promoting innovation*, we quickly realize that there are many ways to do so, even in the face of copying.

We will go a step further: in some cases copying ought to be welcomed, not stopped. Imitation can fuel innovation, serve as a form of advertising for originals, spur more competitive markets, and lead to better, more valuable new creations. In short, as we have shown in a wide range of fields, creativity can persist even in the face of widespread copying. Indeed, in some instances creativity occurs *because* of copying. In the end, the basic message of this book is optimistic. We live in a world of ever-easier copying. Yet, in a surprising number of ways, creativity can survive and even thrive despite copying.

Six Lessons about Innovation and Imitation

The creative industries we have explored clearly differ in important ways. Yet there are some cross-cutting features and lessons that merit special attention. We highlight six in this concluding chapter:

- *Trends and fads* play a powerful role in several creative industries. In the fashion world and elsewhere, the dynamics spawned by trends can turn the conventional view of copying on its head.
- Other industries demonstrate the important role that *social norms* can play in constraining or shaping copying, even when legal actions prove impotent or impractical.
- In some industries creators and owners have blunted the negative effects of copying by redefining the good from *product into performance*—reducing the impact of copying on their economic success.

- Still other creative industries highlight the power of *open-source methods* to lower the costs of innovation—and thereby promote more of it.
- *First-mover advantages* offer enough value to some producers that innovation is profitable, even if those innovations are later copied.
- Finally, several cases illustrate the power of brands and trademarks. Brands can limit the market share of copies, but *copies can also serve as advertisements for brands.* This effect casts the costs of copying in a very different light.

These six lessons are surely not the only ones that can be derived from our case studies. But we think these points are the most important and generalizable. Together, they show that markets like comedy and cuisine have more to teach us than we had realized. And, as we noted earlier, they suggest that the future of the ideas economy is not nearly as bleak as many believe.

Trends and Cycles

Apparel is a global business (and for many, a global art form) with a huge economic impact. Despite the fashion industry's size and cultural importance, its innovation practices have not been widely studied.[13] Yet the fashion world is full of important and interesting features. Maybe the most striking is the paradoxical effects of copying on creativity.

Copying in the fashion world has two unexpected effects, both of which make copying an essential partner to innovation, not an impediment. The first we have called *induced obsolescence.* New designs tend to spread from a small group of fashion followers to the larger mass of consumers. As these designs are copied and then spread throughout the marketplace, they lose their appeal for the earliest adopters. And as a design spreads further, it begins to tip over and, after reaching its peak, rapidly becomes obsolete. This in turn creates demand for new designs to take its place.

This is the familiar fashion cycle. Designs debut, diffuse, decline, and die. The special role of copying in this dynamic is that it accelerates the cycle, pushing the fashion-conscious to more rapidly drop their old look and find a new one. And that in turn incentivizes designers to create new looks. Copying, in short, spurs creativity as designers seek to offer newer, fresher designs to replace those that have saturated the market.

The second important effect is *anchoring*. Fashion is ruled by trends, and trends are made by copying. Trends give consumers important information: they tell us what to wear if we want to remain in style. Trends also make it easier for designers and manufacturers to know what will sell, and to design accordingly. Trends, in short, are a coordination mechanism. They make it possible for many individuals to jump on the same bandwagon—until, by doing so, the trend eventually withers and is supplanted by a new trend.

Together, these two effects help explain what we call the *piracy paradox*. Copying helps, rather than harms, creativity in the fashion world. The piracy paradox, which reflects the fundamentally social nature of fashion, is a powerful reason the apparel industry has remained so creative despite rampant and open copying. There are, of course, limitations to the scope of innovation we see in fashion—clothes do have to fit the human body.* But there is nonetheless a vibrant range of creative designs put forward every season and indeed every week. The paradoxically positive effects of copying help explain how this level of creativity—and commercial success—is possible: by rapidly diffusing a design, copying actually stimulates demand for the next design.

Again, our point is not that there is a fashion cycle: that has been known since Shakespeare's time.* It is that this cycle turns *even more rapidly* in a world of free and legal copying. And this is true because of a key feature of apparel: the consumption of fashion is a public act, not a private one. Fashion, because it is worn and can be seen by others, sends signals about the wearer. Some people, usually the early adopters of new designs, like to signal that they are different, and perhaps trailblazers; others (certainly a larger group) flock to what seems safe and accepted.[14] Given a mix of flockers and differentiators, copying will lead to more rapid change in what is coveted—and that, in a competitive market economy, will lead to more rapid innovation as entrepreneurs seek to supply the new, new thing.

The fundamental dynamic of the piracy paradox is central to understanding how the apparel industry remains so successful in the face of copying. But it has broader implications. Fads and fashions are not limited to clothing; they are present in many pursuits that are social in nature and visible to others—in other words, in which consumption is *external and expressive*.

---

* Though there is some latitude at the upper reaches of fashion. In the 1980s, for instance, Japanese designer Issey Miyake sold three-sleeved sweaters; the third sleeve hung down the back.

* As Conrade says to Borachio in *Much Ado about Nothing*, "I see that the fashion wears out more apparel than the man."

From movies about vampires to soccer fans blowing vuvuzelas, fads come and go, and have done so for centuries if not millennia. While we hesitate to say that copying is essential to the creation of fads, it does seem intrinsic to many fads. Most fads require multiple versions of a central idea—often, it's only when we see many imitators jumping in that we know a particular idea has tipped over into a full-blown fad.[15] And just as copying helps to mark fads, and then to inflate them, it also plays a central role in their demise. When a fad grows too large and too prevalent, it fades, often more rapidly than it arose.

To be sure, many differences exist among trends and fads. Our goal is simply to point out the central tendency and to note that, as in the fashion world itself, copying can serve to both grow and, ultimately, to kill a fad. That dynamic creates opportunity for entrepreneurs. But it also yields a powerful spur to creativity—one that has nothing to do with conventional justifications of IP nor with conventional fears of copying.

We have seen fads at work, for example, in the creation of new fonts. Typeface designs catch on, close copies proliferate, and then, when the look has saturated the marketplace, the font world begins seeking the next design trend. The result is a proliferation of new fonts in a world that offers very little protection against copying. Because fonts are less easily noticed, and less personal a source of expression (though any author or wedding-invitation-sender knows that picking the right font is important), typeface trends come and go much less quickly than in fashion. But the fact remains that fonts are often external and expressive, and unsurprisingly they have fads too. Copying enables those fads to spread and, ultimately, to wither—leading to a need for newer and fresher font designs.

The food world exhibits fads as well, and here too the ability to copy spurs creativity. Some food fashions are general—small plates, nose-to-tail eating—whereas others are specific to certain techniques (think *sous-vide*), tools (the $4,000 Pacojet ice cream maker), ingredients (bacon, fennel pollen), or genres (pie, or earlier, cupcakes). As in fashion and fonts, food trends spread because copying is easy and legal. As we described in Chapter 2, the same is even true of specific dishes, some of which, like the molten chocolate cake pioneered by Jean-Georges Vongerichten, are now ubiquitous. The freedom to copy allows trends and fads to spread quickly. But in turn it prompts creative chefs to seek new and distinguishing dishes, techniques, or ingredients. The culinary world is not nearly as faddish as the fashion world, and as we described, the mechanisms of creativity are a bit different. But there are important overlaps, and food, like fonts and fashion, illustrates that the dynamic of copy-induced creativity is present in many areas.

Music, too, is moving in this direction. The music industry is exploring ways to emulate the dynamic of external and expressive consumption that the fashion industry exploits so well. The current leader in this, as in so much else in the music industry, is Apple. Apple's iTunes gives users the option of sharing the content of their music collection with other iTunes users connected on the same network. In 2010, Apple took another step in this direction when it began not-so-gently nudging its users into its new music-centered social network, Ping. Ping shows people what their friends and favorite artists are listening to, and gives them a very easy way to sample and buy into the trends that Ping highlights.

With these moves, Apple hopes to make music consumption choices external and expressive in the way that fashion trends are, in the hope that consumers will be induced to buy more music to keep up with the trends in which their friends are participating. Like clothing, music is a powerful form of personal expression that can convey identity and establish status. But because music is often so private (especially in today's world of ubiquitious earbuds)* its signaling power is limited. iTunes library sharing and Ping change this by harnessing new technologies to make song choices not just private preference, but public information.

And these features don't just provide information about the music a user buys—pirated music in a user's iTunes library is also grist for the trend mill. If lots of people are pirating the new Bon Iver album, then Apple hopes that by communicating the album's hotness, iTunes library sharing and Ping will lead more of the many law-abiding people to buy it from the iTunes Store. Piracy provides valuable information about tastes and trends. People copy things they desire and share things they respect.

We suspect other creative industries can find similarly powerful ways to leverage the power of external and expressive consumption to make copying work for them. As Apple's moves suggest, the degree to which a product or industry taps into trend-driven innovation is not fixed: it can be altered by the technologies of consumption.

---

* This is yet another way in which technology can alter these dynamics. As Spike Lee depicted in *Do the Right Thing*, in the ancient era of the boombox, owners could broadcast their tastes and identity to everyone nearby (at least as long as the batteries lasted). Radio Raheem would have been a very different character in the age of the iPod.

Social Norms

Social norms can play a significant role in shaping and constraining the effects of copying, whether that copying is legal or not. We found this to be true in the worlds of comedy, cuisine, and magic. Of course, social norms do not prevent all copying, though neither do legal rules about copying. And as the relevant social group grows and disperses, norms—which depend fundamentally on relationships and work best in communities—probably lose their power. But social norms nonetheless can be an important constraint on copying and can help divert copying away from its more harmful forms.

The norms systems we've described share two important features. First, norms deter theft by *rival creators*. They do not map directly onto situations where copying is done on a mass scale *by consumers*. Nonetheless, as we will explain, there is reason to believe that at least some of the lessons of social norms can be adapted to discourage consumer piracy as well. Second, norms probably work best for *individuals rather than firms*. In innovative fields dominated by individuals, which characterizes many of the creative communities we have explored in this book, we see norms working, sometimes very well. In fields where large firms dominate, norms may be much less effective.

Still, several of our case studies show that social norms can be very significant when a creative community seeks to regulate copying among insiders. The check on copying that social norms can provide often makes imitation less harmful to innovators. And norms can also provide an extra-legal means of redress to those whose work has been copied. Norms have one other noteworthy feature: because they are constructed within the relevant industry, they are more likely to reflect the particular nature of that industry and its competition-copying trade-offs.

Comedians offer the most dramatic example of the power of social norms to constrain copying. Among comedians, the norms system operates effectively despite the fact that jokes and routines are formally covered by copyright. Comics prefer the system of norms because it is more tailored to their needs and much more useful to them. For example, copyright law only protects the precise version of a joke or routine; the comedy norms system protects the underlying funny idea or premise as well. So the "rules" in the norms system are quite different from those in IP law. This may be even more true for magicians, where, for example, the rules governing the disclosure of tricks deviate markedly from what the law requires.

In comedy, and in magic, there is also enough of a critical mass of norms-followers to keep the system working well. Comedians and magicians have a high level of agreement about what the norms are and when they are transgressed. Enforcement is social and extra-legal—and sometimes even illegal and violent. But the key is that the norms system is widely agreed upon by insiders, and the public nature of performance helps to deter a lot of copying that would contravene the unwritten rules.

Chefs exhibit some similar traits, though the norms in question appear to be less embedded and well established. Eric von Hippel and Emanuelle Fauchart's study of Michelin-starred French chefs showed that norms about copying and attribution may be significant in the Gallic culinary world.[16] We are less certain about the significance of social norms among American chefs,* who in our interviews demonstrated much more ambivalence about the need for norms against copying—and less clarity on what the norms, if any, are or ought to be. This may reflect the large and dispersed nature of the high-end restaurant world in the United States, a vast country with dozens of truly great restaurants and thousands of merely excellent ones. Or it may simply reflect differing social conceptions of what it means to be a professional chef. Either way, we think the evidence for the role of norms is weaker in cuisine than in comedy. Put differently, there must be other factors in the culinary world that explain why chefs remain innovative in the face of extensive imitation by others.

Still, it is clear to us that many chefs, wherever they may be based, share a broad ethos about appropriate behavior with regard to ownership and attribution. This ethos does not track the rules of copyright and patent, and, as in comedy and magic, in some cases it focuses on different issues. For example, a theme that pervades our study of food is the central role of attribution. Many of the chefs we and others interviewed were not especially concerned about copying per se. They saw execution as central and, in some cases, viewed copying as the price of success—or even a desirable *indicator* of success.

Still, many chefs felt that attribution was essential; they wanted to receive, or give, credit for creation where credit was due. (And to the degree copying

---

* By which we mean American-based; many of those we interviewed are actually foreign-born or foreign-trained.

is thought of as an indicator of success, attribution becomes even more important.) We will return to this theme of attribution and indication in the context of brands. But as this suggests, copying has a complex relationship to credit-claiming—and can serve as a valuable form of advertising for those who are truly innovative.

Again, norms work best among individual producers who see themselves as part of, and seek the respect of, a professional community. Yet norms can play a role even among consumers. Consider the situation in comedy. The norms in the comedy world are developed and largely enforced by comedians themselves. More recently, however, fans have been posting videos of questionable performances and taking sides in disputes over copying. In this way fans shape the ensuing debate over copying—as Dane Cook's complaint to Louis C.K., recounted in the Introduction, made clear.

The ability of fans to play this role is of course driven by technology: it is much less effective to tell a friend that Comedian X copied a bit from Comedian Y than it is to post a cellphone video of the performance online (or to compare two such videos for similarities). The result in comedy, as in food—where fans often blog about and post photos of dishes, sometimes noting copies—is a form of consumer-based policing of the norms governing copying. And the same is even true in some niche forms of music, as we will describe in the epilogue to this book.

In short, norms play an important role in enabling some creative arenas to reduce the harm from copying, just as a wealth of studies have shown that they play an important role in regulating social life, policing specialized markets, and generally providing "order without law."[17] Norms are not a panacea for copying, nor do they work in all areas. Yet a robust norms system can mitigate the downsides of copying, helping to transform copying from a threat to nuisance—and maybe even into a benefit.

Product versus Performance

If an item can be copied perfectly and sold cheaply, or made available free, convincing customers to pay for the original can be difficult. (Just ask the music industry.) But some products simply cannot be copied perfectly. Often that's because the product itself is really analog rather than digital—that is to say, not reducible to a perfectly replicable set of 1s and 0s, or the real-world equivalent. A terrific and innovative dessert is usually a handmade item that is likely to be a little bit different every night it's made. Another chef may copy it, but the copy will rarely be identical to the original, and given that skill is often an important variable, it may well be decidedly inferior. The same can be said of a terrific joke or comedy routine.

There is a second reason, however, that some products cannot easily be copied. It is because they are fundamentally about experiences, and experiences are even harder to reproduce. What we buy in these instances is less a product than a performance. Cuisine is again a perfect example. If a precisely rendered version of David Chang's signature pork belly bun was available at street corner bodegas in Chinatown (and it may well be), what would be the effect on sales at his flagship restaurant, Momofuku?

At some point, if Chang-style pork buns became ubiquitous, like any fad they would peak and then fade away, and perhaps harm Momofuku's reputation and profits in the process.[*] But outside of that somewhat extreme scenario, the bodega pork buns do not really compete with the Momofuku buns, because dining at Momofuku is about more than just eating great pork buns—which, David Chang is the first to admit, is not really a very innovative dish anyway. It is about the clamor and energy of the crowd, the range of dishes available, the entire aesthetic of no reservations, no substitutions, spare décor, loud music, and colliding Asian cuisines that Momofuku represents. A Momofuku pork bun eaten at Momofuku, in short, is a particular experience that customers are willing to pay for (and wait for). A copy is just a really good pork bun.

Even the Supreme Court has noted the centrality of experience in the dining world. In Chapter 2 we described the Taco Cabana-Two Pesos dispute over restaurant trade dress. The issue was whether one somewhat generic Mexican restaurant had copied the décor, and therefore the "trade dress," of another. In the oral argument in that case, Justice Scalia suggested that the underlying issue was not trivial: the atmosphere of a restaurant was a central part of the restaurant experience as a whole. "I don't think it is packaging. I think you're talking about the *substance of what's being sold*," said Scalia. "You're selling atmosphere and food, the two of them. You can have wonderful food in a lousy atmosphere. I'm not going to pay as much money."[18] Neither restaurant in the dispute had wonderful food. But the

---

[*] As alluded to earlier, the greater effect of copies may be to promote the original—in a way akin to advertising—and also to promote the originality of David Chang. We say more on this later in the chapter.

atmospheres were equally nice (or lousy) and Justice Scalia's point was simply that atmosphere was a core element of almost any restaurant's actual product, not just a metaphorical wrapper placed around the product.

The same basic dynamic is present in other industries we have looked at. Bars and high-end cocktails epitomize this phenomenon of performance over narrowly defined product. Why else do people pay upward of $15 for a drink that may cost less than $2 to make? As a sage bartender once said, you are not really buying a drink, you are renting a bar stool. And the rent varies, as you would expect, with the quality of the experience. In short, the high-end bar is a live performance venue. The drink is the ticket to the show. Anything that is a live performance must be experienced to be appreciated, and that experience can shelter creativity from the pernicious effects of copying. Why? Because copying all the facets of the experience is very difficult and often extremely costly—and sometimes impossible, as many would-be restaurateurs and bar owners have discovered to their peril.

The centrality of experience helps explain the co-existence of some otherwise-contradictory trends outside the restaurant industry. Consider the willingness of customers to pay high prices for movie tickets in some theaters, even as streaming video in the comfort of one's home grows ever more common. Why pay to go out to a movie theater when you can watch the exact same film on your widescreen high-definition television, thanks to one of the many torrent Web sites that feature illegal content? One answer is that the experience is different, and many smart theater owners have been rapidly moving to accentuate that difference as dramatically as they can.

The tremendous success of the Arclight theater chain in Southern California is a case in point. The Arclight allows customers to reserve seats in advance and to choose their seat as they do so. The theater seats are big, clean, comfortable, and have good sight lines. The screens and sound are top flight. Inside the complex is a restaurant, bar, and gift shop, and at some showings alcoholic drinks can be enjoyed during the show. The overall experience, in short, is at a much higher level than is available at the average mall multiplex. So are the ticket prices, which can approach $16—about twice the national average. Still, the Arclight has proven successful enough to have expanded in just a few years from its original Hollywood complex to three other locations in Southern California.

The Arclight, and theaters like it around the nation, are far from the norm. Yet they have successfully capitalized on the experiential nature of film. Rather than a product, film becomes a performance. By making the experience one that is very costly to replicate at home, the central good being consumed—the film—becomes just one part of an overall package.* And in turn, that means that copies of the film are copies of but one facet of the overall experience, and therefore are no longer perfect copies, but instead imperfect—and, to many, much less attractive.

The same dynamic helps explain how in the music industry, the record labels can be imploding while the business of live performance is thriving. Live performance cannot be copied in the way that recorded music can. It is true that tribute bands exist, and so in a sense there is a market, albeit very small and quirky, for "copies" of live performance. And there are videos and films of live acts. But no one is going to mistake Mandonna (an all-male Madonna tribute band) for Madonna,* and no video can substitute for the energy or sound of a live concert. Listening to a CD or MP3 is not at all the same thing as going to an actual show. Again, energy, experience, environment—these all are central to performance and cannot be bottled and sold (or digitized and copied) the way a simple song can.

In short, as perfect digital copies proliferate there is a countervailing trend in favor of the unique experience of live performance. In the motion picture industry, reinforcing the desirability of the "live" theater performance feeds Hollywood's box office revenues—which, despite rising worries about copying, reached their all-time high in both 2009 and 2010, in the middle of a major recession, of approximately $10.5 billion in revenues in the United States alone.* In the music world, the major record labels do not have much of a stake in the live performance business. As a result, they cannot (at least yet) recover lost revenues from recorded music via the healthy live performance segment of the industry.

That is unfortunate for the record labels. But the music industry as a whole is not dying; it is changing. Unlike the recording industry, which is shrinking fast, the live music business is growing. Millions of people every

---

* The recent embrace of 3D theater technology only adds to this dynamic—at least until 3D televisions, which are increasingly common, improve in quality and price.

* Though in a strange twist, the occasional tribute band member has crossed over to the original. When in 1992 lead singer Rob Halford left Judas Priest, for instance, he was replaced by Tim Owens of the Judas Priest tribute band British Steel.

* Hollywood's US box office take in 2011 declined by 4.5%; observers blamed a deepening recession and an unusually weak crop of big-budget films. Meanwhile, Hollywood's foreign box office receipts continued to swell in 2011, growing by 7% to a new record of $13.6 billion.

year attend concerts, and between 1999 and 2009, even as the record labels' revenues were plummeting, concert ticket sales in the United States more than tripled in value, from $1.5 billion to $4.6 billion. Total revenues from live shows grew from $7.3 billion in 2006 to $10.3 billion in 2011.[19]

The importance of concert revenues to music is nothing new; for most of history the live show was the musician's main source of support. That point was made with terrific clarity by Mick Jagger in a recent *New York Times* interview:

There was a window in the 120 years of the record business where performers made loads and loads of money out of records," Jagger says. "But it was a very small window—say, 15 years between 1975 and 1990."[20]

As the *Times* article noted, touring is now the most lucrative part of the Rolling Stones' business. (The "Bigger Bang" tour, from 2005 to 2007, raked in $558 million, making it the highest-grossing tour of all time.) The band has also been forward thinking about other pieces of the business, including recruiting sponsors, selling song rights, and flogging merchandise. And this strategy has made it very rich. "The Stones carry no Woodstockesque, antibusiness baggage," a *Fortune* magazine profile noted approvingly back in 2002.[21]

Performance is of course no guarantee of riches. Revenues from touring can be erratic, and most of the biggest grossing tours feature well-established acts. For these acts, however, recordings are but a tiny fraction of their earnings; economist Alan Krueger found for 35 top-earning acts in 2002, live concert revenues exceeded recording revenues by a factor of almost 8 to 1.[22] Figures for acts in the middle of the pack are harder to come by, but there is at least some reason to think that concert revenues are larger than recording revenues for these performers as well.[23]

Growing the live music business is an obvious way to make the industry as a whole less vulnerable to piracy while remaining profitable. There is no good way (yet) to "pirate" a live show.[*] The importance of touring to the industry's post-Internet fate is illustrated by a recent comment

---

[*] As we noted earlier, cover bands are of course an attempt. But they pose little risk to most popular bands and might even be thought to whet the appetite and keep the flame alive for many fans of the real thing.

David Bowie made in an interview with the *New York Times*: "Music itself is going to be like running water or electricity. You'd better be prepared for doing a lot of touring because that's really the only unique situation that's going to be left."[24]

The important point is that concerts are far less vulnerable to copying. And copying plays a very different role in a world in which the primary product is performance. As Sasha Frere-Jones, music critic for *The New Yorker*, has noted, increasingly "recordings have become advertisements for shows."[25] This spurs some artists to give away recordings, and makes the impact of illegal copies very different: an illegal copy or a free giveway can be equally powerful ads for the real product—the performance. And like any ad, the more widely it is heard or seen, the more effective it is.

This is not just true of music, dance, or other obviously performative arts. The more a given creation can be transformed from commodity to experience, from product to performance, the more innovators can effectively ignore imitators. Think back to the Kogi taco truck story that we told in the Introduction. Kogi was an innovator in several respects: it fused Korean and Mexican food, upscaled the lowly food truck, and used Twitter and facebook effectively as marketing tools.

But Kogi's fundamental product was the Korean taco, and that was soon knocked off—legally—by a rash of imitators. What made Kogi remain a formidable competitor was not just that it was the first, and most famous, Korean taco slinger. It was also that (at least initially) finding the Kogi truck and joining the crowd in line was an experience as much as a meal. A stylized picture on Kogi's Web site evokes the late night party vibe that made Kogi such a hit:

FIGURE 5.1 Kogi website image

Kogi's legion of copycats may make a decent short rib taco, but they have never been able to quite match the Kogi experience.

Openness and Innovation

In his brilliant 2009 book *Drive*, Daniel Pink offers a fascinating thought experiment. Pink asks us to travel back to the last millennium—to 1995, to be exact—and to imagine a conversation about, of all things, the future of encyclopedias. He starts the conversation by describing two new encyclopedias that are about to hit the market:

> The first encyclopedia comes from Microsoft. As you know, Microsoft is already a large and profitable company. And with this year's introduction of Windows 95, it's about to become an era-defining colossus. Microsoft will fund this encyclopedia. It will pay professional writers and editors to craft articles on thousands of topics. Well-compensated managers will oversee the project to ensure it's completed on budget and on time. Then Microsoft will sell the encyclopedia on CD-ROMs and later online.
>
> The second encyclopedia won't come from a company. It will be created by tens of thousands of people who write and edit articles for fun. These hobbyists won't need any special qualifications to participate. And nobody will be paid a dollar or a euro or a yen to write or edit articles. Participants will have to contribute their labor—sometimes twenty and thirty hours per week—for free. The encyclopedia itself, which will exist online, will also be free—no charge for anyone who wants to use it.[26]

And then Pink says that in 15 years—that is, in 2010—one of these two will be the biggest and most widely used encyclopedia in the world, and the other will no longer exist. Which is which?

You already know the answer. Microsoft shuttered its proprietary encyclopedia, Encarta, in 2009. The all-volunteer, open-source Wikipedia, on the other hand, has grown like kudzu. At its peak, Encarta had entries on approximately 62,000 subjects. Wikipedia currently has nearly *20 million* entries, all of them written and edited collaboratively by more than 90,000 volunteer contributors around the world. It is estimated that Wikipedia receives almost 3 billion page views monthly from the United States alone. It is not just the world's leading encyclopedia. It is, for anyone under 30, practically the only reference source they have ever used.*

---

* We're old enough to remember using paper encyclopedias, but we used the Wikipedia entry for "Wikipedia" to gather much of the basic information we just gave you about Wikipedia. (And then we fact-checked it using other sources.)

In 1995, of course, virtually no one would have predicted the stunning success of Wikipedia. Most people would have assumed that Microsoft's encyclopedia, backed by millions of dollars of investment from one of the world's largest companies and protected by copyright (facts are outside copyright's domain, but copyright does protect the particular way in which an encyclopedia entry is written), would win out over a start-up enterprise that seemed pretty flaky and even vaguely communist.

Wikipedia doesn't charge for access, doesn't pay contributors, and doesn't take advertising. It relies on voluntary contributions. And Wikipedia *invites* people to copy and to edit the content that their volunteers create—the Wikimedia Foundation licenses, free of charge, all Wikipedia content to whoever wants it. In exchange, users must agree to give Wikipedia credit if they publish that content, and to allow others to share whatever they take, including any content they've adapted, according to the same conditions. Yet Wikipedia beat one of the world's most successful firms, Microsoft, at a game Microsoft was determined to win.

Wikipedia is just one example of a much larger method of innovation: what is usually known as *open source*. Open source is most famously associated with computer software, that is, software developed mostly by volunteer programmers who work without prospect either of salary or—importantly—legal rights in the code they create. (Yochai Benkler and others have written in detail on the stunning success of open-source software.)[27] Open-source software is usually licensed in a way that allows users to tweak it, but bans any attempts to monopolize the code through copyright law. These licenses turn copyright on its head, encouraging copying and blocking ownership.

Open source is important to this book for two reasons. First, it is another very important area in which creative people engage in significant, persistent innovation despite the fact that their work may be copied. Indeed, they *want* it to be copied. But second, open source represents a broad method of creation—open, collaborative, intrinsically focused on sharing—that we find present in some unusual places, such as top restaurant kitchens.

Let's step back and look at the story of open-source software a bit more closely. After a quarter century of enormous growth, there's no longer a serious question that the open-source model works. Mozilla Firefox, the world's second largest browser with over 150 million users, is open source. So is the Linux operating system, which is running on about 25% of all corporate servers. Over half of corporate servers run Apache, the open-source

Web server software. And these are just a few of the many thousands of open-source projects.

What makes software "open source"? The best way to explain it is to distinguish between software that your computer can understand, versus software that *you* can understand. When you purchase a piece of commercial software (say, Microsoft Office) you get the *object code*—the strings of 1s and 0s that your computer understands but you do not. In contrast, when you download open-source software, you get both the object code and the *source code*—that is, human-readable computer code that underlies the object code. Reading source code is a bit harder than reading this book (we hope). You need to understand the computer programming language in which the source code is written. But millions of people do.

Open-source software distributors reveal the source code deliberately. They want you to understand the software, and crucially, *they want you to improve it, extend it, and tweak it.* That's the point of open source—to keep software code *open*, which really means free of restrictions on copying and improving. Open-source proponents believe—with much justification—that copying and modification can spur, not just retard, creativity. Openness leads to more innovation and better software.

How is open-source software better? For one, it's usually free. One consultancy has estimated that open source has saved consumers about $60 billion.[28] But the cost savings, even though substantial, are not the principal benefit. More important is open-source software's transparency and quality. Since everyone can see the source code, anyone can improve the software. And many people do. In other words, open source is an example of how, to use the phrases we employed in the last chapter, tweaking can be as important as pioneering. Pioneers come up with big ideas. But very often pioneering inventions require extensive refinement—tweaking—to actually reach the marketplace, and even more refinement to become truly effective and successful.

A key to the success of open source is the motivation of those who tweak products to make them better. Some expect to make money by selling services or advice to people who adopt a particular piece of open-source software. A prominent example is Fortune 500 company Red Hat. Red Hat is a major contributor to the continuing development of Linux, and it distributes its own version of Linux—to which others are free to make changes. Red Hat also sells Linux consulting services. And this business model—dealing in open-source Linux, and servicing it—has made Red Hat an industry giant with a market capitalization of $7.7 billion. (As *Wired* editor Chris Anderson compellingly details in his 2009 book *Free*, this basic approach—allow others to copy or take for free an underlying good, but make money servicing that good—can be very lucrative.)

Red Hat is unusual; many individual programmers don't hope for or expect riches. They work on open-source projects to learn or to gain a reputation for expertise and innovation among their fellow programmers. Doubtless for some the plan is to turn reputation into dollars—perhaps using connections made working on an open-source project to find a job or get a promotion. But there are others for whom reputation is not a means to an end, but an end in itself. To those for whom the only coin worth having is the metal sort, this may sound strange. But remember the participants in the MathWorks contests; many poured hundreds of hours of work into winning a programming competition whose only prizes are a T-shirt and the admiration of other contestants. Humans are status-hungry creatures, and for many creators, the most important form of status is recognition by other creators. Open source feeds on that desire for reputation. And it provides a way to improve skills and learn by doing.

There is another, and potentially very important, spur to open-source creativity—the competitive interests of rival firms. Take IBM. IBM is heavily involved in open source. IBM has committed hundreds of millions of dollars and over 600 employees to open-source development, especially in Linux. Yet IBM will not own any of the software this effort aids.

Why does IBM do this? The answer is simple: Linux is the principal competitor to Microsoft's Windows Server operating system software. IBM is much better off selling its hardware in a market in which there is vigorous competition among operating systems. Without competition from Linux, Microsoft might be a monopolist in server operating systems, and from that position of strength, better able to suck up more of the profits from selling computer systems to corporations—profits that IBM would like to keep for itself. And so IBM is eager to make sure that Linux succeeds.

Google feels the same way. The Google Android operating system, despite being on the market only since 2007, is now installed in nearly half of US mobile phones and is the biggest mobile platform in the United States (Apple's iPhone is second at about a quarter of the market, and RIM's BlackBerry third at under 20%). Like IBM and Linux, Google pumps enormous resources into development of Android, and yet it licenses the software for free, and licensees can copy and modify the software at will. As people shift more of their Web access to mobile phones, Google wants to make sure that people continue to use its search engine and see the search-related ads that Google sells. By denying Apple dominance in the smartphone market, Google is helping to ensure that Apple does not fundamentally threaten Google's core business.

The open-source approach is most famously associated with software, but is not limited to it. The basic method—free and open copying, and a collective process of incremental improvements—is at play in several of the industries we have explored in this book. Most obviously, we saw the open-source dynamic at work in the MathWorks computer programming experiments described in Chapter 4. A pioneer will establish a basic approach to solving a programming problem. Then the tweakers improve the pioneer's work and expose the flaws that limit its ultimate value. And in doing so, they prepare the ground for the next pioneer. Both flavors of innovation play an important role in the development of a winning program.

We also saw the interplay between pioneers and tweakers in the open-source-like development of new football strategies. Of course, in football there are no open-source licenses (because football formations and plays, unlike software, have not been copyrighted, such licenses are neither necessary nor possible). But the general open-source *method* is important to many teams' success. Mouse Davis (probably) invented the spread offense in the 1970s. A decade later, Mike Leach tweaked it by spreading not just the receivers but the entire offensive alignment. At about the same time, Rich Rodriguez tweaked the spread in another way, mashing it up with more traditional offenses to create the spread-option. And then Chris Ault tweaked the spread-option, moving the quarterback up from the shotgun to the pistol position.

Coaches and offensive coordinators tweak each other's ideas in an effort to create a new twist on an existing formation or play that will allow them an edge next game day. But coaches also share ideas—and not only because, inevitably, their innovations are broadcast for all to see on millions of television sets around the nation. As the *New York Times* vividly described in its profile of New York Jets coach Rex Ryan, coaches from around the nation have come to "take the Ryan cure" by watching his offseason practices.[29]

The culinary world also features some open-source elements. Chefs often say that culinary change is the product not of large inventive leaps, but of collective, incremental processes of innovation. If so, spreading and sharing innovative ideas is essential to creating them. Freedom to copy enables chefs to learn from one another and thereby to keep incrementally improving their offerings.

Adding to this process is the tradition of staging, or apprenticing, in fine restaurants. As we described in Chapter 2, stagiers have access to the inner workings of a great restaurant. Some certainly misuse that access—as did Robin Wickens, if he did indeed try to pass off the creations of Chicago-based chef Grant Achatz and others as his own in his distant Australian restaurant. But for most chefs, staging is a way to gain invaluable experience, to learn from the greats, and to participate in the process of running a top kitchen. For the leading chefs who control these kitchens, stagiers are part of a long tradition of openness and teaching. But stagiers also bring new energy and ideas, and can help improve and revitalize a restaurant's offerings.

That cuisine is an art form characterized by incremental and collective innovation is a widely view held among top chefs. Earlier we noted that three of the world's most famed and innovative chefs—Ferran Adria of El Bulli, Heston Blumenthal of the Fat Duck, and Thomas Keller of the French Laundry (along with acclaimed food writer Harold McGee)—offered a manifesto on cuisine in 2006 in the pages of the British newspaper *The Guardian*.[30] In it, they declared that "three basic principles guide our cooking: excellence, openness, and integrity." The chefs, famously inventive, wrote that they embrace innovation, but built on the bedrock of tradition—and that the best culinary traditions are "collective, cumulative inventions."

Many of the chefs and restaurateurs we interviewed for this book expressed similar sentiments. They endorsed the idea that even truly groundbreaking cooking is necessarily derivative of what came before. And they believed that sharing ideas and techniques is part of the ethos of cuisine. Not all concurred, of course. But for many, openness was essential to innovation, and in any event valuable beyond its creative potential.

In all these settings, then, innovators innovate by tweaking the creativity that another has pioneered. And neither the pioneer nor the tweakers are motivated by the prospect of monopoly rights over their creations. Indeed, it is the *absence* of monopoly rights that makes all this tweaking possible. Without a system of open copying, both the ability and the incentive to tweak are far weaker. In short, the open-source method presents a very different approach to innovation than that embedded in our IP laws. Rather than monopoly control, open source rests on no control.

And in a sense, nearly every story told in this book exhibits a bit of the open-source method: because these are creative industries that lack effective protection against copying, their underlying innovations are open to rivals and partners alike. But as fields as disparate as software and football illustrate, that does not mean that innovation grinds to a halt. Instead, innovation can blossom in an open setting. This innovation may be different: collaborative, incremental, and multipronged. But once we escape the romantic notion that the only innovation that counts is that of the lone inventor with the big breakthrough, we can see that the freedom to copy and improve can be a terrific foundation for innovation.

First-Mover Advantage

First-mover advantage usually refers to the period of de facto exclusivity that an innovator enjoys due to the practical difficulties of copying a particular innovation. In other words, if it takes time for copyists to successfully copy a creation, the creator may have a first-mover advantage—particularly if being first can provide enough of a head start to lock in markets or at least make it hard for latecomers to compete. In some cases, first-mover advantage can offer a sufficient incentive to engage in meaningful innovation, even without the prospect of IP rights to protect that innovation.

It's important to note that first-mover advantage has been employed in different ways by people thinking about different questions. There is a lively debate in the business literature, for example, regarding just how often first-mover advantage gives firms durable market dominance, versus instances where a first entrant loses out to a better organized "fast follower." We're not entering this particular debate. Instead, we use the concept of first-mover advantage simply to capture the idea that even without legal protection against copying, creators can sometimes gain significant benefits from their creations before others imitate them.

In a sense, first-mover advantage is the essence of IP rights: the central premise of these rights is to extend this period of de facto exclusivity by making it illegal to copy an innovation for a set period of time. Patent and copyright are not perpetual; anyone can copy the work of another innovator eventually. But the law is meant to be calibrated so that the gain to the first mover is large enough that it will incentivize continued innovation.

The interesting question here is how much a creator can benefit from "natural" (that is, nonlegal) barriers to copying as opposed to those barriers created by legal restraints. In other words, how much first-mover advantage is there absent IP rights? And is this advantage sufficient to motivate meaningful levels of innovation?

As we saw in Chapter 4, first-mover advantage seems to be enough to maintain substantial innovation in football. New formations and plays can offer meaningful advantages to creative coaches and teams, even though nothing stops other teams from copying those innovations.[*] In fact, many football coaches teach others their plays and approach. In part, coaches keep innovating despite the prospect of copying because they are incredibly short-term thinkers who have to win a game every week; winning now trumps the possibility of losing over the longer term as (hypothetically) their idea spreads.

But there is another reason that copying does not deter innovation in football. Football formations and plays often depend on a certain kind of team and player, and teams cannot be reconstituted quickly. Given this, an innovative coach can achieve substantial success with a new formation even if opponents ultimately adopt it too. The window in which the innovating team is the only one using the new system—or at least, using it well—is large enough to make innovations worthwhile.

Fashion also exhibits some first-mover advantage, though how much is a hotly contested point among those who study apparel markets. It is easy to copy a new design, and it is not hard to find examples of a hot dress appearing quickly in inexpensive stores such as Forever 21. Some even claim that knockoffs have appeared in stores *before* the original.[31] While the instances in which copyists beat or match originators to market are unlikely to be frequent enough to really matter, it is still the case that many copyists are remarkably fast. Hence the lead time enjoyed by originators is often brief.

But—and this is important—it is hard to see how that lead time can shrink entirely. There is no point in knocking off a garment that does not sell well. And most designs do not sell well. The only way to be sure a garment will sell is to see how it fares in the stores. In short, copyists can only be so

---

[*] As we discussed in Chapter 5, while it is theoretically possible to claim that a football formation is a choreographic work, and therefore capable of receiving copyright protection, no one has ever successfully done so.

fast before they are simply making bets on what trends will be hot. And if they are that good at guessing what will be hot, why not just make it themselves and be first—or open a store and sell only those designs guaranteed to sell?

So while copying in fashion can be fast, in reality there is almost always some degree of lead time for innovators. And this lead time, as we explained in Chapter 1, is essential for the operation of fashion's piracy paradox to operate. The freedom to copy a design that is becoming hot helps to create trends and, ultimately, expands the market for that design. For this to work, however, the design must become hot in the first place. Over time this dynamic leads to the diffusion and eventual death of the design and, as early adopters seek something fresh, the debut of a new design. The creative cycle starts anew.

What is special about the piracy paradox in fashion, in other words, is not just that an innovative designer can sell enough units before copies emerge to make innovation worthwhile. If the only advantage to fashion designers was that short window of exclusivity, we would be making a simple first-mover advantage argument. Instead, the heart of the piracy paradox is that *copying drives early adopters to seek new designs.* That in turn gives the innovator a new market to chase. What really matters in fashion is not the first-mover advantage per se. Rather, the lead time a first mover has makes it worthwhile for the fashion conscious to chase new designs. The fashion-following *consumer* is the key player. Since the fashion conscious are differentiators, not flockers, they will only adopt designs that differentiate.[32] And in a system of free and legal copying, that requires some lag between the debut and the diffusion of a design. As a practical matter, that lag continues to exist, no matter how fast copying technologies become.

Databases also exhibit some degree of first-mover advantage. Like an innovative football team deploying a new formation, a successful database can remain competitive due to the need to train users in the new interface. What do we mean? As law professors, we rely heavily on legal databases such as Westlaw. These databases charge paying customers a substantial fee, and they require extensive training to learn to use well.[*] That training begins in

---

[*] In response to a generation of would-be lawyers raised on Google and fed up with complex database programs, the legal databases are moving toward much simpler interfaces that require less training to use effectively—but are likely to produce less stickiness in the user base.

law school, and the big database companies allow students to use their products for free as a way to get them to learn—and to become hooked. Once a law student becomes comfortable with Westlaw (or its primary competitor, Lexis-Nexis) he or she is unlikely to shift to another database. The result is that even if we create a new database tomorrow with all the legal materials contained in Westlaw—and lower prices—we will have a hard time competing with the incumbent firms, who know that lawyers who have spent years, if not decades, using one system are unlikely to start over just to save a few bucks.

Probably the most common example of first-mover advantage is software. Being first—and creating a network of users that all rely on the same program and, as a result, can easily share files and documents—can give decisive and durable advantages to the first mover's product. And that can lead to substantial market control and lasting profits. We wrote this book using Microsoft Word, not because it is the best word processing product in existence, but because we both already had it (and it is plenty good for our purposes). There is not much competition in the word processing world, and that is partly because we all know that if we have a Word document we can send it to virtually anyone and that person too will use Word to open it. We are all part of the Word network, and that makes sharing and communicating easy—and Bill Gates rich.

Only a few industries exhibit such "positive network externalities," as economists call them: benefits that accrue from the fact that others are using the same network. The simplest example of network externalities is a telephone: a single phone is useless, two phones on a network are nice, but hundreds of millions of connected phones are much, much better. Each additional phone on the network makes the other phones more valuable. As we have just discussed, first-mover advantages can certainly accrue in the absence of positive network externalities. But when these externalities exist, the power of first-mover advantage is much greater. The ability to lock consumers in a network that they do not want to leave makes it easier to defeat new entrants into a market, even those that mimic or improve on an existing product.

Think of (the short) history of social networks. Perhaps Facebook, so dominant today, will give way to Google +. But many people do not want to shift over to Google + because their friends are all on Facebook. It is not impossible to dislodge a leading product even when network externalities exist—Friendster and Myspace, after all, were ultimately buried by Facebook. But it is more difficult. When products exhibit positive network externalities, first-mover advantages are very powerful.

In sum, first-mover advantage is a key concept not just in the industries we have explored but in all IP-protected industries. The fundamental purpose of copyright and patent is to create first-mover advantage: IP laws regulate second movers so the first mover has ample time to make money. Our point is simply that first-mover advantage still exists when IP law is absent or ineffective, and in some cases first-mover advantage is powerful enough to sustain a meaningful level of innovation. In others, such as fashion, it is a necessary input into a more powerful dynamic of innovation.

Branding and Advertising

Brands play an important and often unappreciated creativity-inducing role in several of the industries we have explored in this book. By brands we mean familiar names and symbols such as Nike and its swoosh or Apple with its famous apple-with-a-bite-taken image.

Brands are protected by trademark law. The traditional justification for trademark protection has little to do with innovation. Instead, trademark functions to ensure that consumers can identify the source of products and thereby buy the item they want, and not an imitation. Put in economic terms, trademarks reduce the search costs associated with consumption. If you've had a positive experience with basketball shoes from Adidas, then marking them with the trademark-protected three-stripes helps ensure that you can quickly find their shoes the next time you are shopping. And of course it also lets everyone else know which shoes you prefer.

So brands are fundamentally a shortcut—rather than try on lots of shoes, we save time by heading straight for the Adidas rack. Brands can be extremely valuable as a result, and firms take expensive measures to develop and protect them. Legally, trademark law prevents the unauthorized use of a brand in a way that would confuse consumers about the source of products or services. But trademark law goes further. It also aims to prevent anything that would "dilute" consumers' ability to associate a famous brand with the brand's owner, as well as any uses of the brand that might tarnish its image.

Unlike patent and copyright, trademark law is not generally thought of as a spur to creativity. In fact, over a century ago the Supreme Court struck down the Trademark Act of 1870 on precisely this ground. The act was created under the part of the Constitution that authorizes Congress to make patent and copyright law, which are powers given to Congress "To promote the Progress of Science and useful Arts." Trademarks, the Court said, have "no necessary relation to invention or discovery."[33] For that reason, Congress's power to enact a trademark law could not be grounded in the power to "promote . . . Progress."*

While that view has a superficial appeal, it misses some important effects of trademarks. Trademarks can, in fact, function as an incentive mechanism, only in a different manner from that of other IP rights. And as we will describe, trademarks can interact with other creative incentives in important ways.

The power of brands is very apparent in any big drugstore. Walk into a CVS drugstore, as we did recently in Charlottesville, Virginia, and you can buy, for $20.99, 300 tablets of Advil brand ibuprofen. That is just under $0.70 per tablet. The CVS private label ibuprofen—which contains exactly the same dosage of the same medicine—costs $17.79 for 750 tablets, or about $0.24 per tablet. The Advil brand ibuprofen, in other words, is almost three times as expensive as the CVS ibuprofen, despite the fact that they are functionally indistinguishable—they will both get rid of your headache equally well. And this situation is not limited to medicines. On a recent visit to a local grocery in Charlottesville, for example, we found that a 14-ounce box of Cheerios cost $4.59. A 14-ounce box of the store-brand version—the same basic product, except for the packaging—cost $2.75. Despite this significant price differential, Cheerios are the best-selling brand of cereal in the United States.*

As this shows, brands have a strong power over price. And as a result, they wield an unexpected ability to spur innovation. The story of ibuprofen can help explain this relationship. Ibuprofen was invented in the early 1960s by the UK firm Boots, which runs a large chain of drugstores. First patented in

---

* Ultimately, a revised federal trademark law was upheld on other grounds.
* More than 70 years ago, the Supreme Court in *Kellogg Co. v. National Biscuit Co.*, 305 U.S. 111 (1938), held that the shape of Nabisco's shredded wheat biscuit was functional and therefore could not be protected by trademark law. The shape of the Nabisco wheat biscuit was originally patented, as were other famous cereals such as Kellogg's Corn Flakes, but those patent rights have long since expired. And yet these classic branded cereals continue to enjoy a significant pricing premium over unbranded rivals.

1961, it was introduced in the United States as a prescription drug in 1974. In 1984, the FDA approved ibuprofen for over-the-counter (OTC) sale. That same year, Pfizer reached a license agreement with Boots and introduced OTC ibuprofen under the brand name "Advil." Boots's US patent expired in 1986, and soon after other brands of ibuprofen entered the market.

So in all, Pfizer's Advil brand of ibuprofen had less than two years of market exclusivity in the United States. After those two years, many competitors jumped in. And yet today, almost 25 years after the expiration of the ibuprofen patent, Advil still owns *51% of the market*. That's more than twice the combined share of all generic ibuprofen products, despite the fact that Advil is functionally equivalent to its rivals and quite a bit more expensive.

Why are consumers willing to pay so much for certain brands? There is surprisingly little consensus among researchers about this. Part of the brand premium is surely based on perceived quality differences, and some studies suggest that beliefs about quality may account for perhaps 20% of the difference. The degree to which perceptions of quality matter, however, is likely to differ widely based on the product and the amount of information the consumer has about it. For breakfast cereal, where quality is fairly subjective, it makes sense that consumers pay more for those brands they think represent high quality. But this rationale makes less sense in the case of a basic pain reliever like ibuprofen, where the FDA certifies that the generic drug is as safe and effective as the branded pill. The brand itself seems to have some effect on the willingness of consumers to pay more.

So brands can keep prices high and give firms large and resilient market shares. That brands can have such huge effects explains why companies spend so much money promoting them and designing nifty names and symbols. This much is well known. But the power of brands also has important implications for innovation. If an innovator can link her innovation to a successful brand, she can maintain pricing power even after his innovation is copied. This is the key takeaway of the ibuprofen story. The patent on Advil gave only two years of monopoly control. Yet decades later, Advil still dominates the market for ibuprofen. This suggests that whatever the period of exclusivity, once the brand is established the innovator can continue to profit—substantially—even after the entry of copies, and even if the copies are quite literally identical products. The brand, in effect, can substitute for the protection against copies offered by patent or copyright.

Think back to the Two Pesos-Taco Cabana dispute that went to the Supreme Court, described in Chapter 2. In that case, the issue was whether one Mexican restaurant illegally copied the décor of another. The key to the case was the idea that décor can be a kind of trademark: its purpose is to signal that you are at Two Pesos (or Taco Cabana—they were so similar it is hard to tell them apart). The decor serves to indicate source and quality.

By protecting trade dress, as this is formally known, the law allows copies of one very important part of a restaurant experience (the food) while policing copying of another (the décor.) As long as the décor meets the legal standard—that is, as long as the public associates it with the particular restaurant—it is protected. In this way, trade dress protection partially protects innovation, permitting competitors to copy some things but not others—and allowing an originator to keep a larger share of the market than they would otherwise.

The fashion industry offers a twist on this scenario. As we have explained, neither patent nor copyright really protects new fashion designs from copying. And yet the fashion industry is stocked with very valuable brands, and the owners of those brands are often able to demand a giant premium for their products despite the fact that they compete against often very close copies. Some of this price differential is due to quality differences—the $45,000 Patek Phillipe watch is much more expensively made (though perversely, it is often less accurate) than its $45 Canal Street knockoff. But not nearly all of it. A big part of the trademark premium is the excitement, and the perception of increased social status, that comes from owning a real Patek Phillipe.[*] The same can said of a Proenza Schouler dress or Prada coat.

And where does that set of feelings come from? From the meaning that brands, and the advertising associated with them, create. The process of creating this meaning is expensive and difficult. There is no foolproof recipe for it. But if the alchemy succeeds, the result can be astonishing. The monopoly theory of IP suggests that perfect copies will deprive innovators of any significant returns on their investments in creativity. But when an innovation is linked to a valuable brand, copies are never perfect. Indeed, they differ in perhaps the most important feature.

---

[*] No buyer believes that a Canal Street watch is the real thing, but some copies mimic originals in ways that are very hard to detect—and sometimes are not detected until the owner tries to get the item repaired. Elizabeth Holmes, "The Finer Art of Faking It: Counterfeits Are Better Crafted, Duping Even Sophisticated Shoppers," *Wall Street Journal*, June 30, 2011.

The bottom line is this: in the many contexts in which brands are significant but patent and copyright are absent or weak, market share and pricing power will not necessarily disappear. They will just flow from the power of brands, rather than from legal enforcement of a monopoly. Copies may compete with the original, but brands keep them from truly outcompeting the original based only on price. And this, in turn, preserves some of the reward that monopoly power over copying is meant to provide.

Brands have an interesting relationship to copies in another very important way. Copying may serve as *advertising for brands*—advertising that is not only free but arguably more powerful. Why? Because it stems from the authentic actions of consumers rather than the carefully orchestrated efforts of producers.

In a fascinating paper, legal scholar Jonathan Barnett explored the ways in which, in the fashion industry, brand owners benefited even when knockoff artists not only took their designs but also counterfeited their brands. Barnett argued that the presence of counterfeits may actually help brand owners by signaling to high-end consumers the desirability of the original item as part of an emerging fashion trend. Because the counterfeit copies are most often of lower quality, consumers usually can tell they're not the real thing. At the same time, Barnett argues, their presence on the streets signals that the dress, handbag, or shoes they are aping are especially desirable. Counterfeits communicate the fact that even those who can't afford to have the real thing still want it. That's a free ad for the branded product.

Other studies support the power of copies as a form of advertising. A two-and-one-half year study by Renee Gosline of the Massachusetts Institute of Technology looked at people who purchase counterfeit luxury items, like handbags and sunglasses, and found that counterfeits do not hurt the sales of luxury brands so long as consumers can distinguish between them. Indeed, Gosline found that counterfeits are often used as "trial versions" of the high-end genuine branded item, with over 40% of counterfeit handbag consumers ultimately purchasing the real brand.

Gosline's study suggests that fake luxury goods are a very effective form of advertising: people who buy them and live with them have a significant probability of being converted to the brand and buying the real thing once they can afford to do so. Copies, in short, are a kind of "gateway drug" that leads to consumption of the harder (or at least, more expensive) stuff. What's more, every time consumers go out with their fake item, they're publicly displaying the desirability of the brand, sparking trend-driven consumption that spills over—or up—to the original version.

Gosline's and Barnett's findings are broadly reinforced by other recent research. A 2011 study by economist Yi Qian for the National Bureau of Economic Research looked at data from 31 branded shoe companies, as well as a number of counterfeiters, operating in China in 1993–2004. The study likewise found that counterfeiting had a surprisingly *positive* effect on the sales of high-end branded items. The tendency of counterfeits to advertise the desirability of the branded product—what we will call the "advertising effect"—outweighed any substitution effect, by which we mean the effect of consumers purchasing the counterfeit instead of the original. The substitution effect is harmful for creators, and the advertising effect is helpful. And only for low-end branded products did the substitution effect outweigh the advertising effect.

These results lead to two key points. First, trademark can actually provide some of the value to innovators that patent and copyright are designed to offer. Owners of well-known brands can often maintain a stable market share and demand a significant price premium for their products—even when cheap copies are widely available. Pfizer can charge high prices for Advil to those who prefer the brand name; CVS can sell generic ibuprofen to everyone else. Second, copies of branded goods—counterfeits—can have a counterintuitive effect on originals. While these copies can steal away some would-be buyers of the original, they also can help create new buyers through the advertising effect. Some counterfeit buyers "graduate" to the real thing, whereas others who never buy a counterfeit become buyers of the original because the counterfeits serve as advertising.

And importantly, this second point is not limited to formal brands—that is, to the kinds of brands protected by trademark law. The basic dynamic of the advertising effect can also be seen in individual creators, who can build a very valuable name for themselves as innovators.

Los Angeles–based chef Ludovic Lefebvre, for instance, is not a brand in the formal sense. But his name and personality draw big crowds, providing him with several ways, besides actually getting behind the stove, to gain value from his skill as an innovative chef: cookbook author, consulting chef, *Top Chef: Masters* contestant, and so forth. In 2011, he even debuted his own television show, *Ludo Bites America*, on the Sundance Channel. And it is enough to know that a new restaurant is run by Lefebvre—or by any of a number of other famous chefs—for legions of fans to show up.* Like shoppers in the shoe store seeking the Adidas rack, they know what the Ludo Lefebvre brand entails.

Unauthorized copies, in turn, can serve as unintended advertisements in the same way we have described. In some cases the unauthorized copy is a noteworthy dish that soon appears in competitor restaurants and sparks interest in the original. Being copied in this way can reinforce a reputation as an innovator and elevate a chef's standing in the public eye. In other cases, as with Pearl Oyster Bar and Ed's Lobster Bar, what is copied is not a dish (or two) but an entire restaurant or culinary approach. As described in Chapter 2, Pearl Oyster Bar and Ed's Lobster Bar, both located in downtown Manhattan, are pretty similar in look, feel, and menu, though whether Ed's is a direct copy of Pearl's—or simply a co-equal variant of the basic idea of a New England shellfish shack—is a more difficult question that divides the food cognoscenti.

But whatever the true answer—and the dispute settled before going to trial, so no legal ruling on the question emerged—assume for a moment that Ed's is indeed a deliberate copy. It is far from clear that Ed's copying harmed Pearl Oyster Bar, or for that matter that the arrival of Mary's Fish Camp, an earlier offshoot of Pearl Oyster Bar, did any harm either. Despite being within a mile or so of each other, all three restaurants do a brisk business. (Ed's even recently opened a satellite a few blocks away.) And on several recent visits, we found that Pearl Oyster Bar seemed to have far more business than it could handle—a result that, at least according to the 2011 Zagat restaurant guide, is the norm for Pearl. Having competitor shellfish/seafood bars that appear to be knockoffs may simply serve to trigger the advertising effect: to make customers want to try the original, and putatively best, version—or at a minimum to try all three spots and compare.* And maybe the copies have fueled a trend of oyster bar-hopping, spurring the growth of all competitors.

Advertising via copying is perhaps the most powerful endorsement a brand can hope for. Few people believe that the celebrities in glossy product

---

* In fact, Lefebvre's brand is strong enough that he has dispensed with standard features of restaurants altogether (such as fixed addresses), operating only his roving "LudoBites" pop-up operation, whose seats sell out over the Internet almost instantly, and his even-more roving "LudoTruck."

* Not to mention the Mermaid Oyster Bar, which opened maybe 100 yards away from Pearl Oyster Bar. Or Jack's Luxury Oyster Bar, a few blocks farther east.

ads really consume (or are actually willing to pay for) the product they are shilling: we are too jaded for that, even if the halo effect of a celebrity somehow renders the item in question more desirable. In this sense, conventional advertisements are inherently limited because they rarely convey authentic endorsement. A copy, by contrast, is as sincere an endorsement of quality and desirability as any creator could hope for.

Brands, first-mover advantage, norms, the power of performance, trends and fads, and open-source innovation: all are important elements in the many creative industries we have explored in this book. And to varying degrees, they provide new ideas and new approaches to the many creative and often copy-plagued industries we have not discussed. To be sure, we are not offering a guaranteed tool kit of anti-copying strategies. Nor are we Pollyannas who believe that all copying is harmless. But a clear-eyed and realistic look across the many and diverse innovative industries in the world shows that there is substantial reason for optimism, even in a world in which copying is becoming ever easier and more prevalent.

This coming world is sometimes depicted as either a technology-driven utopia in which information finally gets to be free, or a looming cultural wasteland in which "digital parasites" destroy first one, then another, creative enterprise.[34] Both of these positions are overheated and hyperbolic. Rules against copying are essential to our economy; as we have repeatedly emphasized, we do not want to abolish IP.[35] At the same time, the *already-existing* creative fields that we have explored make plain that ever-freer and easier copying is not an inevitable death sentence for creativity and innovation. And as we will describe in the Epilogue to this book, even in an arena such as music, commonly considered the paradigmatic example of a creative industry plagued by pirates and parasites, the reality is different from the rhetoric. *Music* is thriving, though the *major music labels* are not.

In short, creative output is a more complicated process than many assume. Our legal structure of innovation—the IP system—is but one part of that process. We will wrap up this concluding chapter by briefly considering some of the broader factors at work in innovation. These broad factors, such as the tendency, which appears endemic to human nature, to make rosy-eyed predictions about our future success, provide further support for the idea that creativity is more resilient to copying than conventional wisdom suggests.

Costs, Benefits, and Creativity

If we step back from the particular stories we have told and consider what generally drives people to create and innovate, two basic, even obvious, factors are paramount. *How much does it cost to create?* And, *what is the expected return on that creation?* In other words, the rate of innovation broadly reflects the costs and benefits of investing time and money in creative work. Many creators, to be sure, create for the love of it. But in the end, sustained innovation requires adequate incentives. This premise is a foundation of the monopoly theory of innovation. But it is equally central to our account of innovation; in this book we have simply illustrated the many more complex creative incentives that exist, incentives that—as the sustained success of fashion, food, and the like demonstrate—keep creativity alive despite copying.

In this final section, we want to extend the analysis with two points, both of which make us more optimistic about the future of innovation. First, the benefits of innovation are often overestimated *by the innovator*, which serves to induce more innovation than otherwise and may also make innovation more resilient in the face of losses from copying. Second, the costs of creation are dropping in many fields, which has a similar effect on innovation: lower cost generally means more output than otherwise. Together, these two phenomena provide more reason to think that a world of easy copying is not necessarily a world of little creativity.

Consider first the benefit side of the equation. Copyright and patent are fundamentally about ensuring sufficient benefit to creators. Their primary justification is that they raise the expected return on innovation by ensuring that copyists cannot undercut the market for creations after they are made. Discouraging copying allows innovators to reap more of the benefits of their innovations. This much is conventional wisdom, and we agree that IP law generally has this positive effect. But what this underscores is that the key is *return on innovation, not restrictions on copying.* As long as the return is high enough, we will see innovation.

This leads to an obvious, but too often overlooked, point: legal rights are not the only way to raise that return. Innovation can be induced by other things—ranging from social norms to tax credits to prizes.* And some of the

---

* Great Britain created a prize in the 18th century for the first person to develop a reliable way to measure longitude; more recently, Netflix created a $1 million prize to improve its online recommendation feature. The X Prize Foundation has offered several prominent prizes, such as the Google Lunar X Prize for the first privately funded mission to send a robot to the moon.

forces incentivizing innovation are even more fundamental than these—
they arise not from external prods, but from basic human psychology. Consider again the cost-benefit calculation of creating something new. It is not
actual return but *perceived or expected return* that most powerfully shapes
decisions to create. And because there is good reason to think that we all are
prone to overestimate the benefits that will flow from our creativity, we are
likely to overinvest in it. This "optimism bias" is one more reason to think
that creativity and innovation are more resilient in the face of copying than
conventional wisdom would suggest.

Optimism Bias

Conventional thinking about innovation and IP relies on the concept of a
rational innovator. It assumes that innovators calculate, either explicitly
or implicitly, the cost of creation versus the size of the return they will
likely enjoy. A writer might anticipate a certain advance from her publisher; a musician might estimate the sales of a new song. This expected
return shapes how much effort they pour into creation and what kinds of
creation they pursue. Abundant research in economics and psychology,
however, suggest that their judgments are often likely to be wrong—and
systematically so.

As many studies have found, individuals are very bad at assessing their
own future prospects. They have a pronounced optimism bias.[36] They think
they will succeed where others have not, and they heavily discount the prospect of failure. Nearly all newlyweds, for example, believe they will not get
divorced, when in fact a large minority will—and often within a few years.
Likewise, students wildly overestimate their likely grades, even in the face of
stiff competition. Like the residents of Lake Wobegon, we all want to believe
we are above average.

Optimism bias has been shown to apply broadly to life events, and there
is no reason to think it does not also apply to innovation.[37] Indeed, two lab-
oratory studies conducted by one of us (Sprigman) and Christopher Buccafusco of the Chicago-Kent College of Law showed that creative artists
believe their work is far more valuable than do potential buyers.

In the first study, several hundred subjects were given the opportunity to
buy and sell chances to win a haiku contest. The subjects were randomly
assigned to be Authors or Bidders. Authors were told that they would be

competing in a contest with nine other writers. A poetry expert would select the winner, who would receive a $50 prize. Each Bidder wrote down the amount he would be willing to pay to purchase a specific Author's chance to win. Similarly, each Author wrote down the amount she would be willing to accept.[38] On average, Authors were willing to sell their chance of winning the haiku contest for $22.90. But Bidders' average willingness to pay was less than half: only $10.38.

These results are consistent with the hundreds of other studies that have confirmed optimism bias in a wide variety of settings. Authors believed that they were roughly 30% likely to win a contest where in reality they had, on average, a 10% chance. They were irrationally optimistic about the reward they expected.

These results were replicated with would-be professional artists—painting students from the School of the Art Institute in Chicago. The students were invited to enter a medium-sized painting into a contest. The Painters were told that they would be competing with nine other entrants for a $100 prize judged by an expert. Each Painter was matched with one of 10 additional subjects acting as Bidders.

Here too there was a huge gap between bidders and creators—in fact, the gap was quite a bit larger, which suggests that would-be professional creators tend to over-value their work even more than do ordinary people. The Painters demanded on average nearly $75, while the Bidders were willing to pay less than $18. And again, the biggest cause of the widely diverging variations was over-optimism. Painters believed that they had more than a 50% chance of winning the contest. The real number, since there were 10 of them, was (on average) 10%.

We see behavior like this all the time. Most people think they're a better-than-average driver, not to mention smarter than average. And the haiku and painting experiments suggest that creators may be even more prone to this sort of optimism bias. Optimism bias, in short, leads many innovators to think they will gain a greater return from their intellectual creations than they actually do.

Why is this important to understanding the interaction between copying and creativity? Because optimism bias likely acts as a subsidy for innovation. Creators who have an unduly strong belief in their ultimate prospects for success should be willing to invest more in their creativity. And this increased willingness to invest is likely, in turn, to lead to increased creative output as compared with a world in which creators rationally calculated the odds—odds that may include expected losses from copying.[39]

We began this Conclusion by noting that many artists and inventors toil because they are driven to, not because they expect riches. But many do expect—or hope—for some tangible reward. For these people the widely noted phenomenon of optimism bias is as likely to work its magic as effectively in the creative world as it does in assessments of marriage or job prospects. They expect more, and so they work to create more.

Tournament Markets

There is another important, and related, factor that skews how innovators assess their expected return on innovation. Many contemporary markets for creative goods are what economists call "winner take all" or "tournament" markets.[40] In these markets, a huge reward goes to a few at the very top—the superstars—while much less goes to those just below them. This dynamic is easy to see in areas like professional sports: just think about Major League Baseball, where the very best players receive enormous salaries, while those who are merely excellent languish on AAA farm teams, earning a tiny fraction of what the true stars do.

Tournament markets amplify small differences in performance into enormous disparities in reward. Given this basic dynamic, we might expect people to shy away from competing in markets like these—the risk of failure is great, competition can be very intense, and the difference between success and failure hard to determine until years of effort have been invested. Yet we see large numbers of individuals competing to become a sports star, a national politician, a CEO, or, most important for our purposes, a musician, writer, or inventor of the next huge Web concept.

Many markets for creative goods are tournament-like. A hit song can yield huge sums for the right creative artist. Yet the vast majority of songs go nowhere, commercially speaking. Likewise, books and screenplays can rake in enormous revenues if they are truly successful, but New York and Los Angeles are awash in the tens of thousands of authors who tried and failed. Perhaps the best example is in the realm of patent. Whether it is a new drug or a new widget, "the firm that wins the patent race is awarded a patent and even a close second-place finisher earns no reward whatsoever from the patent system."[41]

As this suggests, the tournament nature of creative work is to some degree driven by IP law: patent and copyright, by creating the reward of a lucrative monopoly, help to make the market tournament-like. If others could copy the good without restraint, the size of the "prize" will not be nearly as great, since there will be more and stronger competition. But this is not an all-or-nothing phenomenon: we see tournament effects even in markets featuring a substantial amount of copying.

Fashion, for example, is not a winner-take-all market; it is more like a winner-take-most market, in which the winning designs are effectively "shared" with other competitors, making the entire market a bit less volatile.[42] Yet even in the fashion industry there is a big disparity between the superstars and the also-rans, with the top designers and brands raking in outsized profits. Tournament markets require that winners appropriate at least some of their winnings. But *complete* appropriability is not required. Markets like fashion and food, in which there is relatively little IP, suggest that high levels of IP protection are not essential for the tournament dynamic to take hold.

Like optimism bias, tournaments induce more investment than is rational. So both optimism bias and tournament markets push innovators toward high levels of innovation. And this makes innovation more resilient to copying. Why? Copying may lower individual innovators' return (even if it raises the overall return of a given industry). If creators rationally calculated their returns, the prospect of being knocked off might dissuade them from creating in the first place. But if they instead overestimate their returns, as so many of us seem habitually to do, they may still have sufficient incentive to invest in creation.

To be sure, these effects are hard to measure. There is good reason, however, to think they are not insignificant. With respect to optimism, just think of the painting study, which found that painters were, on average, *five times* more optimistic than they would be if they were accurately calculating the odds.[43] And with respect to tournaments, just think of the ultimate tournament game—the lottery. People are drawn to the lottery in droves, even though it is clearly, on average, a losing bet. Tournament effects are powerful, and even if they cannot be precisely measured, it is hard to believe that they do not drive creative activity as well.

The important point is that both of these effects exaggerate anticipated benefits. And it follows that exaggerated expectations of benefit will tend to keep innovation buoyant, beyond what a rational calculation of return would predict.

The Costs of Creation

The supply of innovation depends not just on anticipated benefits but also on expected costs. As innovation gets cheaper and easier, we should see more of it. As we noted earlier, not all innovation costs the same. Yet these costs are not fixed; technology can lower the costs of innovation in many industries, sometimes dramatically.

Consider music. Not that long ago—as recently as the mid-1990s—producing an album required an expensive studio and skilled engineers. Today artists can produce music at home using a computer loaded with Pro Tools, Abelton Live, or even Garageband, which comes free on Apple computers. These tools have markedly reduced the cost of producing music. Perhaps more important, the cost of distribution has also fallen tremendously. Distribution in the music business used to be complex—recording tapes were transferred to vinyl (or later compact discs) and then shipped around the world to record stores. Today, digital files can be instantly uploaded to an artist's Web site, or to a commercial site like iTunes, and distributed easily anywhere there is an Internet connection.

Sometimes technological advances like these make it possible for one person to do what many did before, as with music recording. Other times they allow many individuals to do what one (or a few) did before, by permitting large-scale tweaking (as in Wikipedia) and more generally what might be understood as open-source production or "crowd-sourcing."[44] Perhaps the most important effect of technological change, however, is how it reduces the cost of making and distributing creative work.

A great example of this is the recent effort by comedian Louis C.K.—he of the Dane Cook joke-copying powwow described in the Introduction—to offer a comedy show directly to fans for download. Louis C.K. produced and filmed the show himself, and sold it for an inexpensive $5 per copy. As he wrote to fans on his Web site, $5 is

> less than I would have been paid by a large company to simply perform the show and let them sell it to you, but they would have charged you about $20 for the video. They would have given you an encrypted and regionally

restricted video of limited value, and they would have owned your private information for their own use. They would have withheld international availability indefinitely. This way, you only paid $5, you can use the video any way you want, and you can watch it in Dublin, whatever the city is in Belgium, or Dubai. I got paid nice, and I still own the video (as do you).[45]

Louis C.K. recently stated that he's collected more than $1 million from sales of his self-released comedy show. The success of efforts like this (and Louis C.K. is not the first nor, surely, the last to try this approach)* is obviously bad news for distributors like record companies. But it is great news for fans, and if Louis C.K. is to be believed, great for artists as well. Similar if less marked changes in film, literature, and even areas like fashion and financial innovations have also significantly reduced the costs of both creation and distribution.

This fundamental shift in the cost of distribution has two very important effects. One, if the *costs* of creation are lower, the expected *returns* that are necessary to spur innovation can also be lower. And that means the creator can absorb more copying-related losses without erasing the incentive to innovate. Two, lower costs permit lower prices, and lower prices make consumers more likely to buy and less likely to copy. The price of an item (like an album or show) can now be so low that many people are happy to just pay it and not bother illegally copying—even if illegal copying is easy to do.* The phenomenal success of Apple's iTunes illustrates this latter principle well. There have been over *16 billion* paid downloads since the service began, in an industry that is the self-proclaimed poster child for illegal, Internet-enabled copying. Make it cheap and easy enough, and crime just doesn't pay any more.

Now, new digital technologies have made illegal copying easier as well, so the aggregate effect of technological change is not clear (and hard to measure accurately, in any event.) Still, the beneficial effects of technology are often ignored, and any serious analysis must consider them.

---

* We discuss Radiohead's famous "pick your price" download experiment in the Epilogue to this book.
* Again Louis C.K.: "I really hope people keep buying it a lot, so I can have shitloads of money, but at this point I think we can safely say that the experiment really worked. If anybody stole it, it wasn't many of you. Pretty much everybody bought it." Of course this needs to be taken with a grain of salt. Lots of research on taxation shows that people are much more likely to comply if they believe others are complying. So Louis C.K. is smart to say that almost no one stole it, whether that is in fact true or not.

The key point here is simple: many of the same technologies that promote piracy also promote creativity. Technological change can and often does make innovation cheaper, and it is Economics 101 to note that lower costs generally lead to higher production. This is one more reason to think that, in our current technological environment, copying is not nearly as fearsome a prospect as many believe.

Wrap Up

Let us recap our argument briefly. In this book we have explored many industries where creativity is sustained even though copying is common and often legal. These industries are not dying; they are thriving. This is a mystery for conventional thinking about innovation and the role of intellectual property, which rests on the belief that imitation kills innovation. Explaining why fields like fashion, fonts, and finance remain creative despite pervasive copying is the major puzzle that animates this book.

We have described these industries and have drilled down into the details of how (and why) they work. In this conclusion, we've sketched six broad lessons drawn from these varied case studies. No one lesson applies to every industry we have looked at. But together, they help explain why there are so many successful industries that exhibit both imitation *and* innovation. And, we hope, they offer a set of ideas for making other creative industries—even those that have traditionally relied heavily on copyright and patent to battle copying—more resilient to copying. Finding workable sources of resilience is essential because, whatever you may think of copying, it is not going away.

In the last few pages we brought two other factors into the equation. First, innovation, like any economic good, is the product of costs and benefits. The benefit side encompasses more than just money; many create out of love or compulsion. But over the long term, financial expectations matter, and there are many reasons to believe that innovators are overly optimistic when assessing benefits. The tournament market qualities of many creative industries accentuate this bias. Like a subsidy, these twin forces act to promote innovation.

Second, in the debate over copying, the cost side of creation has been given little attention. Technology can certainly lower benefits by enabling copying. But it can also lower the costs of innovation and distribution. Like raising returns, lowering costs can turn an "unprofitable" act of innovation or distribution into a profitable one. Which effect is more powerful depends on the industry and the technology. But to date, the focus has almost entirely been on the downside of technology. We see a substantial upside as well.

All of these observations point in the same direction: toward a perhaps counterintuitive, but fundamentally positive, message. As we have shown in a wide range of fields, creativity can persist even in the face of widespread copying. Indeed, in some instances creativity occurs *because* of copying. In short, copying has underappreciated virtues. And even when copying is neither benign nor beneficial, it is often not nearly the threat many perceive. The knockoff economy already exists. The important question is how to understand, and ultimately harness, the power of imitation to further innovation.

EPILOGUE: THE FUTURE OF MUSIC

Sean Parker (co-founder of Napster): I brought down the record
    companies with Napster. . . .
Eduardo Saverin (co-founder of Facebook): Sorry, you didn't bring
    down the record companies. They won.
Sean Parker: In court.
Eduardo Saverin: Yeah.
Sean Parker: You wanna buy a Tower Records, Eduardo?
                                   —*The Social Network, 2010*

Copying has been the bane of the music industry for many years—well
before Napster, or even Sean Parker, were born. But something changed in
1999. That was the year that the first online filesharing service, Napster,
exploded.

Suddenly, millions of people were sharing music freely with one another.
In the eyes of the recording industry, this was mass criminality and a grave
threat. The industry reacted swiftly. It lobbied governments to strengthen
intellectual property protections. It hired more lawyers. And it tried to use
the courts to stop Napster. These strategies had some success. Congress
passed increasingly restrictive laws, and the courts ruled in ways favorable
to the record companies. But these victories were superficial and barely
dented the problem. Filesharing—that is, copying—continues on a mass
scale, and copyright enforcement appears ever more expensive and less
effective. The future path of technology is impossible to predict, but if the
past is prologue, tomorrow's technologies are likely to make copying even
harder to stop.

In this Epilogue, we'll look at the music industry's long-running battle against mass copying. In a decade, the industry's revenues shrank by over 60% (adjusted for inflation) as millions of fans took for free what they used to pay for. Today, the music industry's revenues continue to plummet and piracy continues, largely unabated. And yet—this is crucial—musical creativity is flourishing. It is not far-fetched to say that music, in the midst of its alleged decline, is more creative than ever.

The story of the music industry's war against online piracy has been told at length elsewhere.[1] But we do want to use the basic outlines of the story to make two important points.

First, copying has clearly harmed some parts of the music industry. Yet music itself is not going to disappear. In fact, quite the opposite: some of the very changes that enabled widespread copying of music have also dramatically lowered the costs of producing and distributing new music. That is one reason the supply of new music is up, not down.

Second, the music industry's plight is not irreparable. Perhaps the industry can restructure itself by mimicking some of the practices of industries such as fashion and comedy. This new tack can be a useful supplement to vigorous copyright enforcement or, in some instances, can substitute for it. The music industry can change the way it works, with the goal of building resistance to copying—and perhaps even the ability to benefit from it—into its business model.

A Very Brief History of the Music Industry's Decline

Music and the music industry are not the same. The "music industry" is often just shorthand for the interests of the major record labels, such as the Warner Music Group and Sony Music Entertainment. When people say that Internet piracy is killing "the music industry," they are really talking about the major labels. And, in a sense, they are right. The labels have been deeply harmed by illegal downloading.

Yet music itself is very much alive. As we described in the conclusion to this book, musicians once had to rely on expensive studios and highly trained engineers to record their music, and big companies to manufacture and distribute it. Retail stores—even the biggest of them, like Tower Records—could only carry a small amount of stock. The result was an expensive distribution scheme that excluded most artists and restricted consumer choice.

All of this has now changed—for the better. With a laptop, artists can produce high-quality recordings on their own, and distribute them easily via the Internet. In this more wide-open world, even virtual unknowns can make a living while bypassing the traditional industry players. And because online retailers like Amazon are reachable by anyone with an Internet connection, have unlimited virtual shelf space, and much lower costs than physical retailers, consumers now enjoy much greater choice in what music to buy.* The result is a great flowering of music of all kinds. In fact, judged in terms of the diversity and quality of music available today, the ease of obtaining it, its low price, and the amount of information available to guide consumers to the music they want, we are living in a musical golden age.

This is better not only for consumers. It is also better for many musicians. When success meant distribution through a major label, the market produced a few very rich superstars and a large number of broke nobodies. Today, a wide range of musicians use technologies like home studios, blogs, YouTube, MySpace, Facebook, and Twitter to carve out decent careers on their own. Music, in short, is thriving—even in the face of vast amounts of copying.

Still, it is undeniable that the fortunes of the major labels are declining. This decline is driven by technology, but technology is not the only factor. The labels themselves made some strategic missteps, and they failed to recognize the opportunities, not just the harm, inherent in these technological transformations. We elaborate on this point here because it is underscores an important element: *it is often not copying per se that is a problem, but how copying is understood and addressed.*

To begin, take a look at the following chart, which we have constructed from the industry's own data.[2]

In 1999, total record company revenues hit an all-time peak of $14.5 billion. This followed a decade of vigorous growth in which revenues increased from $6.5 billion to $14.5 billion between 1989 and 1999, a 220% increase (or 170% adjusted for inflation). Yet this growth was deceptive, for it was driven primarily by a one-time event: the format shift from LPs to CDs. CDs, first introduced in 1982, outsold vinyl records by 1988, and in subsequent years consumers spent huge sums replacing their old vinyl records.

---

* This is the fundamental insight of Chris Anderson's book *The Long Tail* (Hyperion, 2006): online, even items that sell in very low numbers can be profitable, because the costs of inventory and distribution are extremely small.

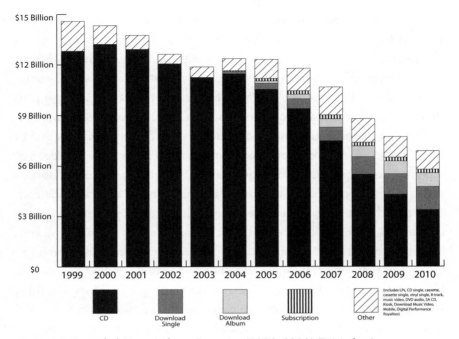

FIGURE 6.1 Recorded Music Industry Revenues (1999–2010) (RIAA data)

But the good times did not last. By the end of 2009, total revenues were down to just over $7.6 billion—a fall of almost 50% over 10 years. And that figure doesn't capture the full extent of the decline. Adjusted for inflation, record company revenues fell by approximately 60% over the last decade. That trend continued in 2010: as the Recording Industry Association of America's (RIAA) latest figures show, total revenues dropped by another 11%, to just under $7 billion. And there's no end in sight.

Enter Napster

What happened? Napster happened. The creation of Shawn Fanning, then a 19-year-old college student, Napster was the first music filesharing service to gain a huge following. Napster attracted almost 50 million users within months of its release. It was appealing because it was so easy to use: Fanning's elegant design made it simple to go online and find exactly the song you wanted. But by far the biggest reason for Napster's viral growth was that it had everything: pretty much any song you wanted, instantly and free.

The huge amount of music available on Napster was, in turn, due mostly to the system's "peer-to-peer" architecture. Napster didn't collect music on a server. Instead, it used the Internet to connect the computers of millions of users. When a user asked for a song, Napster consulted its constantly updated list of music files and then connected the requesting user with another user's computer that had the relevant file.

The music industry's reaction was unsurprising and, given the scale of the copying Napster was enabling, understandable. In 1999, the RIAA sued Napster, asking for $100,000 for each song downloaded—billions of dollars in total—and a court order directing Napster to shut down. In 2001, a federal court agreed, ordering the company to remove all unlicensed content from its network—which quickly led to Napster's shutdown. Facing extinction, Napster offered the major labels a deal worth about $1 billion to license their catalogs. The envisioned "Napster 2.0" service would charge users between $2.95 and $9.95 per month and use the revenue to fund yearly payments to the record companies of $200 million.[3]

The labels turned down Napster's offer. And in retrospect, this looks like a major mistake. If Napster had become a pay service, some of its users would certainly have left to find new sources of free music. But the runaway success, years later, of Apple's iTunes shows that a lot of people are perfectly willing to pay for music, at least if they are getting what they want conveniently (and safely) at a fair price. A Napster pay service would have enjoyed a significant head start. So many people were using Napster in 2001—especially young people, the biggest consumers—that the labels would have at least been able to make a case that paying a reasonable price for convenient online music was better than stealing it. That case would have been more powerful if the labels had embraced the new technology, and trumpeted a Napster settlement as the beginning of a new and better deal for consumers.

Instead, Napster was shut down. But the genie could not be put back in the bottle. New services arose in Napster's wake, including Grokster, Kazaa, and BitTorrent, and millions of Napster users migrated to the newer networks. The music industry again went to court. In 2005, in a major decision, the Supreme Court held that Grokster could be held liable for "inducing" copyright infringement. Here too, however, the victory was more apparent than real. Grokster was not found guilty of directly infringing copyrights—unlike

Napster, when Grokster users shared digital files, they did so without any direct assistance from Grokster. Instead, Grokster was found guilty of essentially provoking piracy. The Supreme Court held that the company had induced copyright infringement by intentionally choosing a name that sounded like Napster, and then encouraging Napster users to use Grokster to download free music.

These acts amounted, in the Court's view, to an open invitation to break the law. They are also unlikely to be repeated. Unsurprisingly, the decision in *Grokster* had little lasting impact. Grokster shut down, but new platforms quickly emerged, and filesharers migrated again. The RIAA's litigation strategy, in short, was like playing Whack-a-Mole, only in this version new and faster moles kept appearing.

A current example is BitTorrent. By some accounts, files shared over Bit-Torrent comprise as much as one-third of current Web traffic. Users can search BitTorrent using public search engines like the Pirate Bay. However, an increasing amount of BitTorrent filesharing occurs via "closed" search engines that are accessible only by invitation—basically, clubs that share files among their members. New technological tools make detection of file-sharing much less likely and more expensive.

And even newer technologies are coming online, such as the file-hosting and "cyberlocker" sites. To distribute music via a file-hosting site, a user uploads a file to a site like Rapidshare, and then distributes a Web address that permits visitors to download the file. The large number of file-hosting sites, their independence, and the fact that many are located in foreign jurisdictions with weak legal systems makes cracking down on them very difficult.

The music industry, in short, has remained one step behind the technologies used for illegal downloading. And while it has won many court victories, these have been largely Pyhrric. The copying of music is more prevalent today than when Napster was invented.

IF YOU CAN'T BEAT THEM, JOIN THEM

The major labels likely would have done better had they struck a deal with Napster when they had the chance. Providing an attractive legal alternative to copying would not have stopped piracy altogether. Yet the market for paid online music is very big indeed: as we noted in the Conclusion, iTunes has provided well over 16 billion paid song downloads. Perhaps if the labels had co-opted the Napster model, as Napster proposed in its settlement offer, that would have helped to reduce piracy to a level that would no longer be a fundamental threat.

Such a system implies a different business model, of course: one much more like iTunes than A&M Records. Consumers would buy their music one song at a time rather than in higher priced bundles of a dozen or so songs. And they would pay less. These changes would mostly benefit consumers.

In the longer term, however, the labels likely would have benefited as well—certainly relative to the disastrous losses they've suffered over the past decade. Not least, the industry's costs of distribution would have fallen dramatically. Napster would have functioned, in effect, as an efficient and scalable retailer. There was another, perhaps even more important, potential gain—*information*. Napster's network was based around a central server that could have been used to store customer identification information and transactions. Millions of music fans had gathered in one place, Napster's central server knew how to find them, and the labels could have used this to target products and services to the Napster user base. In one stroke, a deal with Napster would have allowed the record labels to adjust their business model to account for the rise of the Internet.*

Instead Napster was shuttered. The technologies that rose up to take its place were much less promising as potential business partners. These networks were decentralized, and so were much harder to control or coopt.[4] The simple fact is that Napster made music incredibly easy to find, and it was the first example of filesharing to really hit it big. That made Napster the perfect partner.

From P2P to Personal

As it became clear that downloading technologies would not disappear, the record labels tried a second strategy. Beginning in 2003, the labels filed suit against 261 individuals who had shared music illegally. Under US law, those

---

* Some have suggested that the labels failed to make a deal with Napster because the labels didn't have the legal right to license online distribution of their artists' recordings. Major label contracts are not public, but the evidence we've seen suggests that most contracts included "all media" clauses, which appear to have given labels the right to contract for online delivery. The fight over online delivery at the time between artists and labels was less about whether the labels had the right to license for online distribution, and more about whether artists would be compensated at the royalty rate applied to distribution via CD, or via a lower royalty rate applied to new media.

defendants were liable for damages of up to $150,000 per song shared. Ulti-mately, the labels would file or threaten suits against more than 30,000 people, including a dead person and a 13-year-old girl.

Most of these suits never reached a courtroom, because the very stiff dam-ages available led the defendants to settle. And yet this strategy too failed to pay off. The cases that did go to trial cost millions in lawyers' fees and gener-ated a significant popular backlash. Nor did the individual lawsuits dis-courage much filesharing. Filesharers numbered in the tens of millions in the United States alone, so any individual's chance of getting sued was minus-cule. Like a lion attacking a huge herd of gazelles, most simply got away. By late 2008, the labels announced that the consumer lawsuits would stop.

APPLE'S RISE TO MUSIC DOMINANCE

The labels have little to show for their frontal attack on copying. But the real long-term damage is not just about money, but control. While the industry was locked in a futile struggle against ever-easier copying, the late CEO of Apple, Steve Jobs, was quietly positioning his company to be the next king-maker in the music business.

Apple's first move was the iPod. Introduced in 2001, it was a runaway hit. Then, in 2003, Apple struck a deal to license music from the major labels. The labels thought that they could control Apple, which seemed at the time like a failing company with a tiny share of the personal computer market. Less than a decade after its iTunes Store opened for business, however, Apple controls almost 75% of the US market for paid downloads. Indeed, Apple's business is so large that it controls more than a quarter of all sales in the *total* US music market. That's more than the combined share of the #2 and #3 players, Walmart and Amazon.

iTunes had another trick up its sleeve, and the labels another fumble. Consumers who purchased music from iTunes became effectively locked into Apple's platform. If a consumer wanted to move to a rival portable music player, his music would no longer be playable. He could work around this by burning his music to a CD and then transferring it, but this is a very labor-intensive process. So once consumers start to use Apple's platform, they are almost certain to stay with it.

The labels had an opportunity to break Apple's lock-in when, in 2006, Microsoft introduced its competing music player, the Zune. If they had vigorously supported Zune, that might have put into play a company with the resources to challenge Apple's dominance. But Zune faced a serious problem—consumers who had built iTunes libraries could play these only on their iPods. Why switch to the Zune if doing so meant walking away from their music collections?

The labels could have helped Microsoft solve the music lock-in problem by offering to license to Zune users, for perhaps a penny a song, replacement copies of all of the music they had bought on iTunes. This did not happen, with the predictable result that the Zune—have you ever seen one?—never caught on.* Apple's dominance remained secure.

Where does this story lead? To a critical point about the respective roles of copying and copyright. Copying certainly hurt the labels. But *copyright* is also to blame. Instead of being a tool the labels used as part of their overall business strategy, strengthening rules against copying became the principal focus of their business strategy. That strategy won a few battles but largely lost the war. It created bad publicity and proved a distraction from the task of reforming the industry's business model to survive in a world that had been changed irreversibly by the Internet. And in the end, it delivered up the music business not to the pirates, but to Apple.

What happens next? Copying is not going away. Indeed, it seems to be getting easier by the day. The entire music industry is increasingly living—whether they like it or not—in the copy-friendly environment that characterizes the other creative industries we've examined in this book. Understanding how creativity thrives in these industries can point toward a future in which the music industry might adapt and even prosper.

LOOKING AHEAD

There was nothing inevitable about this tale of decline. Hollywood, for example, has fared better. To be sure, Hollywood worries a lot about piracy. But while there is plenty of it, especially overseas,* piracy has yet to threaten

---

* In the fall of 2011, Microsoft threw in the towel and canceled Zune.
* According to the Motion Picture Association (the international counterpart of the MPAA), in 2005 losses due to piracy were 80% overseas and only 20% domestic. It will surprise no one that China was identified as public enemy #1; http://mpa-i.org/pdf/leksummaryMPA%20revised1.2008.pdf.

the existence of the major film studios. Box office revenues have increased steadily for years, and even given some ups and downs are now almost double what they were in 1992, when the Internet first began to take off as a social phenomenon.[5] These figures also don't account for DVD releases, a major income stream over the past two decades, though decreasingly important today.

Why has the movie industry's fate been different? For one, technology gave them a few years' reprieve. Video files are much larger than music files. As a result they were, until recently, relatively difficult to download and upload. More important, Hollywood learned some lessons from the music industry's straits. Hollywood fought copying, but as a part of a broader overall strategy aimed at capitalizing on the opportunities the Internet offered, while blunting the effect of piracy. We will examine some of the details of Hollywood's thus-far more successful strategy as we consider music's future.

That future is bound to be different from music's past. Copying music is easy and the risk of getting caught minimal, and this is unlikely to change. But easy piracy does not mean the death of creativity in music. Nor does it mean the end of profits from music. Here are some ways that the music industry could adapt—and in some cases already is adapting—that mimic strategies we've seen deployed by other copy-prone creative industries.

MUSIC AS AN EXPERIENCE

The most obvious adaptation is changing what the music industry sells from product to performance. We argued in the Conclusion that products often are easy to copy, but performances are not. One of the reasons chefs remain so creative is that competitors can copy a restaurant's signature recipe but they cannot so easily copy the quality of the preparation or the restaurant's ambience or service.

We won't repeat the discussion here, but we do want to underscore the centrality of performance. Millions of people every year already attend concerts. A greater shift to performance will never replace all the revenues that currently flow from recording. But shifting the business model away from the easily copied product (the song or album) and toward the hard-to-replicate performance (the concert) can help to stabilize the fortunes of musicians.

In many ways, this is simply a return to the reality of the last two centuries of popular music. As Mick Jagger rightly noted, the era of making riches off of recording was really just a brief window in the history of music. The past was, and the future is going to be, much more about performance. In this new world, recordings often function more as ads for concerts than as money-makers themselves. (And sometimes they are bundled with concert tickets, as Madonna's latest album was.) As a result, copying looks a lot less fearsome. An illegally copied ad is just as effective—and maybe much more so—than the original.[6]

MUSIC AS A SOCIAL NETWORK

As the cost of producing and distributing a product falls, basic economics predicts that more of it will be produced and consumed. This axiom certainly applies to music: as digital technologies have slashed the cost of producing and distributing music, we see an unprecedented amount and variety of music on offer. But there's another change. Digital technologies also change how the rewards of the music industry are distributed. In the heyday of the labels, a lot of revenues unsurprisingly went to them. This system produced some very successful stars, but a lot of musicians—even very talented ones—made little or nothing.

This picture is changing, and where it is heading is uncertain. Yet, while mega-stars still exist, there are signs that a larger and more stable musical middle class may be emerging—artists who are able, by making recordings, touring, and selling merchandise, to sustain a decent living. Because it costs these artists less to produce music, a viable career is possible at a smaller scale. And this can be done with less reliance on intermediaries like record labels. The same technologies that have made pirating music so easy also facilitate direct communication between musicians and their fans.

Just ask pop singer Colbie Caillat. Caillet's music career began in 2005 when a friend posted several of her home-recorded songs to MySpace. One song, *Bubbly*, began to get word of mouth among MySpace users, and within a couple of months went viral. Soon Colbie Caillat was the No. 1 unsigned artist on MySpace. Two years after posting *Bubbly*, Caillet had more than 200,000 MySpace friends, and her songs had been played more than 22 million times. Caillet had built a global fan base while never leaving her Malibu home. In 2007, Universal Records released her debut album, *Coco*, which peaked at No. 5 on the *Billboard* charts and reached platinum status.

Or ask rap artists Mac Miller, Wale, and J. Cole. Each of these artists built up a fan base by releasing free material on the Internet and interacting with fans on social media and blogs. And in a space of two months in 2011, each released a debut album that rose high in the charts (Mac Miller's debut charted at No. 1 and sold 144,000 copies in its first week; Wale debuted at No. 2 the week prior and sold about 164,000 copies in its first week; a month earlier J. Cole's album debuted at No. 1 and sold 217,000 copies in its first week).[7] Fans could have pirated these albums—and doubtless some of them did. But thousands ponied up the money to buy them, perhaps partly out of appreciation for the free mixtapes that they'd downloaded previously.

Social media and the fan base it enabled made the music careers of Colbie Caillat, Mac Miller, Wale, and J. Cole. Social media also broke UK stars Lily Allen, Kate Nash, and Arctic Monkeys, among others. This illustrates an important facet of the relationship between music and copying. Music fans love music, and they often want to support those who make the music they love. The Internet turns some fans into pirates. But it also turns fans into promoters. And the same technologies that enable piracy are also restructuring the industry in ways that create an entirely new relationship between creator and listener.

The 2007 release of UK band Radiohead's album *In Rainbows* is an intriguing example. The previous year, Radiohead had terminated its recording contract, and the band decided to release its new album itself. Thom Yorke, Radiohead's lead singer, explained the reasons for that decision: "I like the people at our record company, but the time is at hand when you have to ask why anyone needs one. And, yes, it probably would give us some perverse pleasure to say 'Fuck you' to this decaying business model."[8]

The particular way in which Radiohead released the album was unprecedented. They put up a Web site, and allowed fans to pay whatever they wanted to download the album—including $0.00. And then about two months later, the band released a limited made-to-order "discbox" that contained 2CDs and two 12" heavyweight 45-rpm vinyl records with artwork and lyric booklets. The overall set, packaged in a hardcover case, was priced at approximately $80. The CD itself was also released in normal packaging and with standard pricing.

So how did Radiohead's experiment work out? Exact figures have not yet been released, but about a year after *In Rainbows'* release, the band's licensing agent confirmed that Radiohead made more money from paid downloads of *In Rainbows* than they made in total on their previous EMI-released album, *Hail to the Thief.* In all, there have been 3 million purchases of *In Rainbows* (including CDs, vinyls, box sets and digital sales). Radiohead has admitted that more people downloaded the album for free than paid for it. Still, the 3 million in total sales—100,000 of which came from the $80 box sets—is a hugely successful number considering that the album was both given away for free and was actually *downloaded more times via BitTorrent than legally through Radiohead's own site.*

Radiohead's experiment garnered enormous publicity. And it likely is not the last stab at a new way of selling music, because the music industry is changing in ways that make a variety of business models possible. There are two changes that are, in our view, the most salient, both of which flow from digital technologies. First is the *fragmentation* of the audience into smaller and smaller groups, as more music becomes more available and hence the universe of choices far more diverse. Second is the ability of these smaller groups effectively to *communicate* both with one another and with the artists they like.

What is likely to flow from these changes? These are the conditions—relatively small groups, able easily to communicate—under which social norms can help to regulate behavior. As we described in Chapter 3, this is precisely what we see in the world of stand-up comedy—there are a few thousand touring comedians, and because they often appear together in the same comedy clubs, they communicate readily. These conditions allow comedians to control copying not by relying on copyright law, but through norms.

The problem of piracy in music is, of course, very different from the problem in comedy. Stand-up comics worry most about a rival, not a fan, copying their jokes. Still, the reduction of consumer copying of music via norms may be possible, and will become more imaginable if the music industry experiences ever-greater fragmentation and communication. There is already an interesting example of norms playing a substantial role in controlling copying in music. In the culture of jambands, we see the fans themselves taking action to deter pirates.

What are jambands? In a fascinating 2006 article,[9] legal scholar Mark Schultz studied the unique culture of a group of bands that belong to a musical genre, pioneered by the Grateful Dead, characterized by long-form improvisation, extensive touring, recreational drug use, and dedicated fans. Although acts like Phish, Blues Traveler, and the Dave Mathews Band vary in their styles, they are all recognizably inspired by the progenitors of jam music, the Dead. But the Dead's influence is not only musical. Most jambands adhere to a particular relationship with their fans that also was forged by the Dead.

Touring is central to the jamband culture, and most allow fans to record their live performances. Many even encourage fans to share the live recordings they make. Some bands even set up special "tapers" sections at live shows, and occasionally even allow fans to make recordings directly from the soundboard. And many jambands also set rules whereby some recordings—the band's studio albums, and some special live recordings intended for commercial distribution—cannot be freely shared. The Grateful Dead's statement on taping is a typical example of these rules:

> The Grateful Dead and our managing organizations have long encouraged the purely non-commercial exchange of music taped at our concerts and those of our individual members. That a new medium of distribution has arisen—digital audio files being traded over the Internet—does not change our policy in this regard. Our stipulations regarding digital distribution are merely extensions of those long-standing principles and they are as follows:
>
> No commercial gain may be sought by websites offering digital files of our music, whether through advertising, exploiting databases compiled from their traffic, or any other means.
>
> All participants in such digital exchange acknowledge and respect the copyrights of the performers, writers and publishers of the music.
>
> This notice should be clearly posted on all sites engaged in this activity.
>
> We reserve the ability to withdraw our sanction of noncommercial digital music should circumstances arise that compromise our ability to protect and steward the integrity of our work.[10]

Schultz documents how jambands and their fans interact on the basis of a strong and long-standing norms system. The fans are often very invested in the bands that they follow, and they believe that because the bands give them freedom to record live shows and to share those recordings, they are valued as community members and treated fairly. And in return, fans largely adhere to the rules and discourage others from violating them.

Technically savvy jamband fans have even built music-sharing systems that express the community's norms. One such system is Furthurnet, which is open only to bands that allow sharing, and which allows fans only to upload music by those bands, and to report those who break the rules. Another such system—surprisingly—is BitTorrent, which was written by programmer Bram Cohen to help his friends share their recordings. Much of the press that

BitTorrent receives these days relates to those who use it to pirate music and films. But at the network's inception, it was dominated by jamband fans, and these users kept an eye out for illegal filesharing, and reported it.

While the jamband ethos is unlikely to take over all forms of music, it may spread beyond its original home. And the changes in the industry we noted earlier may make this more likely. Digital technologies allow for smaller, more closely knit fan groups, and easier communication between bands and their fans. Facebook provides a virtual way for fans to interact, and of course live concerts allow a real-world version to develop. The jamband experience suggests that bands cannot simply set rules and demand compliance; Schultz argues that the fans must feel that they are getting something in return. For jambands, it is wide access to recordings of live shows. Given the likely importance of live performance in the future, this may be a workable strategy for a range of musical genres.

Norms are not a panacea for pervasive copying. The casual fan who treats music as a disposable pleasure is unlikely to respect the norms of any particular musical community. So for some types of music, norms are unlikely to have much effect. The pop music of the moment, for example, is unlikely to create the kind of enduring community that can form and sustain a norms system. And the very improvisation that is at the heart of jambands—the jam—makes copying generally less harmful, since no single performance is quite like another. Still, there is no reason to believe that a successful norms system is limited solely to jambands.

In any event, much of what we've said here is about possibilities, not current reality. The power of norms has been noticed by the music industry already, albeit often clumsily. Most music industry discussion of norms thus far has focused on emphasizing the moral wrongness of illegal downloading and declaring downloading to be theft. That approach has had little effect on fans. What the jambands' story—as well as our explorations of chefs and comedians—suggests is that norms that rest on a shared sense of community can have much more power than those that are issued as edicts.

EMPHASIZE QUALITY

The previous chapters in this book suggest additional strategies that the music industry could explore. For music, the pleasure is in the listening. Yet the record labels have done surprisingly little to make listening quality an important part of the music experience. Quality, however, has not been ignored by other creative industries in which rules against copying are ineffective. It is one of the important ways in which chefs maintain their capacity to innovate when others may freely copy their recipes—they focus on achieving the best preparation of that recipe and compete based on quality. We also see quality figuring importantly in the fashion industry. High-end fashion originators face knockoffs very quickly, but the sumptuous materials, precise cut, and meticulous construction of some of their garments rarely can be reproduced at the imitator's price point. The music industry could take a cue from chefs and fashion designers and focus on quality as a way of blunting the effect of piracy.

Despite massive technological change generally, there has been little recent innovation in the provision of quality sound. Indeed, many audiophiles believe the quality of music reproduction has actually gone backwards. Despite the introduction of the CD in 1982, vinyl records never went away, and lately are having a renaissance. Look again at the chart of music industry data shown earlier in this chapter. Since 2006, sales of vinyl more than quadrupled, making the reappearance of the LP a rare music industry success story.

Why are people still buying LPs, a 1940s technology? One reason is that the record industry's mainstay, the CD, has many problems. It comes in packaging that's hard to open, easy to break, and too small to reproduce cover art and lyrics people that can easily read. But the CD has another problem—its sound quality. Invented at a time when computing power was expensive, CDs are encoded at the low bitrate that inexpensive electronics were capable of processing in the late 1970s. The result is a small, airless sound that lacks the warmth and presence of an LP.

That explains, in part, why so many consumers who care about music are returning to LPs: the older technology sounds better.[*] For the vast majority of listeners who do not migrate back to vinyl, however, the CD's infirmities have an important consequence. Because CDs are not a sonically great experience, consumers copying compressed mp3 files from the Internet weren't

---

[*] There is undoubtedly an element of trend and fashion attached to the resurgence in vinyl—young people in particular, who never experienced the heyday of the LP, may be attracted to the older technology simply because it's novel to them and looks cool. And for older listeners, the act of slipping the record out of the sleeve and dropping the needle is special in a way that clicking a mouse will never be.

missing much. And so the fact that mp3 files sound even worse than CDs wasn't the barrier to piracy that it might have been.

You would think that making music sound better was one of the things the record labels would be most eager to do. Yet the labels made only the most superficial attempt to improve fidelity. A decade ago the industry flirted briefly with two new formats, DVD-Audio and Super Audio CD, that offered superior sound. But as consumers shifted to (mostly pirated) downloads, these efforts withered. Revenues from Super Audio CDs peaked in 2003 at a comparatively minuscule $26 million; revenues from DVD-Audio peaked at less than a third that level. Both formats are now dead.

What can we learn from this? The story is mostly one of a path never taken. There has always been a small group of consumers who value musical fidelity. Then there are legions of consumers who care very little about sound quality. One strategy that might have been pursued, but never was with any vigor, is to try to enlarge the size of the first group by creating new audiophiles.

The renewed popularity of LPs suggests that a well-presented physical medium with high-quality sound can succeed. Perhaps not surprisingly, some higher quality downloads are already available on p2p networks. And recently, a couple of labels have been working with Apple to offer downloads at CD quality. By making them available on iTunes, at least people who are willing to pay can get the same quality that the pirates get.

All Roads Should Lead to Your Content

For years, the record labels had a business model that was consistent and single-minded: (1) bundle together a dozen songs on a CD, (2) ship the discs out to retailers, and (3) collect money. The labels' business became even simpler following the shift from LPs to CDs—it was at that time that the labels killed off the singles market. Why ship CD singles when, for virtually the same cost, you could ship an album and charge at least three times the price?

But it turns out that by killing the single, the record labels made the Internet piracy problem, when it arrived, even worse. One of the major attractions of filesharing was that it brought back singles. Consumers wanted the one or two songs on the album that they liked, and not the ten they didn't. Look again at the music industry data chart. The market for singles downloads is much larger than the album downloads market. It is enormously larger by units sold—so much so that it's almost twice as large *by revenues,* even though, on average, albums cost ten times as much.

What we learn from this is unsurprising. Consumers like choice, and new technologies frequently offer more choice than the old. In this case, Hollywood's very different, more profitable, and more piracy-resistant approach is instructive. The movie industry has long managed releases according to a series of "windows." Films are first released at the box office—and at a premium price. Then, after a few months, films are released to the DVD sales and rental market. Shortly after that, they are available via video-on-demand, pay-per-view, and on airlines. And later still, the films are released to pay-TV cable channels like HBO and Starz. And then, finally, they go to basic cable and broadcast channels.

This system gives consumers a wide variety of ways to watch movies. And different ways of watching movies appeal to different types of consumers. For those with willingness to pay, there is the new release in the theater. And for those willing to wait, there is video rental, pay-TV, and commercial television.

The rental channel in particular has long been a very important piece of the industry's overall revenues, and it is growing in importance as Netflix (the current market leader), Amazon, and other competitors introduce "all-you-can-eat" streaming video plans. Video rental may be Hollywood's biggest anti-piracy tool. Take Netflix, which offers consumers unlimited streaming from a substantial library of licensed content. The allure of Netflix and other streaming services is that they get Hollywood's content immediately into the hands of people who want it. And people want it. In the United States, movies streamed over Netflix now represent more Internet traffic than does piracy over BitTorrent.[11] The rental channel, moreover, is expanding as both Amazon and iTunes expand their video rental and download offerings.

Hollywood's release windows system was conceived long before the Internet arrived. For our purposes, however, the system matters because it functions as an anti-piracy tool. Hollywood did not attempt to enforce a one-size-fits-all business model. Instead, it realized that different consumers would have different willingness to pay, and so it developed a distribution model that gave consumers more choice.

Importantly, this system can accommodate technological changes. The gap between theatrical and home video release has shrunk as ever-improving streaming technology encourages more people to watch movies at home.

And, on occasion, the system can be upended entirely when a particular film calls for a different marketing approach. One recent example is a documentary based on the best-selling *Freakonomics* book.[*] The Freakonomics documentary was released online via iTunes *before* it appeared in theaters. Why? Because a big part of the anticipated audience was comprised of people who prefer to get their video online.

In sum, like the recording industry, Hollywood views copying—especially in its growing markets abroad, such as China—as a grave threat. But unlike the recording industry, Hollywood has responded, at least so far, in ways that effectively blunt piracy's impact. It focuses on the experience—watching a movie in a theater is different and, for many people, better than watching a pirated copy on a computer monitor. It focuses on quality, both in the theater (new digital projection and 3-D technologies) and for the home viewer (high-resolution Blu-Ray). It offers multiple ways for viewers to access content. What Hollywood does is not precisely the same as any of the other industries that we've studied. But Hollywood has taken a page out of several of their playbooks.

There is much the music industry could learn from this openness to new approaches to creation and distribution. Until very recently there has been no real music equivalent to Netflix, for instance. Rhapsody, the largest of the subscription services, claims 750,000 subscribers, but that number is hotly disputed and, even if taken at face value, has been flat for a couple of years. For comparison, Netflix has over 20 million subscribers. Subscription streaming service is transforming the movie business. And yet—until recently—it barely figured in music.

That may be changing with the US introduction of the Spotify music subscription service. Spotify has been available in some European countries since 2008, but licensing negotiations delayed its US launch until mid 2011. Spotify's catalog of approximately 15 million songs is now available for streaming. Users have the choice of a "free" service featuring restricted access to the catalog and advertising, or a $5 per month service that removes ads and gives users unlimited access to the full catalog.

So will Spotify emerge as the music version of Netflix? It's too early to tell. In mid-October 2011, *Billboard* magazine reported that Spotify had gained

---

[*] We are both bloggers for Freakonomics but were not involved in the film.

approximately 2 million US users, of whom 250,000 were paid subscribers.[12] That's a promising start, but important questions remain—including whether streaming is as appealing to music consumers as it is to movie fans. Some, including the late Steve Jobs, have suggested that music subscription services are failing because consumers want to own music rather than stream it. That is probably true for many (and Steve Jobs, of course, was not neutral in the matter). But for others, music is fairly disposable—they listen to a song for a few weeks or months, and then move on. For these people, subscription music may be a good fit.

Much the same can be said for Internet radio. Services like Pandora allow users to discover new music by telling the service a bit about what kind of music they like—if they're into a folky female singer like Feist, Pandora may expose them to Charlotte Gainsbourg and Cat Power. Unlike services such as Rhapsody, users cannot request specific songs—Internet radio is about exposing listeners to new music, and as such these services should be record label sweethearts. But until recently, subscription radio was struggling. The problem isn't lack of popularity: Pandora alone has 48 million users even though it has a smallish catalog of only about 700,000 songs. Internet radio has been stifled by very high music licensing fees. These license fees are set by a government-run royalty board, and, prompted perhaps by fierce record company lobbying, the royalty board's first round of rulings in 2007 set fees much higher than most Internet radio outfits could afford.

The result might have been the shuttering of services like Pandora. But after a sustained campaign by Pandora's users, Congress passed legislation that pressured the labels to negotiate a new deal. What followed has been a series of contentious negotiations that have resulted in short-term royalty deals. Whether the record labels ultimately strike a longer-term deal that allows subscription streaming and Internet radio services to thrive is a vital question for the future of the music industry. Stay tuned.

SUMMING UP

Today, copying is a fact of life in the music world. Yet music is not dying. Even without any changes, music is vibrantly creative today. From a consumer point of view, life has never been better: more musical choices, more easily obtained, than ever before.

Still, the music industry can change further to better survive a world of easy copying. Rely more on the live show, an experience that cannot be copied. Attempt to woo customers away from piracy by emphasizing the quality of the legitimate product. Create (or bolster) social norms about copying. And diversify the ways in which consumers can access music. The result will be a very different music industry. But it will be a world with a lot of great music.

ACKNOWLEDGMENTS

We could not have written this book without a huge amount of help from a large number of people. First are Lara Stemple and Anne Metz, who heard (without complaint) an awful lot about this book as it was gestating, and who read, commented on, and helped improve many pieces of it. Thanks are due also to our parents, who have supported us in everything we've done. And now for some gratitude on a more specific level . . .

Thanks to Steven Levitt and Stephen Dubner for taking us onboard as regulars at the *Freakonomics* blog—we first developed many of the ideas in this book in blog posts we wrote there.

We thank our colleagues Chris Buccafusco, Michael Heller, and Larry Lessig for their very helpful input on our first draft of the book, and Doug Lichtman and Neil Netanel for great comments on our concluding chapter. We also thank our editor, Dave McBride, for his careful reading and incisive comments.

For very helpful input on the world of financial innovation we thank George Geis, Paul Mahoney, and Peter Sweeney. We are grateful to Dick Stemple, Josh Swartz, Siva Vaidhyanathan, and Dave McBride for talking to us about football. We thank Dana Foley, Eric Wilson, Cathy Horyn, Ilse Metchek, and the members of the California Fashion Association for sharing their knowledge of the fashion industry. Laurent Torondel, Drew Nieporent, Joachim Splichal, Kerry Heffernan, Ludo Lefebvre, Jonathan Gold, Evan Kleiman, Josiah Citrin, Nancy Silverton, David Chang, Roy Choi, and many other chefs and food writers from Los Angeles to New York did the same for cuisine—and their input was invaluable. Michelle McNamara and the many unnamed comics quoted in the chapter on comedy gave us terrific insight into the tribe of stand-ups.

A host of others provided comments and conversations that helped us make this book better: we thank Amy Adler, Lu Alvarez, Nathalie Atkinson, Willoughby Anderson, Margo Bagley, Shyam Balganesh, Jonathan Barnett, Jon Baumgarten, Stefan Bechtold, Barton Beebe, Laura Bradford, Michael Carroll, Julie Cohen, Dan Crane, Troy Dow, Rochelle Dreyfuss, John Duffy, Dave Fagundes, Kathleen Fasanella, Terry Fisher, Brian Fitzgerald, Brett Frischmann, Jeanne Fromer, Blake Fry, Lolly Gasaway, Lauren Gelman, Daniel Gervais, Jennifer Granick, Joe Gratz, Adam Gutterman, Ned Gulley, Kathryn Hashimoto, Scott Hemphill, Terry Ilardi, David Jacoby, Mark Lemley, Jessica Litman, Lydia Loren, Glynn Lunney, Michael Madison, Peter Menell, Robert Merges, Joseph Scott Miller, Tom Nachbar, David Nimmer, Tyler Ochoa, Dotan Oliar, Dan Ortiz, Frank Pasquale, Mitch Polinsky, Elizabeth Rader, Tony Reese, Blake Ellis Reid, Glen Robinson, Judith Roth, Zahr Said, Mark Schultz, Jule Sigall, Kate Spelman, Lior Strahilevitz, Katherine Strandburg, Jeannie Suk, Michael Traynor, Rebecca Tushnet, Siva Vaidhyanathan, Charles Valauskas, Molly Shaffer Van Houweling, Polk Wagner, Tara Wheatland, Jeremy Williams, Adam Winkler, Del Wood, and Tim Wu. Special thanks are due to Pam Samuelson for learning she's provided over the years that undergirds a lot of this book.

We also thank a wonderful group of librarians who were invaluable to this project, including Kristin Glover, Kent Olson, Jon Ashley, Leslie Ashbrook, Michelle Morris Beecy, John Wilson, Amy Atchison, June Kim, and Ben Doherty, and a great group of student research assistants, including Shaun Bockert, Louis Shernisky, Isaac Wood, Jack Wickham, Lucas Beirne, Nell Moley, April Reeves, Phil Rucker, Lillian Park, Robert Wu, Marie Lamothe, Sonya Paskil, China Irwin, Tim Cook, Sean FitzGerald, and Demetra Karamanos.

We also thank colleagues at USC Law School, the University of Michigan School of Law, Washington University Law School, Stanford Law School, Berkeley Law School, UCLA Law School, the University of Chicago School of Law, George Washington University School of Law, ETH-Zurich, the University of Pennsylvania School of Law, the University of Virginia School of Law, the Copyright Society of the USA, the Corcoran Gallery, and the Los Angeles Copyright Society for hosting workshops and talks at which we presented work that ended up in this book.

NOTES

INTRODUCTION

1. Faviana, www.faviana.com/catalog/category-celebrity-dresses (accessed January 5, 2012).
2. There have been many attempts to change this, however, most recently the Innovative Design Protection and Piracy Prevention Act, S. 3728, 111th Cong. (as reported by Senate Committee on the Judiciary, December 6, 2010). Fabric prints are copyrightable, on the theory that they are akin to two-dimensional drawings (which are copyrightable). But the main aspect of a garment—its overall design—has never been legally protected in the United States. Some other nations do protect fashion designs, and this contrast has for nearly a century been invoked (thus far unsuccessfully) as a reason to change American law.
3. The relationship between competition and IP is complex and has been developed in different areas of American law, including antitrust law and unfair competition law. The basic structure of our legal system is of course pro-competitive. IP rights represent a deliberate and temporary deviation from that pro-competitive stance. This deviation is required, it is thought, by the need to protect and thus spur innovation. As one court aptly put it, "there exists a fundamental right to compete through imitation of a competitor's product, which right can only be temporarily denied by the patent or copyright laws." *In re Morton-Norwich Products, Inc.,* 671 F.2d 1332 (C.C.P.A. 1982). The line between acceptable competition and IP violation is not written in stone; American law has shifted over time to prohibit some kinds of copying that formerly had been permitted. See, e.g., the Architectural Works Copyright Protection Act of 1990, codified at 17 United States Code, sections 101, 102, 120 (1990).
4. Though moral claims crop up occasionally in debate over IP law and policy, they play a minor part in the American legal framework. As the Supreme Court explained in *Sony Corp. v. Universal City Studios,* IP rights "are neither unlimited nor primarily designed to provide a special private benefit. Rather, the limited grant is a means by which an important public purpose may be achieved. It is intended to motivate the creative activity of authors and inventors by the provision of a special reward," 464 US 417 (1984) at 429. Moral justifications for IP protection have somewhat greater

purchase in Europe. Since our topic is American law, in this book we focus on the primary American rationale for rules against copying, which is economic and instrumental in nature.

5. Thomas Jefferson, *Letter to Isaac McPherson*, August 13, 1813. On the historical understanding of the balance between protection and competition, and an excellent close reading of Jefferson's letter, see James Boyle, *The Public Domain: Enclosing the Commons of the Mind* (Yale, 2008).

6. A word about the words "monopoly" and "innovation." We use "monopoly" deliberately, though we recognize that there is controversy over the degree to which IP technically rests on monopoly power. Most patents and virtually all copyrights don't grant the sort of power that an economist would recognize as a textbook monopoly—i.e., a position as the only provider of a product or service for which there are no ready substitutes. Yet, quite a few patents and copyrights provide their owners with very substantial market power, including the ability to charge prices substantially above what a competitive market would otherwise allow. Indeed, this is precisely the reason the American legal system contains patents and copyrights— they are intended to give creators the ability to charge a price higher than would be possible in a market with free copying. A firm that owns a patent on a useful drug will be able to charge a higher price, and to sell more of its drug at that high price, than if it faced competition from generic versions (i.e., copies) of the drug. The same is true of copyright. The copyright on this book will allow us (really, our publisher) to charge a higher price for this book than we would be able to charge in a market where everyone was free to copy the book and sell a competing version.

We use "innovation" broadly, to refer not just to new patentable inventions, such as machines, drugs, and the like, but also to new literary and artistic works, which are covered not by patent but by copyright. We recognize that copyright rests on a relatively lax originality requirement, whereas patent has a much stricter "novelty" standard. Yet both copyright and patent are mechanisms for encouraging creative effort, with the goal of producing new knowledge and culture. In this broader sense, patent and copyright both produce innovation, albeit of different types.

7. The political economy of IP tends to be dominated by the interests of those who possess IP, since the "other side"—that is, the public interest—is diffuse and usually disorganized. The result is a tendency toward the expansion of these rights. In the patent context that tendency is less strong, since there are many powerful economic actors who have an interest in restraining patents so they can use the inventions they describe. But in copyright the large corporate owners of IP have a powerful organizational advantage, and as a result the scope of copyright has expanded markedly.

8. Robert Levine, *Free Ride: How Digital Parasites Are Destroying the Culture Business, and How the Culture Business Can Fight Back* (Doubleday, 2010).

9. We favor having an IP system, unlike some prominent critics who counsel abolition. See, e.g., Michele Boldrin and David K. Levine, *Against Intellectual Monopoly* (Cambridge, 2008). We certainly agree with Boldrin and Levine that IP law is a monopoly, government-issued at that, and that it inhibits competition. Where we part ways with Boldrin and Levine, whose arguments we respect, is in their call for

dismantling the system. We take a more measured and we think more prudent tack, favoring reform over revolution.

10. As we discuss further in the conclusion, one of the key differences is the cost of creation. Higher cost industries are more vulnerable to copying's harms. At the same time, however, many technological changes are transforming the costs of creation and of distribution in ways that upend traditional assumptions about cost.

11. "New Football a Chaos, the Experts Declare: Ground Gaining by Carrying the Ball Made Impossible; Onside Kick Is Only Hope," *New York Times*, September 30, 1906.

12. A common argument, with which we generally agree, is that without confidence that copyists will not undercut the market for innovative works, distributors (publishing companies, film studios, etc.) will not invest in bringing creative works to market. As we will describe, this is sometimes true but not always. In some cases intermediaries play a small role. And even when intermediaries are important, changes in technology can create new modes of distribution that can be very significant and much less sensitive to the effects of copying. And finally, there are important markets in which intermediaries do their job of marketing and distributing creative works without the motivations of IP. We'll look at all of these instances in this book.

13. Edward J. Epstein, *Hollywood Demystified, The Reel Show*, Winter 2005, www.scribd.com/doc/5885934/How-film-studios-make-money (accessed May 24, 2011). The case was *Sony Corp. of Am. v. Universal City Studios, Inc.*, 464 U.S. 417 (1984).

CHAPTER 1

1. Eric Wilson, "Simply Irresistible," *New York Times*, May 21 2008.
2. Serena French, "Knock It Off!! Fashion Fights Back at Year of the Copycat," *New York Post*, May 1, 2007.
3. Marie Claire: Splurge vs. Steal, www.marieclaire.com/fashion/tips/splurge-vs-steal/ (accessed May 31, 2011).
4. See, e.g., Dana Thomas, *Deluxe: How Luxury Lost Its Luster* (Penguin, 2007).
5. Pankaj Ghemawat and Jose Luis Nueno, "Zara: Fast Fashion," *Harvard Business School Case #9-703-497* (2003).
6. See, e.g., Francois Baudot, *Fashion: The Twentieth Century* (Universe, 1999) and Teri Agins, *The End of Fashion: How Marketing Changed the Clothing Business Forever* (Harper, 2000). Of course, apparel dates back millennia, but scholars generally view the Renaissance as the birth of fashion, by which they mean clothing used to distinguish individuals from one another in terms of status. See, e.g., Jean Baudrillard, who wrote that fashion is "born with the Renaissance, with the destruction of the feudal order by the bourgeois order and the emergence of overt competition at the level of signs of distinction." Quoted in Veronica Manlow, *Designing Clothes: Culture and Organization in the Fashion Industry* (Transaction, 2007), 9.
7. Manlow, *Designing Clothes*, 35. See also Nancy Green, *Ready to Wear and Ready to Work* (Duke University Press, 1997), 45, and Paul Nystrom, *Economics of Fashion* (Ronald Press Company, 1928), chapter 16.
8. Eric Musgrave, *Sharp Suits* (Pavilion, 2009), 97.
9. Manlow, *Designing Clothes*, 47,
10. Baudot, *Fashion*, 123.

11. Agins, *The End of Fashion*, 34.

12. Thomas, *Deluxe*, 4.

13. Thomas, *Deluxe*, 316. Zara changes three-fourths of its merchandise every month, or less. Ghemawat and Nueno, "Zara," 13.

14. *See* "Fashion Scoops: Vigilante Justice," *Women's Wear Daily*, September 11, 2007, 13.

15. Nystrom, *Economics of Fashion*, 190. Nystrom's book is a treasure trove of information about early 20th-century fashion, both in Europe and the United States, and Nystrom thought systematically about several of the issues we discuss here.

16. Copyright is not entirely consistent in this regard. Despite being highly functional, maps and charts have been copyrightable since the first US copyright statute in 1790.

17. See, e.g., *Galiano v. Harrah's Operating Co., Inc.*, 416 F.3d 411, 422 (5th Cir. 2005) (casino uniforms unprotected; expressive element not marketable separately from utilitarian function); *Poe v. Missing Persons*, 745 F.2d 1238 (9th Cir. 1984) (copyright found in "three dimensional work of art in primarily flexible clear-vinyl and covered rock media" shaped like a bathing suit; evidence suggested article "was an artwork and not a useful article of clothing").

18. 35 U.S.C. 102. See also *In re Application of Bartlett*, 300 F.2d 942, 49 C.C.P.A. 969, 133 U.S.P.Q. 204 (C.C.P.A. 1962) ("The degree of difference required to establish novelty occurs when the average observer takes the new design for a different, and not a modified already-existing, design").

19. We recognize that this pattern of "remix" innovation may be endogenous; in other words, if not for the practical barriers sharply limiting the availability of design patents, it is at least theoretically possible that the fashion industry would engage less in the endless reworking of existing designs and turn attention toward designs that would meet patent's novelty requirement.

20. Not all are cheap; the quality of knockoffs can be extremely good, and distinguishing imitations from originals difficult. "Counterfeit for Christmas: Gift Givers Tap New Source as Travel to China Eases, Knockoff Quality Improves," *Wall Street Journal*, December 9, 2005, B1. For further discussion of the links between trade, fashion, and IP generally see Jonathan M. Barnett, "Shopping for Gucci on Canal Street: Reflections on Status Consumption, Intellectual Property, and the Incentive Thesis," 91 *Virginia Law Review* 1381 (2005).

21. Lanham Act, Sec. 2(e)(5). The nonfunctionality requirement for trade dress may be somewhat lower than in copyright, because most courts have held that functional design elements may be protected as trade dress if they are part of an assemblage of trade dress elements that contains significant nonfunctional items. See *Fuddruckers, Inc. v. Doc's B.R. Others, Inc.*, 826 F.2d 837, 842 (9th Cir. 1987) ("Our inquiry is not addressed to whether individual elements of the trade dress fall within the definition of functional, but to whether the whole collection of elements taken together are functional").

22. *See*, e.g., *Knitwaves, Inc. v. Lollytogs Ltd.*, 71 F.3d 996 (2d Cir. 1995) (aesthetic features of girls' sweaters that were not source designating were not part of protectable trade dress). See also *Wal-Mart Stores, Inc. v. Samara Bros., Inc.*, 529 U.S. 205, 213 (2000) (product design cannot be "inherently distinctive," and "almost invariably serves purposes other than source designation").

23. *Samara*, 529 U.S. at 213.

24. *Inwood Laboratories, Inc. v. Ives Laboratories, Inc.*, 456 U.S. 844, 851 n.11 (1982) (emphasis ours).

25. *Jack Adelman v. Sonners & Gordon*, 112 F. Supp. 187 (S.D.N.Y. 1934).

26. Arnold Plant, "The Economic Aspects of Copyright in Books," 1 *Economica* 167–192 (Blackwell, 1934). See also Nystrom, *Economics of Fashion*, for a similar discussion.

27. Cathy Horyn, "Is Copying Really a Part of the Creative Process?" *New York Times*, April 9, 2002; Manlow, *Designing Clothes*, 95.

28. Robert Merges, "Contracting into Liability Rules: Intellectual Property Rights and Collective Rights Organizations," 84 *California Law Review* 1293, 1363 (1996).

29. *Fashion Originators' Guild v. FTC*, 312 US 457 (1941).

30. "Dress War," *Time*, March 23, 1936.

31. Ibid.

32. *Fashion Originators' Guild v. FTC*, 312 US 457 (1941), 467. Simultaneous with its action against the Fashion Originators' Guild, the Federal Trade Commission also successfully struck down a similar cartel that organized makers of women's hats. See *Millinery Creators' Guild, Inc. v. FTC*, 109 F.2d 175 (2d Cir. 1940).

33. The Filene's case was significant, however, as we discuss below. The Supreme Court noted in its first footnote that it agreed to hear the case because of the difference in opinion on the legality of the Guild between the First Circuit, which heard Filene's claim, and the Second Circuit, which agreed with the FTC that the Guild was illegal.

34. "Fashion Designer Asks 'Piracy' Ban," *New York Times*, July 22, 1947.

35. Thomas, *Deluxe*, 269.

36. Thanks to the latest amendments, named for Sonny Bono, the singer and former Congressman, the standard copyright term is now life plus 70 years for the creations of individuals and 95 years after first publication or 120 years from creation for those of corporations.

37. On this shift, see Jamie Boyle, *The Public Domain* (Yale University Press, 2008); Adrian Johns, *Piracy: The Intellectual Property Wars from Gutenberg to Gates* (University of Chicago, 2010).

38. The comparison with France dates back to at least 1928. Nystrom described France's legal protections for fashion design favorably, noting that "style-creating houses, both in this country and in Paris, would like to see such a law provided, so as to stop American copying of both American and French designs." Nystrom, *Economics of Fashion*, 191.

39. Press Release, "Delahunt, Goodlatte and Nadler Reintroduce Legislation to Combat Design Privacy," April 30, 2009, www.cfda.com/index.php?option=com_cfda_content&;task=news_display_all.

40. Biography of Allen B. Schwartz, www.absstyle.com/allen.asp. See also Sarah Childress, "Proms Go Hollywood," MSNBC.com, May 18, 2005, www.msnbc.msn.com/id/7888491/site/newsweek/?GT1=6542 (discussing Schwartz's history of design copying).

41. Eric Wilson, "Before Models Can Turn Around, Knockoffs Fly," *New York Times*, September 4, 2007.

42. Vanessa Lau, "Can I Borrow That? When Designer 'Inspiration' Jumps the Fence to Full-On Derivation, the Critics' Claws Pop Out," *W Magazine*, February 2008.

43. Cara M. DiMassa, "Designers Pull New Styles Out of the Past," *L.A. Times,* January 30, 2005; see also Cathy Horyn, "Defying Knockoffs and Inviting Them," *New York Times,* October 2, 2009. Cathy Horyn, "Is Copying Really Part?"

44. Horyn, "Is Copying Really Part?"

45. *Societe Yves Saint Laurent Couture S.A. v. Societe Louis Dreyfus Retail Management S.A,* [1994] E.C.C. 512 (Trib. Comm. (Paris)) ("YSL"). Interestingly, Yves Saint Laurent's position was illustrative of the significant measure of legitimacy copying enjoys in the fashion industry. According to St. Laurent: "It is one thing to 'take inspiration' from another designer, but it is quite another to steal a model point by point, as Ralph Lauren has done." Ibid., 519, 520. See also Agins, *The End of Fashion* (quoting a fashion consultant as saying that "Yves Saint Laurent has blown the whistle on the dirtiest secret in the fashion industry. None of them are above copying each other when they think they can make a fast buck").

46. Lau, "Can I Borrow That?"

47. *International News Service v. Associated Press,* 248 U.S. 215, 250 (1918) (Justice Brandeis dissenting) ("The noblest of human productions—knowledge, truths ascertained, conceptions, and ideas—become, after voluntary communication to others, free as the air to common use," and should have "the attribute of property" only "in certain classes of cases where public policy has seemed to demand it").

48. Thorstein Veblen, *The Theory of the Leisure Class* (Macmillan, 1899).

49. "Economics A–Z," *The Economist,* at www.economist.com. See also Juliet Schor, *The Overspent American: Why We Want What We Don't Need* (Harper, 1999) and Robert Frank, *Luxury Fever: Why Money Fails to Satisfy in An Era of Excess* (Princeton, 1999) (portraying much consumer purchasing as an arms race, in which each new purchase spurs others to engage in similar purchasing, with no gain in status since status is inherently relational). Barnett, "Shopping for Gucci," focuses on this literature to create a three-tiered model of utility: snob utility, aspirational utility, and bandwagon utility. An early treatment with regard to fashion is Paul M. Gregory, "An Economic Interpretation of Women's Fashions," 14 *Southern Economic Journal,* 2 (1947).

50. In this respect, two-sided positional goods are very different from those goods subject to positive externalities and network effects. Goods like fax machines or computer operating systems are continually more valuable as they are more widely used. The rate at which these goods increase in value may slow past a certain threshold of distribution, but there is no inflection point at which the good begins to decline in value as it is more widely spread.

51. *New York World Telegram & Sun,* August 21, 1960.

52. Manlow, *Designing Clothes.*

53. Gregory, "An Economic Interpretation," 161.

54. "Symbolic Exchange and Death," 2000 at 98.

55. See Lorrie Grant, "UGG Boots a Fashion Kick," *USA Today,* December 10, 2003, www.usatoday.com/money/industries/retail/2003-12-10-ugg_x.htm.

56. "Ugg Poncho, the New Ugg Evil," *Defamer,* August 9, 2004, www.defamer.com/hollywood/culture/ugg-poncho-the-new-ugg-evil-019192.php.

57. Tad Friend, "Letter from California: The Pursuit of Happiness," *New Yorker,* January 23–30, 2006.

58. Georg Simmel, "Fashion," 10 *International Quarterly* 130, 138–39 (1904). See also Nystrom, *Economics of Fashion*, who devotes an entire chapter to the mechanisms of the fashion cycle, replete with detailed graphs of hemline changes and the like.

59. We borrow the language of differentiation and flocking from Scott Hemphill and Jeannie Suk, "The Law, Culture, and Economics of Fashion," 61 *Stanford Law Review* 1147 (2009).

60. The exceptions, such as inventions of new fabrics that wick moisture or retain heat, are usually limited to outdoor and technical apparel and moreover tend to be patented—not for the design, but for the fabric itself.

61. We thank James Suroweicki for this analogy. Earlier economic analyses, such as economist Paul Gregory's in the 1940s, have noted the obsolescing quality of apparel, but have not drawn the link to copyright. Instead, Gregory stressed factors like deliberately poor quality. Paul M. Gregory, "A Theory of Purposeful Obsolescence," *Southern Economic Journal* (July 1947). See also the discussion in Nystrom, *Economics of Fashion*. Nystrom notes that "imitation is the most essential element in fashion" (26). But he nonetheless opposed the freedom to copy and favored the French model of design protection, as did Maurice Rentner years later. For Nystrom, the "evil of copying" was a central problem for the apparel industry (190).

62. In interviews, the designers told us of a woman returning to the store in tears with her dress, after discovering the existence of the Forever 21 version.

63. We mention this retail outlet and this brand for illustrative purposes only. We do not mean to suggest that data from this outlet and brand are included in the BLS data, which is confidential.

64. Nystrom, *Economics of Fashion*, 26.

65. David Colman, "Choices, Up to Your Knees," *New York Times*, August 25, 2005, E1.

66. Lauryn Howard, "An Uningenious Paradox: Intellectual Property Protections for Fashion Designs," 32 *Columbia Journal of Law & Arts* 333 (2009).

67. Horyn, "Is Copying Really a Part?"

68. Ibid.

69. Lau, "Can I Borrow That?"

70. Lau, "Can I Borrow That?"

71. A classic treatment of first mover advantages is Marvin B. Lieberman and David B. Montgomery, "First Mover Advantages," *Strategic Management Journal* 9, 1 (1988).

72. "Dress War," *Time*.

73. Kenneth D. Hutchinson, "Design Piracy," *Harvard Business Review* 191, 198 (1940).

74. Nystrom, *Economics of Fashion*.

75. Barnett, "Shopping for Gucci," 30.

CHAPTER 2

1. Complaint at 1:3, *Powerful Katinka, Inc. v. McFarland*, 2007 WL 2064059 (S.D.N.Y. 2007). This was not the first dust-up between Charles and a former co-worker; Mary's Fish Camp, a little further uptown, engendered a similar dispute a few years earlier.

2. Pete Wells, "Chef Sues over Intellectual Property (the Menu)," *New York Times*, June 27, 2007.

3. Figures drawn from National Restaurant Association, *Restaurants by the Numbers* (2011), www.restaurant.org/pdfs/research/2011forecast_pfb.pdf.

4. David Kamp, *The United States of Arugula: How We Became a Gourmet Nation* (Random House, 2006), 15.

5. Ibid. After the outbreak of World War II kept many French staff from wanting to return home, The Pavillion at the Fair became Le Pavillion in Manhattan.

6. Malla Pollack, "Intellectual Property Protection for the Creative Chef, or How to Copyright a Cake: A Modest Proposal," *Cardozo Law Review* 12.5 (1991): 1477, 1490.

7. For the full story see Jennifer 8 Lee, *The Fortune Cookie Chronicles: Adventures in the World of Chinese Food* (Twelve, 2008).

8. Kamp, *The United States of Arugula*, 70–71.

9. Figures in current dollars from the National Restaurant Association, www.restaurant.org/pdfs/research/2011forecast_pfb.pdf.

10. Lauren Sherman, "The Most Unusual Restaurants in the World," *Forbes*, December 19, 2006.

11. A quick (if that is possible) look at *Modernist Cuisine: The Art and Science of Cooking* (Cooking Lab, 2011), a nearly 2,500-page tome by Nathan Myrhvold, Chris Young, and Maxime Bilet, will explain what all the fuss is about.

12. Adria himself disclaims the phrase, as do others. Along with Thomas Keller, Heston Blumenthal, and writer-scientist Harold McGee, Adria wrote an open letter to the UK newspaper *The Guardian* stating, "The fashionable term molecular gastronomy was introduced relatively recently, in 1992, to name a particular academic workshop . . . that workshop did not influence our approach, and the term molecular gastronomy does not describe our cooking, or indeed any style of cooking." Ferran Adria et al., "Statement on the 'New Cookery,'" *Guardian Observer*, December 10, 2006,
www.guardian.co.uk/uk/2006/dec/10/foodanddrink.obsfoodmonthly.

13. Katy McLaughlin, "That Melon Tenderloin Looks Awfully Familiar . . .," *Wall Street Journal*, June 24, 2006, http://online.wsj.com/article/SB115109369352989196.html.

14. Whether Vongerichten or Matsuhisa are really the inventors of these dishes is of course another question, about which there is some controversy. We have already noted that miso cod probably was not really pioneered at Matsuhisa; the same may be true for the molten chocolate cake. For example, Michel Richard, Michel Bras, and Jacques Torres have all been touted at some point as the true originator of the molten chocolate cake.

15. www.recipesecrets.net/forums/recipe-exchange/23906-chilis-molten-chocolate-cake.html.

16. Under US law the medium in which a work is fixed need not be especially durable. Any fixation of the work that is perceptible for more than a "transitory duration" is sufficient. We recognize that molten chocolate cake is usually consumed pretty quickly, but since the cake nearly always lasts for more than a transitory duration it would seem qualified to receive a copyright. As we explain, however, this is not the case.

17. Architectural Works Copyright Protection Act (AWCPA), Pub.L. 101–650, Title VII, 104 Stat. 5133, December 1, 1990.

18. *Publications Int'l, Ltd. v. Meredith Corp.*, 88 F.3d 473 (7th Cir. 1996) at 476.

19. Ibid., 480. Very similar reasoning, based on *Meredith*, appeared a few years later in *Lambing v. Godiva Chocolatier*, 142 F.3d 434 (6th Cir. 1998).

20. U.S. Copyright Office, *Recipes*, www.copyright.gov/fls/fl122.html (accessed September 14, 2006).

21. Nigella Lawson, *Nigella Bites—Comfort Food*, http://www.channel4.com/life/microsites/N/nigella/bites2.shtml (accessed June 2, 2011).

22. See U.S. Copyright Office, *Recipes*, 101. See also Pollack, "Intellectual Property Protection,". As David Nimmer pointed out to us, instructions merged with explanation in a cookbook are typically copyrightable. Thus when Lawson writes, apropos the Halloumi bake, "Season with black pepper, but no salt as the cheese will make it salty" that passage would probably qualify for copyright. Interview with David Nimmer, author of *Nimmer on Copyright* (Matthew Bender, 1978).

23. "To say that a recipe is an uncopyrightable procedure or process is the same as saying that a schematic rendering of dance steps is a procedure or, more clearly, that the required instruments and notes for a symphony constitute [an uncopyrightable] process. In truth, the recipe, the drawing, and the musical notation are simply means for fixing a work (the dish, the dance, or the symphony) in a tangible medium of expression." Christopher J. Buccafusco, "On the Legal Consequences of Sauces: Should Thomas Keller's Recipes Be per se Copyrightable?" *Cardozo Arts & Entertainment Law Journal* 24.3 (2007): 1121, 1131.

24. Nimmer, *Nimmer on Copyright*, § 2.18[I].

25. Unless somehow the aesthetic appeal of the dress or the dish is "separable" from its function. For both dresses and food, the aesthetic appeal—the lovely appearance, the delicious taste—is infused into the article itself, and thus is not separable, and that fact defeats copyright protection. For this reason, food simply falls outside the scope of contemporary copyright law.

26. Complaint, *Powerful Katinka, Inc. v. McFarland*. In addition, Charles claimed that McFarland had violated his fiduciary duties as a sous-chef at Pearl Oyster Bar.

27. Trade dress is generally divided into packaging and product design. Trade dress that is only packaging does not always require secondary meaning to be protected, whereas trade dress that is part of product design must have it. See *Walmart Stores v. Samara Bros.* 529 U.S. 205 (2000).

28. *Two Pesos v. Taco Cabana*, 505 U.S. 763 (1992).

29. Ron Ruggless, "Taco Cabana Buys Rival Two Pesos," *Restaurant News*, January 25, 1993.

30. On February 23, 2012, a jury handed down a mixed verdict but nonetheless found that Phillipe Chau had engaged in unfair competition and false advertising. Details of the feud can be found in Aaron Gell, How Now Mr. Chow? The Sweet and Sour Saga behind the City's Epic Food Fight, *New York Observer*, February 28, 2012, www.observer.com/2012/02/mr-chow-02-28-2012/5/.

31. Sara S. Munoz, Patent No. 6, 004, 596; "Peanut Butter and Jelly Sandwich," *Wall Street Journal*, April 5, 2005.

32. Pete Wells, "New Era of the Recipe Burglar," *Food & Wine*, November 2006.

33. Ibid. The review in *The Age* appeared in March 2004; John Lethlean, "Interlude," *The Age*, March 16, 2004, www.theage.com.au/articles/2004/03/15/1079199150268. html.

34. McLaughlin, "That Melon Tenderloin," reports that Wickens said that he would tell patrons of Interlude that the dishes in question originated in American restaurants. The apology is noted in the eGullet commentary, by an Alinea staff member.

35. *Campbell v. Acuff-Rose Music*, 510 U.S. 569 (1994).

36. Quoted in Buccafusco, "On the Legal Consequences of Sauces," 1152.

37. Ibid., 1153.

38. Interview with Joachim Splichal, Chef, Patina Catering Company.

39. Interview with Laurent Torondel, Chef, Bistro Laurent Torondel.

40. With the exception of the Buccafusco and Von Hippel/Fouchart papers, which we've noted elsewhere in this book.

41. Robert Ellickson, *Order without Law: How Neighbors Settle Disputes* (Harvard University Press, 1994).

42. Emmanuelle Fauchart|Eric von Hippel, "Norms-Based Intellectual Property Systems: The Case of French Chefs," *Organization Science* 19.2 (2008): 187.

43. Eric von Hippel, "Cooperation between Rivals: Informal Know-How Trading," *Research Policy* 16.6 (1987): 291.

44. Emily Cunningham, "Protecting Cuisine under the Rubric of Intellectual Property Law: Should the Law Play a Bigger Role in the Kitchen?" *Journal of High Technology Law* 9.1 (2009): 21.

45. *Pete Wells*, "New Era of the Recipe Burglar."

46. Fauchart and von Hippel, "Norms-Based Intellectual Property," 191.

47. *Bridgeport Music, Inc. v. Dimension Films*, 410 F.3d 792 (6th Cir. 2005).

48. Bret Thorn, "Catch-22: For Celebrity Chefs, the Bigger They Are, the Less They Usually Cook," *Nation's Restaurant News*, April 26, 2004.

49. Fauchart and von Hippel, "Norms-Based Intellectual Property."

50. Michel Orecklin and Laura Locke, "Food for Thought," *Time*, 2004, www.time. com/time/magazine/article/0,9171,994185,00.html (quoting Nancy Seryfert of the California Culinary Academy); *Chefography* (Food Network Broadcast).

51. James Hibberd, Cable Year End Ratings, *The Live Feed*, November 30, 2011, www. hollywoodreporter.com/blogs/live-feed/cable-year-ratings-usa-hbo-52808.

52. Michael Pollan, "Out of the Kitchen, Onto the Couch," *New York Times Magazine*, August 2, 2009.

53. Ibid.

54. Katy McLaughlin, "Chefs Gone Wild: Where to Eat this Fall," *Wall Street Journal*, September 17, 2005.

55. *Twentieth Century Music Corp. v. Aiken*, 422 U.S. 151 at 156 (1975).

56. Adria et al., "Statement,".

57. Jonathan Gold, "The New Cocktailians," *L.A. Weekly*, March 4, 2009.

58. Chantal Martineau, "The Era of Copyrighted Cocktails?" *The Atlantic*, August 31, 2010.

59. Jonathan Miles, "The Right Stuff (By Law)," *New York Times*, July 2, 2009.

60. Nick Fauchald, "Secrets of a Cocktail Master," *Food & Wine*, www.foodandwine. com/articles/secrets-of-a-cocktail-master.

61. Martineau, "The Era of Copyrighted Cocktails?".

CHAPTER 3

1. Melvin Helitzer, *Comedy Writing Secrets: How to Think Funny, Write Funny, Act Funny and Get Paid For It* (Writers Digest Books, 1987), 4.
2. This chapter is adapted from Dotan Oliar and Christopher Sprigman, "There's No Free Laugh (Anymore): The Emergence of Intellectual Property Norms and the Transformation of Stand-Up Comedy," *Virginia Law Review* 94.8 (2008): 1787. All interview excerpts in this chapter are taken from the Oliar/Sprigman article, unless noted otherwise.
3. Silo360, Joe Rogan and Carlos Mencia Fight, www.youtube.com/verify_age?next_ url=http%3A//www.youtube.com/watch%3Fv%3D5gVYfDCgYxk (accessed June 6, 2011).
4. *See* Silo360, Joe Rogan and Carlos Mencia Fight; nomencia, Mencia Steals from Cosby? www.youtube.com/watch?v=lCixAktGPlg at 1:18–2:03 (accessed June 6, 2011) (comparing Mencia and Cosby versions of a bit); deadfrogcomedy, George Lopez v. Dave Chappelle: Is This Joke Stealing? www.youtube.com/watch?v=-OHMeDqhAgU at 0:15–1:16 (accessed June 6, 2011) (comparing Mencia and Chappelle versions of a bit); deadfrogcomedy, Whose Joke Is It? Carlos Mencia? D.L. [*sic*] Hughley? George Lopez? www.youtube.com/watch?v=kPuu_VE7KOA at 0:14–0:27 (accessed June 6, 2011) (comparing a bit used by multiple comedians).
5. Oliar and Sprigman, "There's No Free Laugh (Anymore)."
6. These joke files were valuable property and were sometimes sold. Joey Adams and Henry Tobias, *The Borscht Belt* (Bentley Pub. Co., 1966), 61 ("When [Henny] Youngman and Henry Tobias heard that the file of one of the funniest standup comics in vaudeville, Richy Craig, Jr., was on the block, they begged and borrowed and sold their clothes to get enough money to grab it. Then they split it between them. It was like an investment. Not only did they have fresh material, but they made copies and peddled them to other emcees at a profit").
7. Milton Berle also maintained a large joke file. He published only its crème-de-la-crème in two heavy volumes, which he had the chutzpah to copyright. See Milton Berle, *Milton Berle's Private Joke File* (Three Rivers Press, 1992); Milton Berle, *More of the Best of Milton Berle's Private Joke File* (Book Sales, 1996). Bob Hope also maintained his own joke file, which he contributed before his death to the Library of Congress. *Bob Hope and American Variety: Joke File* (December 29, 2004), www.loc. gov/exhibits/bobhope/jokes.html (accessed June 6, 2011).
8. See, e.g., Adams and Tobias, *The Borscht Belt*, 61 ("[Henny] Youngman's style of delivery kept him joke broke. Like all Toomlers his need for new, fresh material was complicated by the fact that he worked to repeater guests season after season. The usual method of obtaining material (by most Social Directors) was to lift from the best. Any opening day at Loew's State or the Palace found a dozen comics in the audience, pencils akimbo.").
9. See Thrilling Days of Yesteryear, http://blogs.salon.com/0003139/2004/02/22. html (February 22, 2004) (containing transcript of *The Milton Berle Show* from January 20, 1948).
10. *See* deadfrogcomedy, Whose Joke Is It? Carlos Mencia? D.L. [*sic*] Hughley? George Lopez? www.youtube.com/watch?v=kPuu_VE7KOA at 0:14–0:27 (accessed June 6, 2011).

11. Ibid.

12. Much of this part of the chapter draws on this work, originally published as Oliar and Sprigman, "There's No Free Laugh," 60.

13. See nomencia, Mencia Steals from Cosby? www.youtube.com/watch?v=lCixAktGPlg at 1:18–2:03 (accessed June 6, 2008) (comparing Mencia and Cosby versions of bit).

14. Ibid. at 0:09–1:17.

15. See Robert W. Welkos, "Funny, That Was My Joke," *L.A. Times*, July 24, 2007, A1 (quoting Cosby as saying that joke stealing involves the performer accepting acclaim under "false pretenses" of originality and that whenever Cosby would use other comedians' material he would give public attribution).

16. See Lopez, www.redban.com/audio/lopez.mp3 at 0:40–1:46 (accessed June 6, 2011) (providing George Lopez's description on the Howard Stern radio show of his physical attack on Mencia); see also Q&A 12-01-06, www.redban.com/audio/dco.mp3 at 27:23–27:50 (accessed June 6, 2011) (providing the account of Jamie Masada, owner of the Laugh Factory in Los Angeles, who claimed to have witnessed Mencia and Lopez "almost killing each other").

17. See deadfrogcomedy, George Lopez v. Dave Chappelle: Is This Joke Stealing? www.youtube.com/watch?v=-OHMeDqhAgU at 0:15–1:16 (accessed August 18, 2008).

18. *See* Judy Carter, *The Comedy Bible: From Stand-up to Sitcom—the Comedy Writer's Ultimate How-to Guide* (Touchstone, 2001), 56. See also Dave Schwensen, *How to be a Working Comic: An Insider's Guide to a Career in Stand-Up Comedy 16* (Back Stage Books, 1998) ("What you never want to do is plagiarize another act. In other words, don't be a carbon copy of someone else. It could haunt you in more ways than one. Comedians are very protective of their material. . . . [W]hat they perform onstage is the basis of their careers and it's not for someone else to 'steal' and profit from. Beginners sometimes fall into the plagiarism trap because they don't understand what's expected from them when they first walk onstage. . . . A major point of this book is that to make it as a stand-up comic, you must be an original.").

19. Here is one comedian's description of such a cooperative dispute resolution:

> What you learn as a child is if you have a problem with someone you go and you talk to them. . . . So if somebody has a joke that sounds like mine . . . I'll just go up to the person and say "Hey, listen, I do this joke, that joke sounds a little bit similar," and then we talk it out. And they'll say blah, blah, blah. And then one of us will say, "all right I'll stop doing it." And that's that. It's done.

20. *See* Dean Johnson, "Stop! Thief!: Comics Say They're Getting a Bad Rap," *Boston Herald*, August 14, 1998, S03, available at 1998 WLNR 270264.

21. *See* Brian McKim, "Stolen Goods," *SHECKYmagazine.com*, December 2002, www.sheckymagazine.com/mckim/mck_0301.htm.

22. Ibid., 78.

23. This discussion is largely adapted from Jacob Loshin, "Secrets Revealed: How Magicians Protect Intellectual Property without Law," in *Law and Magic: A Collection of Essays*, Christine A. Corcos, ed. (Carolina Academic Press, 2010), 123.

24. The famous "Metamorphosis" illusion is an example. Nineteenth-century magician John Nevil Maskelyne invented the trick, but Harry Houdini popularized it. Nevil

Maskelyne and David Devant, *Our Magic: The Art in Magic, the Theory of Magic, the Practice of Magic* (George Routledge and Sons Limited, 1912), 67.

25. Ibid.

26. Rice v. Fox Broadcasting Co., 330 F.3d 1170 (2003).

27. Eriq Gardner, "Teller of Penn & Teller Breaks Silence to Sue Over Magic Trick," The Hollywood Reporter, April 15, 2012.

28. Additionally, to the extent that the pantomime is truly necessary to the performance of the uncopyrightable trick, a long-established element of the copyright law known as the "merger doctrine" very likely nullifies any copyright in the pantomime.

29. *Goldin v. Clarion Photoplays, Inc.*, 202 A.D. 1, at 4 (N.Y. App. Div. 1922).

30. Paul Brownfield, "What's This Guy Got Up His Sleeve?" *L.A. Times*, March 3, 1998.

31. "Criss Angel Makes Magicians Disappear—With Help from Security," *Radar Online*, September 10, 2010, www.radaronline.com/exclusives/2010/09/criss-angel-makes-magicians-disappear-with-help-security.

CHAPTER 4

1. www.vanguard.com/bogle_site/lib/sp19970401.html.

2. "Bill Walsh and Joe Montana: The Genius and the Gun," *Football Digest*, December 1982 Interestingly, back in 1986, a federal appeals court held that a baseball game is a protectible work of authorship. See Baltimore Orioles v. Major League Baseball Players Association, 805 F.2d 663 (7th Cir. 1986). By 2005, however, the same court signaled that it was no longer following its previous holding. See Toney v. L'Oreal USA, 406 F.3d 905 (7th Cir. 2005) (noting that the holding in the Orioles case had been "widely criticized by our sister circuits and by several commentators.").

3. Ibid.

4. For more on the importance of tweaking, see Malcolm Gladwell, "The Tweaker: The Real Genius of Steve Jobs," *The New Yorker*, November 14, 2011.

5. Tim Layden, *Blood, Sweat and Chalk, The Ultimate Football Playbook: How the Great Coaches Built Today's Game* (Sports Illustrated Books, 2010).

6. Pete Thamel, "Nevada's Runaway Offense," *New York Times*, October 10, 2010.

7. Nicholas Dawidoff, "Rex Ryan: Bringing It Big," *New York Times Magazine*, September 12, 2010.

8. 209 U.S. 1 (1908).

9. Gladwell, "The Tweaker."

10. Ibid. Gladwell draws on Ralf Meisenzahl and Joel Mokyr, "The Rate and Direction of Invention in the British Industrial Revolution: Incentives and Institutions," NBER Working Paper 16993 (April 2011), www.nber.org/papers/w16993.pdf. They note that patent played a small role in this process; instead "many workmen relied on secrecy and first-mover advantages to reap the benefits of their innovations. Over 40% of the sample here never took out a patent." Ibid., abstract.

11. *Madey v. Duke University, 307 F. 3d. 1351 (2002)*. The court found Duke liable for patent infringement when Duke continued to use Madey's patented laser for research purposes after Madey had left the university. Previously, courts had allowed researchers to use patented technologies for basic scientific research that was not directly aimed at commercial use. *Madey v. Duke University* made clear that this exception would be construed very narrowly—any experimental use that was motivated by more than

"mere curiosity" and could lead eventually to a commercial use was out of bounds. This is a narrow exception, and it makes it difficult to tweak a patented invention without the threat of liability. Moreover, the courts' constriction of experimental use creates a big tension in patent law. On the one hand, patent law grants some rights to Tweakers who make an improvement. But on the other, it makes it hard for Tweakers to do the basic research necessary to make that improvement in the first place.

12. One long-standing exception to this general rule was the high-end art world, where tweaking was fairly common (under the guise of "appropriation") and rarely prosecuted. In 2011, however, a ruling against the artist Richard Prince cast considerable doubt on this practice, sending shock waves throughout the art world and prompting protests from many quarters, including the Metropolitan Museum of Art and Museum of Modern Art.

13. Calligraphy, the predecessor to fonts, allows this too, but the range of variation is narrower and replicability more difficult to achieve.

14. Released in 2007; see www.helveticafilm.com/.

15. H.R. Rep. No. 94–1476, at 55.

16. *Eltra v. Ringer*, 579 F.2d 294 (4th Cir. 1978); *Leonard Storch Enters., Inc. v. Mergenthaler Linotype Co.*, No. 78-C-238, 1979 WL 1067 (E.D.N.Y. 1979).

17. Fonts are not "inherently distinctive"—i.e., the trademark law (correctly) does not presume that consumers looking at a font will associate it with a particular producer. And it would be difficult, if not impossible, to show that any particular font has acquired distinctiveness out in the marketplace.

18. Alexander Lawson, *Anatomy of a Typeface* (Godine, 1990), 386–89.

19. Anthony Cahalan, *Type, Trends and Fashion: A Study of the Late Twentieth Century Proliferation of Typefaces* (Mark Batty, 2008), 61.

20. Randall Rothenberg, Computers Change the Face of Type," *New York Times*, July 23, 1990, D1.

21. Caitlin Liu, "Creating a New Generation of Vivid Typefaces," *New York Times*, August 5, 1996, D5.

22. Cahalan, *Type, Trends and Fashion*.

23. See, e.g., Philip W. Snyder, "Typeface Design after the Desktop Revolution: A New Case For Legal Protection," 16 *Columbia-VLA Journal of Law & the Arts* 16.1 (1991): 97, 98 n.3.

24. Blake Fry, "Why Typefaces Proliferate without Copyright Protection," *Journal on Telecommunications & High Technology Law* 8.2 (2010): 425.

25. See http://seekingalpha.com/article/216283-stock-market-capitalization-exceeds-gdp.

26. Peter Tufano, "Financial Innovation and First Mover Advantages," 25 *Journal of Financial Economics* 25.2 (1989): 213.

27. *State Street Bank and Trust Co. v. Signature Financial Group Inc.*, 149 F.3d 1368 (Fed. Cir. 1998).

28. Robert M. Hunt, "Business Method Patents and U.S. Financial Services," *Contemporary Economic Policy* 28.3 (July 2010): 322–52.

29. Robert P. Merges, "The Uninvited Guest: Patents on Wall Street," *Economic Review* Q4 (2003): 1–14.

30. Josh Lerner, "Trolls on State Street? The Litigation of Financial Patents, 1976–2005," mimeo, Harvard Business School (2006).

31. Hunt, "Business Method Patents," p. 333.
32. Ibid.
33. Peter Tufano, "Financial Innovation," in George M. Constantindes, Milton Harris and René M. Stulz eds., *The Handbook of the Economics of Finance* (Elsevier, 2003).
34. Ibid.
35. Ibid.
36. Merges, "The Uninvited Guest."
37. See Sugato Battacharyya and Vikram Nanda, "Client Discretion, Switching Costs, and Financial Innovation," *Review of Financial Studies* (Winter 2000): 1101–127.
38. Robert C. Merton, "On the Application of the Continuous-Time Theory of Finance to Financial Intermediation and Insurance," *The Geneva Papers on Risk and Insurance* 14 (July, 1989): 225.
39. See www.ncbi.nlm.nih.gov/omim.
40. 499 U.S. 340 (1991).
41. www.dialog.com.
42. Commission of the European Communities, *DG Internal Market and Services Working Paper, First Evaluation of Directive 96/9/EC on the Legal Protection of Databases*, at §1.4, Brussels, 12 December 2005, http://ec.europa.eu/internal_market/copyright/docs/databases/evaluation_report_en.pdf.
43. Ibid., § 4.2.1
44. See ibid., Figure 7.
45. http://projects.latimes.com/value-added/faq/#database_grades.

CHAPTER 5

1. See Dennis Dutton, *The Art Instinct: Beauty, Pleasure and Human Evolution* (Bloomsbury Press, 2009).
2. Douglas G. Lichtman, "The Economics of Innovation: Protecting Unpatentable Goods," *Minnesota Law Review* 81.3 (1997): 693.
3. The nature of that monopoly varies; under copyright law, for instance, if someone else independently creates the same work, they have not "copied" the first work and therefore have broken no laws. Patent has a stricter standard. A second inventor who unwittingly (and without copying) invents the same device or method cannot use it commercially without violating the first inventor's patent.
4. E.g., Robert Levine, *Free Ride: How Digital Parasites Are Destroying the Culture Business, and How the Culture Business Can Fight Back* (Doubleday, 2011).
5. This is not to say that there are not serious criticisms of our IP laws. For some of the best work in this vein see, e.g., Jamie Boyle, *The Public Domain: Enclosing the Commons of the Mind* (Yale, 2008); Neil Netanel, *Copyright's Paradox* (Oxford, 2008); and Larry Lessig, *Free Culture: The Nature and Future of Creativity* (Penguin, 2004)
6. Present in this hypothetical are also what economists call positive and negative externalities. *The New Palgrave Dictionary of Economics* (Palgrave Macmillan, 2008) defines externalities as "indirect effects of consumption or production activity, that is, effects on agents other than the originator of such activity which do not work through the price system." The interaction between copying and externalities is interesting. The second café might enjoy positive externalities from the first, especially if the first has more business than it can handle at certain times and hence

customers "spill over" into Café #2. And the later followers of both cafés enjoy the positive externalities of the first two as the street transforms into a destination spot. But the owner of Café # 1 also experiences negative externalities as the second owner outcompetes him for some customers. Customers, of course, are the overall winners as they experience more choice and, eventually, better quality and lower prices induced by competition.

7. *The Sopranos*, "46 Long" (1999).

8. While Paulie's views on who owns the cappuccino may seem extreme, this is actually a live issue in intellectual property thinking today. It usually falls under the banner of "traditional knowledge" or "cultural property." See generally Steven Munzer and Kal Raustiala, "The Uneasy Case for Intellectual Property Rights in Traditional Knowledge," *Cardozo Arts and Entertainment Law Journal* 27.1 (2009): 37; Kristen A. Carpenter, Sonia K. Katyal, and Angela R. Riley, "In Defense of Property," *Yale Law Journal* 118.6 (2009): 1022; Susan Scafidi, *Who Owns Culture: Authenticity and Appropriation in American Law* (Rutgers, 2005); Michael Brown, *Who Owns Native Culture?* (Harvard, 2004).

9. *In re Morton-Norwich Products, Inc.*, 671 F.2d 1332 (C.C.P.A. 1982).

10. Congressional Budget Office, *Research and Development in the Pharmaceutical Industry* (October 2006), 2.

11. Brooks Barnes, "'Avatar' Is No. 1 but without a Record," *New York Times*, December 20, 2009.

12. Hearings before the Subcommittee on Courts, Civil Liberties, and the Administration of Justice on Home Recording of Copyrighted Works, April 12, 1982.

13. For some notable exceptions, see Paul Nystrom, *Economics of Fashion* (Ronald Press, 1928); Paul M. Gregory, "An Economic Interpretation of Women's Fashions," *Southern Economic Journal* 14.2 (1947): 148; Wolfgang Pesendorfer, "Design Innovation and Fashion Cycles," *American Economic Review* 85.4 (1995): 771; Jonathan Barnett, "Shopping for Gucci on Canal Street: Reflections on Status Consumption, Intellectual Property and the Incentive Thesis," *Virginia Law Review* 91.6 (2005): 1381; Kal Raustiala and Christopher Sprigman, "The Piracy Paradox: Innovation and Intellectual Property in Fashion Design," *Virginia Law Review* 92.8 (2006): 1687; and C. Scott Hemphill and Jeannie Suk, "The Law, Culture, and Economics of Fashion," *Stanford Law Review* 61.5 (2009): 1147.

14. Hemphill and Suk coined these useful terms in their *Stanford Law Review* article. They treat the two as simply different types, though of course there is a social class dimension to this, and in the past this was far more apparent. The great French historian Fernand Braudel quotes a story of a Sicilian nobleman in Paris in the early 18th century who noted that "nothing makes noble persons despise the gilded costume so much as to see it on the bodies of the lowest men in the world . . . so the upper class had to invent new 'gilded costumes.'" See Pesendorfer, "Design Innovation and Fashion Cycles," 771–72.

15. Identifying the tipping point is a task for Malcolm Gladwell, *The Tipping Point: How Little Things Can Make a Big Difference* (Back Bay Books, 2002).

16. Emmanuelle Fauchart and Eric von Hippel, "Norms-based Intellectual Property Systems: The Case of French Chefs," *Organization Science* 19.2 (2008): 187.

17. Robert Ellickson, *Order without Law: How Neighbors Settle Disputes* (Harvard, 1994); Eric Posner, *Law and Social Norms* (Harvard, 2002); Lisa Bernstein, "Opting Out of the Legal System: Extralegal Contractual Relations in the Diamond Industry," *Journal of Legal Studies* 21.1 (1992): 115.

18. Oral Argument, *Two Pesos, Inc.*, 505 U.S. 763, 1992 WL 687823 *16 (Scalia, J. speaking; emphasis added).

19. "Having a Ball: What's Working in Music," *The Economist*, October 7, 2010.

20. Zoe Heller, "Mick without Moss," *New York Times*, December 3, 2010.

21. Quoted in ibid.

22. Marie Connolly and Alan B. Krueger, "Rockonomics: The Economics of Popular Music," in *Handbook of the Economics of Art and Culture*, Victor Ginsburg and David Throsby, eds. (Elsevier, 2006), 670; "Music Industry Decides that All the World's a Stage," *The Independent*, January 3, 2009.

23. Connolly and Krueger, "Rockonomics," 673.

24. Jon Pareles, "David Bowie, 21st Century Entrepreneur," *New York Times*, June 9, 2002.

25. Sasha Frere Jones, "Critic's Notebook: Pay Scale," *The New Yorker*, March 23, 2009, 9.

26. Daniel H. Pink, *Drive: The Surprising Truth about What Motivates Us* (Penguin, 2009), 15–16.

27. To learn more about open source, see Yochai Benkler, *The Penguin and the Leviathan: How Cooperation Triumphs over Self-Interest* (Random House, 2011); Steven Weber, *The Success of Open Source* (Harvard, 2005); Eric S. Raymond, *The Cathedral and the Bazaar: Musings on Linux and Open Source by an Accidental Revolutionary* (O'Reilly Media, 2001).

28. Richard Rothwell, "Creating Wealth with Free Software," *Free Software Magazine* (August 2008), www.freesoftwaremagazine.com/community_posts/creating_wealth_free_software#. See also the discussion in Chris Anderson, *Free* (Hyperion, 2009), chapter 7.

29. Nicholas Dawidoff, "Rex Ryan: Bringing it Big," *New York Times*, September 8, 2010.

30. Ferran Adria et al., "Statement on the 'New Cookery,'" *The Guardian*, December 9, 2006.

31. Eric Wilson, "Before Models Can Turn Around, Knockoffs Fly," *New York Times*, September 4, 2007; see also Paul Nystrom, *Economics of Fashion* (Ronald Press, 1928) for an early version of this claim.

32. Hemphill and Suk, "The Law," 24.

33. Congress responded to the Trade-Mark Cases by enacting the Trade Mark Act of 1881. It did so based on its power under the Constitution's Commerce Clause to regulate interstate commerce. That enactment later passed constitutional muster.

34. Levine, *Free Ride*.

35. Michele Boldrin and David K. Levine, *Against Intellectual Monopoly* (Cambridge, 2008).

36. There are scores if not hundreds of studies demonstrating the existence of optimism bias. Russell Korobkin and Thomas Ulen, "Law and Behavioral Science:

Removing the Rationality Assumption from Law and Economics," *California Law Review* 88.4 (2000): 1091; Neil Weinstein, "Unrealistic Optimism about Future Life Events," *Journal of Personality and Social Psychology* 39.5 (1980): 806.

37. Christopher J. Buccafusco and Christopher J. Sprigman, "Valuing Intellectual Property: An Experiment," *Cornell Law Review* 96.1 (2010): 1.

38. The participants were told that they would be selling only the chance to win the prize, not the poem itself—in adopting this structure, the experiment modeled an IP transaction, in which the author of something like a poem, which is what economists call "nonrival" property, sells some opportunity to use the poem (for example, to publish it), but does not divest himself of the poem completely. Contrast this with a transaction involving "rival" property, like a coffee mug. In the latter, the seller loses all access to the good he has transferred—you don't drink out of a mug once you have sold it to someone else.

39. These experiments do not empirically demonstrate increased effort, but instead increased ex ante valuations of goods. But the same is largely true for the incentive basis of copyright or patent: both rest on the belief that larger expected rewards will result in more output of innovation. A potentially more important caveat is that firms may be institutionally structured to reduce optimism bias and have more rational and reasonable valuations in mind when engaging in innovation. How individuals differ from firms in this regard is an interesting question not addressed by these experiments.

40. Sherwin Rosen, "The Economics of Superstars," 71.5 *American Economic Review* (1981): 845; Robert H. Frank and Philip J. Cook, *The Winner Take All Society* (Free Press, 1995).

41. Doug Lichtman et al., "Strategic Disclosure in the Patent System," *Vanderbilt Law Review* 53.6 (2000): 2200. Whether the second and third place finishers truly wasted their efforts is a hard question, since there may be useful spillovers from these efforts. But the central point remains.

42. Jonathan Barnett et al., "The Fashion Lottery: Cooperative Innovation in Stochastic Markets," *Journal of Legal Studies* 39.1 (2010): 159.

43. Buccafusco and Sprigman, "Valuing Intellectual Property," 7. Loss aversion may also play a role here, as a counter-countervailing force against the countervailing force of optimism bias and tournament effects. We are not claiming that the overall effect of various psychological biases is clear; rather, we simply want to point out that there is good reason to think that there are some, possibly significant, forces that lead creators to overestimate their incentives to create.

44. These have slightly different connotations but share a reliance on an open innovative system in which many actors, often formally unconnected, participate. On crowd-sourcing, see James Suroweicki, *The Wisdom of Crowds* (Anchor, 2005).

45. https://buy.louisck.net/statement (accessed December 16, 2011).

EPILOGUE

1. Greg Kot, *Ripped: How the Wireless Generation Revolutionized Music* (Scribner, 2009); Steve Knopper, *Appetite for Self-Destruction: The Spectacular Crash of the Record Industry in the Digital Age* (Free Press, 2009); Donald Passman, *All You Need*

to Know about the Music Business (7th ed., Free Press, 2009); M. William Krasilovsky et al., *This Business of Music: Definitive Guide to the Music Industry* (10th ed., Billboard Books, 2007).

2. Recording Industry of America, www.riaa.com (accessed July 8, 2011).

3. "Napster: A Cool Billion," *The Economist*, February 22, 2001.

4. Indeed, the record label's anti-piracy campaign appears to have provoked innovation in the technology of filesharing that made future anti-piracy campaigns less effective. Had the industry made its peace with Napster, these developments would likely still have happened, but they may have happened less rapidly and been less salient to ordinary users.

5. Statistics drawn from domestic release figures at Box Office Mojo; http://boxofficemojo.com/yearly/?view2=domestic&view=releasedate&p=.htm.

6. Zoe Heller, "Mick without Moss," *New York Times*, December 3, 2010. On albums as ads, see Frere Jones, in Conclusion. On Madonna, see Sean Michaels, "Madonna Records Biggest Second-week Sales Drop in US Chart History," *The Guardian*, www.guardian.co.uk/music/2012/apr/11/madonna-second-week-sales-drop.

7. Jon Caramanica, "For Some, Free Music Is an Investment that Pays Off," *New York Times*, November 18, 2011.

8. Josh Tyrangiel, "Radiohead Says: Pay What You Want," *Time* Magazine, October 1, 2007, www.time.com/time/arts/article/0,8599,1666973,00.html.

9. Mark F. Schultz, "Fear and Norms and Rock & Roll: What Jambands Can Teach Us about Persuading People to Obey Copyright Law," *Berkeley Technology Law Journal* 21.2 (2006): 651.

10. Schultz, "Fear and Norms," 680–81.

11. Ryan Singel, "Netflix Beat BitTorrent's Bandwidth," *Wired*, May 17, 2011, www.wired.com/epicenter/2011/05/netflix-traffic/.

12. Glenn Peoples, "Spotify Has 250,000 U.S. Subscribers," *Billboard*, October 14, 2011, www.billboard.biz/bbbiz/industry/digital-and-mobile/spotify-has-250-000-u-s-subscribers-report-1005411992.story.

INDEX